CHINA IN TRANSITION

Also by David C. B. Teather

HIGHER EDUCATION IN A POST-BINARY ERA

INFORMATION TECHNOLOGY IN EDUCATIONAL MANAGEMENT FOR SCHOOLS OF THE FUTURE (*co-author*)

Also by Herbert S. Yee

THE POLITICAL CULTURE OF THE MACAU CHINESE (*co-author*)

MACAU BEYOND 1999

A STUDY OF MACAU'S POLITICS AND PUBLIC POLICY

A TALE OF TWO CITIES: A Comparative Study of Political, Economic and Social Developments in Hong Kong and Macau

THE MODERNIZATION OF TIBETAN REGIONS: Theory, Practice and Policies

THE POLITICAL CULTURE OF CONTEMPORARY CHINESE UNIVERSITY STUDENTS

China in Transition

Issues and Policies

Edited by

David C. B. Teather
Professor and Dean
Faculty of Social Sciences
Hong Kong Baptist University
Hong Kong

and

Herbert S. Yee
Associate Professor
Government and International Studies
Hong Kong Baptist University
Hong Kong

Consultant Editor: Jo Campling

First published in Great Britain 1999 by
MACMILLAN PRESS LTD
Houndmills, Basingstoke, Hampshire RG21 6XS and London
Companies and representatives throughout the world

A catalogue record for this book is available from the British Library.

ISBN 0–333–73133–6 hardcover
ISBN 0–333–73134–4 paperback

First published in the United States of America 1999 by
ST. MARTIN'S PRESS, INC.,
Scholarly and Reference Division,
175 Fifth Avenue, New York, N.Y. 10010

ISBN 0–312–21964–4

Library of Congress Cataloging-in-Publication Data
China in transition : issues and policies / edited by David C.B.
Teather, Herbert S. Yee
p. cm.
Includes bibliographical references and index.
ISBN 0–312–21964–4
1. China—Politics and government—1976– 2. China—Economic conditions—1976– 3. China—Social conditions—1976– 4. China––Foreign relations—1976– I. Teather, David C. B. II. Yee, Herbert S.
DS779.26.C473524 1999
951.05—DC21 98–45611
CIP

This book is printed on paper suitable for recycling and made from fully managed and sustained forest sources.

10 9 8 7 6 5 4 3 2
08 07 06 05 04 03 02 01 00

Printed and bound in Great Britain by
Antony Rowe Ltd, Chippenham, Wiltshire

Contents

List of Tables and Figures

Tables

Figures

Acknowledgements

Several years before the return of Hong Kong to China, the Civil Service Training and Development Institute of the Hong Kong Government contracted the Hong Kong Baptist University to provide two short courses on understanding contemporary China. Since that time six of these courses have been offered each year, with each course attracting over a hundred civil servants of all ages and from all branches of government. The editors of this book organised these courses, and most of the authors of the chapters contributed the lectures.

Hong Kong was then, and is still, a unique vantage point from which to view China. Apart from the villagers of the New Territories, most Hongkongers or their immediate forebears migrated here from other parts of China – many from neighbouring Guangdong Province, some from much further afield. Since the open-door policy of 1978, family ties and business connections have been re-established, so information about China gleaned from the news media is complemented by personal experience. Academics from Hong Kong are frequent visitors to other parts of China.

Yet Hong Kong, the most modern of Chinese cities, looks also to the West. Its universities are staffed by academics who have studied and worked overseas, and who would be equally at home in the universities of Chicago, London, Toronto or Sydney. It is this combination of, on the one hand, intimate knowledge of China and, on the other hand, familiarity with Western ways, that enables the contributors to this volume to communicate so insightfully and effectively to English-language readers.

The editors would like to thank all those who have contributed to this book. In addition to the authors of the chapters themselves, we thank those other academics who participated in two workshops, 15 months apart, in which drafts of all the chapters were presented and critiqued. Among these participants were Professor Sung Yun Wing of the Chinese University of Hong Kong; Professor Leonard Chu, Dr Larry Chow, Professor Ma Hing Keung, Dr Danny Paau, Professor Herbert Tsang, Mr To Yui Ming and Mr Woo Tun Oy of Hong Kong Baptist University; and Dr Guo Zhenglin of Zhongshan University.

Many people helped with the organisation of these workshops, and with the wordprocessing of the individual chapters. Ms Ada To,

Secretary of the China Studies Programme of Hong Kong Baptist University, contributed throughout, and not least in the preparation of the final typescript. She was assisted by colleagues and students from the Faculty of Social Sciences office.

Special thanks are due also to Jo Campling who, following a visit to Hong Kong Baptist University, encouraged the editors to prepare the typescript for publication and who, together with Annabelle Buckley and colleagues at Macmillan, provided both generous professional advice and practical help in transforming the typescript into the published book.

We hope that the publication of this book will help towards real understanding of contemporary China in the English-speaking world.

DAVID C. B. TEATHER
HERBERT S. YEE

Notes on the Contributors

CHEN Yu Hsi is Associate Professor of Journalism, Hong Kong Baptist University. He was a journalist in Taiwan and the US for more than ten years. From 1982 to 1987 he was Deputy Chief Editor and Chief Editorialist of *Centre Daily News* in New York City. He writes extensively on political and socioeconomic issues relating to Greater China. He is the author of *Dependent Development and Its Sociopolitical Consequences: A Case Study of Taiwan* and *Nation Divided: Selected Essays and Papers on Greater-China Political Economy*.

Luk Tak CHUEN is Lecturer in Sociology, Hong Kong Baptist University. His research interests include organizations, stratification, work and industry, Chinese society, and labour studies. He has contributed book chapters and articles to scholarly journals.

LI Si Ming is Professor of Geography, Hong Kong Baptist University. His research interests include urban studies and housing, both economic and social aspects. He has contributed book chapters to edited books, and articles to a number of international journals. He has recently edited or co-edited three books entitled *Perspectives on the Regional Economy of China, The Other Hong Kong Report* and *Social Development in China: Analysis of Hong Kong Scholars*.

Carlos W. H. LO is Associate Professor in the Department of Management at the Hong Kong Polytechnic University. His area of interests are in Chinese law and government, environmental management, and public sector management. He has recently published a book entitled *China's Legal Awakening: Legal Theory and Criminal Justice in Deng's Era*. He has contributed articles to *Environmental Management, Public Administration & Development*, and *Journal of Contemporary China*.

Sonny S. H. LO is Lecturer in Politics, University of Hong Kong. His research interests include the politics of China, Hong Kong and Macau. He is the author of two recently published books entitled *Political Development in Macau* and *The Politics of Democratization in Hong Kong*. He has contributed articles to *China Quarterly, Asian Survey, Journal of Contemporary China, Pacific Affairs* and other scholarly journals.

Werner MEISSNER is Professor of Government and International Studies, Hong Kong Baptist University. A specialist in Chinese political thought he is the author of *Philosophy and Politics in China: The Controversy on Dialectical Materialism in the 1930s*. His recent publications include *Western Philosophy in the People's Republic of China, 1987–1992: A Bibliography* and *Western Political Science in the People's Republic of China, 1987–1992: A Bibliography*.

SIU Yat Ming is Associate Professor of Sociology, Hong Kong Baptist University. His research interests include population studies and Chinese society. He has contributed a chapter to *China Review 1993* and articles to scholarly journals. He has edited (with Li Si Ming and Mok Tai-kee) a book entitled *Social Development in China: Analysis of Hong Kong Scholars.*

David C. B. TEATHER obtained batchelor and doctoral degrees at University College London. He subsequently held academic appointments at the Universities of London, Liverpool, Otago and New England, before taking up the post of Professor and Dean of the Faculty of Social Sciences at Hong Kong Baptist University. His recent books include *Higher Education in a Post-Binary Era* and (with Alex Fung and Others) *Information Technology in Educational Management for Schools of the Future*.

TING Wai is Associate Professor of Government and International Studies, Hong Kong Baptist University. His research includes the domestic politics and foreign policies of China, and China–Hong Kong relations. His latest publications include a monograph entitled *The External Relations and International Status of Hong Kong*.

WANG Jinhong is Lecturer in Politics, South China Normal University, Guangzhou. His research interests include the politics of Chinese peasants and national minorities. He is the co-author of a book entitled *Chinese Public Policies: Theories and Practices*. He has contributed articles to scholarly journals published in mainland China.

K. K. WONG is Lecturer in Geography, Hong Kong Baptist University. His research interests include man–environment interaction, environmental policy, sustainable development, environmental and landscape perceptions, housing satisfaction and environmental education. He publishes widely in international journals and in edited books.

Herbert S. YEE is Associate Professor in Government and International Studies at the Hong Kong Baptist University. He has authored or edited several books on Chinese politics (all in Chinese). He has contributed book chapters to edited books and articles to international journals.

ZHANG Xiaohe is Lecturer in Economics, Hong Kong Baptist University. His research interests include Chinese political economy, international trade, and foreign investment in China. His recent publications appear in *Journal of Development Studies, Industry and Development* and *China Economic Review*.

Abbreviations

APEC	Asia Pacific Economic Cooperation
APL	Administrative Procedure Law
ASEAN	Association of South East Asian Nations
BOC	Bank of China
CASS	Chinese Academy of Social Sciences
CCP	Chinese Communist Party
CDIC	Central Discipline Inspection Commission
CMC	Central Military Commission
CPPCC	Chinese People's Political Consultative Conference
DPP	Democratic Progressive Party (Taiwan)
EU	European Union
FDI	Foreign direct investment
FFE	Foreign funded enterprise
FIE	Foreign invested enterprise
FRG	Federal Republic of Germany
GATT	General Agreement on Tariffs and Trade
GDP	Gross domestic product
GDR	German Democratic Republic
GIOV	Gross industrial output value
HKSAR	Hong Kong Special Administrative Region
ICAC	Independent Commission Against Corruption (Hong Kong)
IMF	International Monetary Fund
KMT	Kuomintang
LDC	Less developed country
LGEDPA	Leading Group for the Economic Development of Poor Area
MDC	More developed country
MFN	Most favoured nation
MTCR	Missile Technology Control Regime
NCNA	New China (Xinhua) News Agency
NEPA	National Environmental Protection Agency
NPC	National People's Congress
NPT	Nuclear Non-Proliferation Treaty
PADO	Poor Area Development Office
PAP	People's Armed Police

PLA	People's Liberation Army
PPP	Purchasing power parity
PRC	People's Republic of China
PSB	Public Security Bureau
RMB	*Renminbi* (Chinese currency)
RMRB	*Renmin ribao* (*People's Daily*)
ROC	Republic of China
SEZ	Special economic zone
SIPC	Shenzhen Intermediate People's Court
SOE	State-owned enterprise
TIM	Taiwan independent movement
TVE	Township and village enterprise
UK	United Kingdom
UNDP	United Nations Development Programme
US	United States
USSR	Union of Soviet Socialist Republics
VAT	Value-added tax
WCED	World Commission on Environment and Development
WMD	Weapons of mass destruction
WTO	World Trade Organization
ZGTJNJ	*Zhongguo tongji nianjian* (*Statistical Yearbook of China*)

Introduction

The last two decades of the twentieth century are the turning point in contemporary Chinese history. After two decades of reform and the open door policy, China has accomplished achievements on all fronts. To many people China is a rising world power and may even overtake the United States in GNP by or before the middle of the twenty-first century.[1] Indeed, according to the Purchasing Power Parity (PPP) calculations, China has already become the world's second or third largest economy. Yet accompanying the process of reform and the open door policy many problems became apparent. Many are related to the policy formulation and implementation process, but a significant proportion of problems are institutional, caused by inherent contradictions within the Chinese political and economic systems. The objective of this book is selectively to analyse some of the problems and issues confronted by the Chinese leaders. We believe that the policy issues selected in this volume are quite representative of the current political, economic, and social situations in China.

From the perspective of long-term political development, the political changes of the last two decades of this century are crucial. In order to rectify the radical leftist mistakes of the 'Cultural Revolution' (1966–76), Deng Xiaoping, after he came to power in 1978, adopted a pragmatic, unorthodox approach towards politics. Deng downgraded the importance of ideology and refused to hold any mass political campaigns or to undertake class struggle. Deng's stress on economic development has no doubt contributed to the rapid economic and social development in the last two decades, yet his neglect of ideology had contributed to the 'confidence crisis' or 'authority crisis' of the Chinese Communist Party (CCP). The prestige and authority of the CCP reached an all-time low in the 1980s among the Chinese populace. The legitimacy of Communist rule was at stake. Deng and his supporters included the 'Four Cardinal Principles' in the 1982 constitution, the core of which was to ensure the dictatorship of the CCP. The Dengists were also actively involved in searching for a new ideology or model of government to replace the increasingly unpopular orthodox Marxist–Leninist–Maoist model. At different times in the 1980s, the European model of 'social democracy' and a Singaporean model of 'neo-authoritarian' government were proposed and seriously discussed among academics and officials.[2] Yet the disintegration of the former Soviet Union and the downfall of Zhao Ziyang, the former CCP general secretary, whose associates had proposed the notion of 'neo-authoritarianism', abruptly ended the discourse in searching for an appropriate political model for the regime. The post-Deng leadership merely holds on to the fading shell of socialism.

The perennial crisis facing the Communist regime is leadership succession. China does not yet have an institutionalized system for leadership succession. The final outcome is often the result of a power struggle or political compromises among different Party factions. After the death in 1997 of Deng Xiaoping, China's Paramount Leader, Jiang Zemin, the Party Secretary and the Chairman of the Central Military Committee, gradually assured his grip of the military and Party. Jiang Zemin became more assertive after ousting former Beijing mayor Chen Xitong in a corruption scandal. Jiang foced Qiao Shi, Chairman of the National People's Congress and Jiang's arch rival in the power struggle to succeed Deng, to an early 'retirement' in the First Plenum of the Fifteenth CCP's Central Committee, held in September 1997. Then some high-level officials and cadres in Beijing publicly referred to Jiang as 'Chairman' (*Zhuxi*) or 'Leader' (*Lingxiu*) without the surname, which was reminiscent of the 'Cultural Revolution' era when Mao Zedong was indisputably regarded as the 'Chairman' or 'Leader' of China. However, unlike his predecessors Mao and Deng, Jiang does not have charismatic appeal and is more likely to rely on collective leadership to take China into the twenty-first century.

China has enjoyed an unprecedented period of economic growth since the early 1980s. Inflationary pressures sparked by an overheated economy in the early 1990s are apparently under control. The Chinese economy has achieved a 'soft-landing' after policy measures taken by the central government to control money supply and to restrain the further development of over-expanded infrastructures. However, many problems remain to be tackled such as, *inter alia*, income disparities between the coastal regions and the hinterland provinces as well as between the cities and the rural areas, the perennial problems of the state-owned enterprises, and the issue of environmental protection. Rapid and sustained economic growth has also brought enormous social changes in Chinese cities and villages. The new wealthy have enjoyed high social status and played an increasingly important role in local politics. Yet poverty in the less developed regions and the issue of population control will continue to haunt the Chinese leaders who put top policy priority on maintaining political and social stability.

China's foreign policy orientation, on the other hand, underwent substantial change in the 1990s. In the new post-Cold War era, China is no longer confronted with military threats on its borders. Indeed, China enjoys an unprecedented peaceful global and regional environment. Beijing has made friends with all countries, regardless of ideology, which are willing to terminate their diplomatic relations with Taipei. Hong Kong became part of China in 1997 and Macau followed suit in 1999. Taiwan is the only Chinese territory outside Beijing's control. Understandably, the Taiwan issue remains the major concern of the Chinese leaders. The other important foreign policy issue is China's relations with the United States. After the collapse of the former Soviet Union, the United States became the only military superpower in global politics. Washington's policy strategies in the Asian–Pacific region, particularly its attitudes towards the disputes in the Taiwan Straits and the South China Sea, are closely watched by Beijing. Jiang Zemin's official visit to the United States and his summit meeting with President Clinton in October 1997 was hailed as an important breakthrough in Sino–American relations. Beijing has established a 'strategic partnership' with Washington, Moscow, London, and Paris. A more assertive China will certainly play an increasingly important role in regional and global politics.

This book comprises four parts, addressing respectively politico-legal, foreign policy, economic and social issues. In Chapter 1, Werner Meissner examines the intellectual developments in searching for an appropriate political ideology for China. Since the middle of the last century, the intellectual history of China has been characterised by the oscillation between rejection and acceptance of Western thought. Meissner describes the four periods of this development until the late 1970s and mentions briefly the main currents that developed during that time. Since the beginning of the 1980s the policy of the Four Modernisations (agriculture, industry, defence, and science and technology) has triggered off a completely unexpected new move to adopt Western thought. Before the backdrop of the decline of Maoism, five intellectual developments can be observed: (1) the renaissance of Western political science; (2) the renaissance of non-Marxist philosophy; (3) the revival of Western political liberalism; (4) Neo-authoritarianism; and, in particular, (5) the renaissance of Chinese traditional philosophy.

The chapter provides data regarding the translation of books and articles on Western political science and Western philosophy since the 1980s into Chinese. Between 1987 and 1992 about 500 books and articles on Western domestic politics were translated from Western languages; during the same period about 3500 translations of works by Western authors and by Chinese authors on Western philosophy were published. The chapter concludes by pointing out the possible emergence of a 'National-Confucianism' in China. According to the author, the rehabilitation of Confucianism in recent years has served a dual purpose: (1) Confucianism means order and obedience to one's superior, devotion to the State, and puts the interests of the group above the interests of the individual and thus helps to promote the desperately needed social order and stability; and (2) Confucianism as an ideology could provide the Chinese people with some sort of national identity. In short, National-Confucianism could serve as a bulwark against the ideological incursions from the West.

In the next chapter Herbert Yee and Wang Jinhong examine grassroots political participation in rural China. The authors describe the socio-economic changes that have been taking place in China's villages since the late 1970s and that have caused the rising aspirations for political participation among the peasants. Defining political participation as an attempt by citizens to influence government policies, Yee and Wang analyse the different channels and methods of influence as well as the motivations and efficacies of political participation in China's villages. Unlike the years of the communes and brigades, when the peasants were mobilized during the mass political campaigns, political participation in the 1980s and 1990s was largely spontaneous. Rapid economic growth brought a new middle, capitalist class and a phenomenal rise of traditional clan and kinship associations in the villages. Yee and Wang argue that the intriguing collaborations between the new wealth and the clan and kinship organizations have played a constructive role in developing the rural economy and maintaining social order and stability in the villages. In the long-run, however, the rise of 'unofficial' organizations may threaten the legitimacy of the official organizations of Party and government.

In Chapter 3, Sonny Lo investigates the problems of corruption and public maladministration and their remedies in China. Lo explains the relationship between corruption and maladministration. According to Lo, there are three major approaches to tackling public maladministration, including various characteristics of poor government, such as abuse of power, mismanagement and bureaucratic corruption. Lo argues that, in the Maoist era, China adopted a political approach to tackling public maladministration. This Maoist approach was an ideological one, focusing on the use of study groups and political campaigns. The unintended consequence of ideologization in Maoist China was that there developed a kind of public service ideology, which was shaped by socialism and which emphasized the necessity of officials to serve the public. Deng Xiaoping, Mao's successor, de-emphasized the role of ideology in tackling maladministration. The Dengist approach to public maladministration tends to focus on managerial and legal aspects. Managerially, civil service reform has been implemented. Legally, administrative laws have been enacted to check the power of 'street-level' bureaucrats. However, managerial and legal reforms in Deng's China encounter political obstacles. The alliance between the capitalists and bureaucrats, the unclear boundary between the private and public sectors, the weaknesses of the anti-corruption organ (Central Discipline Inspection Committee), and the opposition of elites constitute the stumbling blocks for managerial and legal remedies for public maladministration. Ultimately, Lo argues, a third approach that includes political reforms directed towards making the legislature (National People's Congress) more assertive, enhancing the channels for citizen participation, allowing the media more autonomy to criticize the government, and perhaps reactivating part of the Maoist ideological approach, could best tackle the problem of public maladministration in the long run.

In the last chapter of Part I, Carlos Lo examines the legal reform in socialist China since the June-Fourth 1989 Tiananmen Square Incident. The author argues that, despite the tragic outcome of the June-Fourth Incident and the ensuing purge which threatened the very existence of the socialist legal system, once the political fever had subsided and the economic reform had been revived, China managed to return to the track heading for a legal society. This chapter examines the legislative activities, the development of legal institutions, the promotion of the nation's legal awareness, and law enforcement in the post-Tiananmen crisis China. It indicates that China has recorded some significant advances in legislation, legal institutional building and raising the legal awareness of the population. Most of the legislative endeavours have centred on developing a system of economic law for introducing and operating a socialist market economy. Other major areas of legislation include criminal justice, public and social administration, and institutional reform. Institution building has a wide coverage, with efforts to tighten Party control over the judicial system, build a clean and honest image, upgrade the quality of legal personnel, strengthen judicial structures, improve logistic support and institutionalize the lawyers' system. The nation-wide campaign to develop a national legal culture has been intensified with the objective of educating both cadres and the public to manage their activities by means of the law. In the administration of justice, Lo shows that the growth of judicial capacity has lagged behind the actual demand for law implementation. This affects the effectiveness of the legal system. In criminal justice, little success has been recorded as both corruption and criminal activities show no sign of being checked. In the non-criminal sector, the judicial organs have been active in settling administrative, civil and economic disputes.

Chapters in Part II address foreign policy issues. Ting Wai critically examines how China's perception of the United States' role and the latter's perception of the Chinese role in the post-Cold War world order affected the two countries' respective evaluations of Sino–American relations. To what extent are these perceptions influential in the two countries' foreign policy decision-making processes? What kinds of structural constraints of the new international political order are imposed on the future development of Sino–American relations? China's further reforms are in the interests of the United States, which is seeking a comprehensive and constructive engagement with China. The paradox is: China would like to integrate into the global economic system, but she declines to become part of the order dictated by the US. An increasingly prosperous China, facing the challenges and pressure from the West, is becoming more and more self-assertive and nationalistic. Ting argues that difficulties will persist, while limited cooperation may also be possible in the future of Sino–American relations. Issues in the domestic political ecology of the two countries, including the political succession in China, and public opinion in US regarding a democratic Taiwan and the June-Fourth bloodshed in China, could increase uncertainties that affect the policy imperatives of the two governments.

Chen Yu Hsi examines the disputes across the Taiwan straits. Strictly speaking, or at least from the standpoint of Beijing, the Taiwan issue is a matter of domestic politics. Chen provides a discourse on how the disputes over national sovereignty between mainland China and Taiwan have evolved, and seeks to identify the nature and root causes of the disputes in different phases of this evolution in the light of both domestic and international politics. Chen argues that, despite the changes in its mainland policy and political rhetoric, the basic position of the Taiwan government on the sovereignty issue cannot be understood in terms of a dichotomy between reunification and Taiwan independence; the Taiwan government merely wants to maintain the status quo and intends to preserve Taiwan as a distinct political entity separate from the communist-oriented mainland polity. He also points out that the Taiwan government has, since the beginning of the 1990s, shifted its mainland policy towards the 'two-China' model, not only out of a need to improve its relations with the mainland but, more importantly, to lay a legal foundation for democratic political reforms.

Chen argues that the only way Beijing and Taipei can resolve their sovereignty disputes peacefully is to revert to the 'two-China' model. The successful economic development and democratic reforms in Taiwan have enhanced the legitimacy of its political system and the awareness and identity of the 'Republic of China on Taiwan' as a distinct sovereign state, to the extent that both the people and government of Taiwan would refuse to consider peaceful reunification unless Beijing accepts Taipei as a legal government. The author suggests that Beijing should accept the concept of 'sovereignty sharing' and the 'one nation, two political entities' model as proposed by Taipei. He stresses the importance of making mutual political concessions and compromises in the long-term interests of the Chinese nation.

Chapters in Part III address the economic issues. Li Si Ming examines the issue of regional development. Li argues that in China there has been a felt need for rapid industrialization ever since the late nineteenth century. Alongside this and central to the communist ideology, however, are the emphases on egalitarianism and equity. China's massive size, varied physical geography and 5000 years of history suggest that enormous differences exist between regions. An integral part of the egalitarianism agenda is the elimination of spatial disparity. Industrialization, especially the development of capital-intensive 'basic industries', however, requires a concentration of resources in selected urban centres. The spatial reallocation exercise often results in a development strategy that favours not only the urban areas at the expense of the vast rural hinterlands but also regions that are already endowed with resources, especially in terms of industrial and human capital. Adding to the quest for industrialization and the egalitarianism ideology is the concern for national security and integration. China is a country with many 'nationalities'. Some of these, notably the Mongols, Uygurs and Tibetans, have attempted secession.

There is therefore a need, Li argues, to design specific policies that can enhance the cohesiveness of the minority groups, including the transfer of resources from the more developed regions populated by Han Chinese to the frontier regions with large concentrations of minority population.

Li points out that the history of regional development in the PRC is one full of self contradictions and ironies, reflecting competing objectives. At times, as was the case during the Cultural Revolution, it appeared that egalitarian considerations had taken precedence over the drive for industrialization; however, the reality was that, through such means as the household registration system and the 'scissors difference'[3] in pricing, resources continued to be siphoned from the rural areas to the urban centres, and from the lagging interior of the country to the more prosperous coastal provinces. At other times, such as during the late 1980s, there was an obvious policy bias favouring the coastal region; however, the greater autonomy given to the provinces allowed them to exert a greater influence over the flow of resources over space, thus inhibiting the geographical transfer of value. The end result was a rapid decline in the degree of regional income disparity amidst a re-orientation of the national economy towards the outside world. The fiscal reform of 1993 was meant to end the particularistic treatment of individual provinces and to bring about a more equitable distribution of resources over space. Yet the massive inflow of foreign capital since Deng's southern tour of early 1992 has worsened the degree of spatial disparity.

Zhang Xiaohe examines the development of the township and village enterprises (TVEs) and their contributions to China's export growth. The growth of China's rural enterprises had been very impressive in the 1980s and early 1990s. The total output of the township and village enterprises grew at an average annual rate of 30 per cent from 1980 to 1995. In 1994, these enterprises produced about 47 per cent of the national total industrial product and provided employment for 120 million people. The growth of output of the township and village enterprises and their capability to provide employment far exceed those of the state owned enterprises (SOEs). Along with the foreign funded enterprises (FFEs), TVEs have become a main component of the so-called non-state sector. One distinguishing feature of the township and village enterprises is the significant role they played in foreign trade. In 1994, there were more than 130 000 outward-looking TVEs, of which more than 320 firms have been vested with the right of direct international transactions. The export value of the TVEs reached US$40 billion in 1994, accounting for more than one-third of the national total. The participation of these enterprises in international trade greatly contributed to China's export growth.

Two questions are raised by Zhang. First, is the emergence of rural industrial exports a main source of the rapid growth of China's international trade? Second, how and to what extent has the development of TVEs' exports changed China's export composition? Applying standard international trade and development theory, Zhang provides some different insights on these issues, in contrast to previous studies. He attributes the rapid growth of China's labour-intensive exports and radical changes in its export composition to the nature of China's partial economic liberalization in general, and to the features of labour-intensive rural enterprises in particular.

Kenneth Wong examines the tensions between economic growth and environmental protection in China. Beijing incorporated the concept of sustainable development, which demands raising the standard of living of people without incurring uncompensated costs to future generations, in the *Ninth Five-Year Plan (1996–2000) and the Long-term Goals for the Year 2010*. On paper at least, the present regime seems very eager to pursue a policy of sustainable development. However, Wong argues, China's current economic development strategy is still one that takes the increase of gross national product or per capita income as its ultimate goal, a strategy that places its emphasis on quickening the pace of industrialization. Such growth has put even greater pressure on the already meagre resources and fragile environment. Moreover, the current regime regards economic growth as the manifestation of national strength and wealth, and the symbol of national prosperity and national pride. China's dilemma is that it has a huge population but a far smaller slice of the world's resources. For instance, with one fifth of the world's population, China has only 7 per cent of its fresh water and cropland, 3 per cent of its forests, and 2 per cent of its oil. According to the current trend of China's economic development, it can no longer rely solely on its own resources to sustain its economic growth. It will inevitably impose pressure on world resources. Wong comments on some of the sustainable development programmes put forward by the Chinese government in recent years. He argues that if China does not want to be trapped into the unreconcilable conflict between economic growth and environmental protection, it must pursue a policy of steady, sustainable and balanced development.

Part IV addresses the social issues. Luk Tak Chuen examines rural poverty and the Chinese Government's poverty alleviation policies. The Chinese Government pronounced a mission in 1994 to raise the living standards of the poorest 65 million of the population to acceptable levels by the year 2000. With the National Seven Year Poverty Eradication Programme, a series of poverty alleviation policies had been formulated to mobilize the various bureaucracies as well as the public to participate in this campaign. Luk, however, argues that the effectiveness of these anti-poverty programmes is severely handicapped by bureaucratic decentralization, bureaucratism, and the onslaught of the market economy in Chinese state socialism. The chapter explores how politics and economics enter into the process of poverty definition, policy formulation and implementation of poverty alleviation programmes, and thus affect the effectiveness of these anti-poverty efforts.

According to Luk, the obscure and unsystematic official poverty line prevents the Chinese Government from obtaining accurate measures of poverty. The Chinese Government does not make clear the rationale behind the standard of poverty definition. The standard of the official poverty line that China adopts is far below the international convention of absolute poverty; the number of the poor is severely underestimated. The official poverty line even fails to take inflation into account and cannot reflect change in the size of the poor population amidst the raging inflation of recent years. The obscure and unsystematic definition of poverty allows the central government and related bureaucracies to manipulate the numbers of the poor for administrative as well as political purposes. Amidst market reform and bureaucratic decentralization, the poverty alleviation programmes do not regulate the regional inequalities, but instead strengthen the disparities by administrative intervention. Loans and grants are channeled to industries rather than to agriculture, to better-off regions and better-off households rather than to the needy households and regions. Poverty alleviation programmes leave the poorest peasant households and regions untouched and even worse off amidst the inflationary pressures of market reform. Moreover, bureaucratic politics hinders the effectiveness of poverty alleviation programmes. The large numbers of ministries, mass organizations and various levels of bureaucracies taking part do not constitute a concerted campaign against poverty. The multiplicity of bureaucracies involved fragment authority in the formulation and implementation of poverty alleviation programmes.

Siu Yat Ming examines the issue of China's birth planning policies. The population of China was estimated to be 542 million at the founding of the People's Republic in 1949; that figure was more than doubled when the fourth census was taken in 1990 with the count then recorded at 1134 million. The number passed the 1.2 billion mark in 1995. This figure, though large in size, was smaller than that expected by many demographers and China observers. The major reason for this low figure was the reduction in the rate of natural increase as a result of the declining birth rate, despite the increase in the number of women at their prime child-bearing age. The major cause of China's fertility decline can be attributed to the continuing success of the state-operated birth planning programme. Since the implementation of the national birth planning programme in 1973, about 300 million births had been averted by 1995. Siu analyses the evolution of China's birth planning policies since the 1950s in the political and social context. It was not until the early 1970s that a consensus on the population problem was reached in the Chinese government. A nationwide birth planning programme was then implemented, leading to an unprecedented rapid decline in fertility. Despite the changing economic conditions and declining fertility, the present tightened policies of birth control are not likely to change.

The author points out, however, that there are two major demographic consequences accompanying the fertility decline. One is the rapid ageing of the population, which is an unavoidable consequence of rapid fertility decline. This problem is particularly acute in China because the speed of the fertility decline is much faster than that experienced by the more developed countries, and China's economy is not sufficiently developed to provide old-age security to all needy persons. The other demographic consequence is the increasing imbalance in the sex ratio in young children, especially in babies, starting from the 1980s. There were numerous reports of female infanticides. Pre-natal sex determination and sex-selective abortion have been widely practiced since the mid-1980s. The underlying reason for this change in the male/female ratio in favour of males is a limit on the number of children one can have in a culture in which sons have been preferred.

DAVID C. B. TEATHER
HERBERT S. YEE

Notes and References

1. See, for example, William H. Overholt, *The Rise of China: How Economic Reform is Creating a New Superpower* (New York & London: W. W. Norton, 1993); and Laurence J. Brahm, *China is No. 1: The New Superpower Takes Centre Stage* (Singapore: Butterworth-Heinemann Asia, 1996).
2. Yan Sun, *The Chinese Reassessment of Socialism, 1976–1992* (Princeton, New Jersey: Princeton University Press, 1995).
3. Before economic reforms, the Chinese Government treated the agricultural sector as a source of surplus products for industrialization. The price of agricultural products was set at a low level while the price of industrial products was set at a high level; this is called the 'scissors difference'.

Part I
Political and Legal Issues

1 New Intellectual Currents in the People's Republic of China

Werner Meissner

Since the 1980s the intellectual development in the People's Republic of China has been characterized by several deep changes related to the opening up of the country towards the West. These changes have been so profound, compared with the time after 1949 that it is not exaggerating to speak of a new period in the history of Chinese thought. For a better understanding of this development a brief survey of the periods of intellectual development before 1978 is necessary.

INTELLECTUAL DEVELOPMENTS BEFORE 1978

Since the middle of the last century, the intellectual history in China has been characterized by an oscillation between rejection and acceptance of Western thought as it has developed in the sciences and parts of philosophy since the European Renaissance. This process of rejection and convergence, of the related attempts either to keep Western thought away from China or selectively to integrate parts of it into the traditional world view, or to dismiss this world view in the course of reception, took place in five historical phases.

The first phase comprises the period from the middle of the nineteenth century up to 1895. During this period, the attempt was made primarily to adopt the military technology and the knowledge for the establishment of an industrial infrastructure. The political leadership had still not perceived the background to the military and economic strength of the West at that time. A reception of the political ideas of the West did not take place. The failure of this *partial* and at the same time conservative modernization was expressed in the defeat in the war against Japan in 1894.

In the second phase, from 1895 to the revolution in 1911, parts of the political leadership had by this time recognized that the military of the West was not just founded on its technology but also on its political systems, and that the two areas obviously belonged together. As a result, the ideas of constitutional monarchy, of parliamentarianism and nationalism met with their first response in China. The country experienced the first attempts at political and institutional reforms: The *Reform of 100 Days* of 1898, the abolition of the examination system in 1905 and the attempts to introduce a constitutional monarchy at the end of the dynasty. Yet these attempts at political reform were unsuccessful, and the development ended with the fall of the Qing Dynasty and the establishment of the Republic in 1911.

The third phase from 1912 to 1949, that is the period of the first Chinese republic, brought for many Chinese intellectuals the realization that the reasons for the military and economic strength of the Western nations lay much deeper, namely in the development of logical and analytical thought in Europe since the Renaissance, above all in the fields of the natural sciences and of political philosophy.

In the twenties, a main stream of interest thus began to focus on the fundamental differences between Western and Chinese thought, between Western and Chinese culture. Many Chinese intellectuals were convinced that the answer to the Western challenge could only lie in a completely open confrontation with all aspects of Western thought. Indeed this should comprise, if possible, a comprehensive 'scientification' (*kexuehua*) of Chinese thought and a complete 'Westernization' (*quanpan xihua*) of Chinese culture, as they called it. In the subsequent intellectual controversies of the 1920s (controversies concerning 'Eastern and Western culture' and concerning 'science and view of life', 1922–3), these ideas were the subject of an extremely intense discussion. To use a popular expression, these were the 'Golden Twenties' in China as far as the free discussion and examination of Western ideas was concerned. As a result of the dictatorship of the national government and the implementation of Sunyatsenism as the state ideology, with the civil war between the Communists and the Nationalists, and also as a result of the Sino–Japanese War 1937–1945, the discussion abated in the thirties to fall almost totally silent after the Second World War.

The fourth phase of the encounter with the West followed the triumph of Chinese communism. It stretches from 1949 to about 1976, the year Mao Zedong died. Firstly, it was marked by a comprehensive eradication of the remnants still present of the political ideas of middle-class liberalism and of Western influence. The numerous and often bloody 'mass campaigns' among the intellectuals primarily served this purpose. Secondly, it was characterized by the institutionalisation of Maoism as the new state orthodoxy. Maoism and Marxism-Leninism formed the ideological counterpart of the re-established central state. Their writings, raised to the status of a canon, contained the ideology of the new centralist bureaucracy. Thirdly, the Soviet model of development was extensively adopted in the fields of economy, the military and culture at the same time. From around 1957, the country then began to loosen itself from the Soviet model and to go a Maoist special way to Socialism, which found its provisional climax in the catastrophe of the 'Great Leap Forward' in 1958 and the 'Great Proletarian Cultural Revolution' between 1966 and 1969.

The fifth period began at the end of the seventies, and again aimed at a cautious opening up to the West. It is connected with the concept of the 'Four Modernizations' (*sige xiandaihua*), that is the modernization of agriculture, of industry, of science and technology, and of the military. In this context the Chinese leadership determined that certain areas were not to be modernized at all or were excluded in principle: the political system, the prevailing structure of ownership, the ruling ideology and the one-party dictatorship. This was called by Deng Xiaoping the 'Four Cardinal Principles' (*sixiang jiben yuanze*).[1]

Deng Xiaoping's ideology was thus again an attempt at *partial* modernization, initiated and implemented from above, while at the same time this modernization should only be carried through within the frame-work defined by the 'Four Cardinal Principles'.

It cannot be ruled out that the period from 1978 to 1989 has only been an interlude, and that with the suppression of the Democracy Movement in Beijing and other Chinese cities in June 1989 we are on the verge of a new phase.

In the first three periods, that is from the second half of the nineteenth century up to 1949, four main ideological currents were developed in principle, all of which essentially sought to answer the same question: how the cultural, economic and military challenge from the West should best be encountered, and in what areas modernization should take place:

Traditionalism and neo-traditionalism. This was represented by orthodox Confucians such as Zeng Guofan (Tseng Kuo-fan), reform Confucians such as Kang Youwei (K'ang Yu-wei) and adherents of Neo-Confucianism such as Zhang Junmai (Chang Chün-mai). Their attitude towards Western ideas ranged from rejection to a limited readiness to receive.

The adherents of Western sciences. To this group belonged in particular Hu Shi (Hu Shih), the main representative of a political liberalization in conjunction with American pragmatism, the geologist Ding Wenjiang (Ting Wen-chiang) and large numbers of the students educated in England and America. They all stood for a radical criticism of the cultural heritage and for the 'scientification' (*kexuehua)* of Chinese thought. I would therefore like to designate them as adherents of *universal* modernization.

Sunyatsenism, the state ideology of the National People's Party under Sun Yat-sen and later Chiang Kai-shek. It represents up to now the only self-contained system which sought to unite both Confucian elements and elements of Western parliamentarianism and the constitutional state in a national state ideology and which was in a position to establish a military and political power base.

Socialism, anarchism and finally Chinese Communism. In particular the latter, characterized in its Chinese form as 'Mao Zedong ideas' (*Mao Zedong ssu-hsiang*), stood for a comprehensive rejection of and fight against both the intellectual and cultural heritage – above all Confucianism, Buddhism and Taoism – as well as Western influence, with the exception of Marxism, Marxism-Leninism and the natural sciences.

INTELLECTUAL DEVELOPMENTS SINCE THE 1980s

Between 1949 and 1978 the prevailing ideology had been of course Marxism-Leninism/Mao Zedong-thought or what the party-ideologists understood by Marxism. During this period and compared with the development in the West, the intellectual life in China looked like a desert, controlled by Maoism.

Since the beginning of the 1980s the policy of 'Four Modernizations' triggered a completely unexpected new move to adopt Western thought. Furthermore, the 1980s showed a striking renaissance of the ideological currents of the 1920s and 1930s. But it also is no exaggeration to say, that by virtue of a tremendous effort the Chinese intellectuals have been successful in getting a far-reaching overview of the main currents and fields of Western thought and ideologies within a few years.

One can establish the following five main currents which shaped the intellectual developments since the 1980s. These five currents took place before the backdrop of the successive decline of Maoism:

(1) the renaissance of Western non-Marxist philosophy; (2) the renaissance of political science; (3) the revival of political liberalism and the idea of 'complete Westernization' (*quanpanxihua)*; (4) the emergence of neo-authoritarianism (*xin quanwei zhuyi*); (5) the renaissance of Chinese traditional philosophy and the emergence of Neo-Conservatism.

(1) The renaissance of non-Marxist Western philosophy

Since the 1980s, several bibliographies of Chinese publications on Western culture, politics and economy appeared, which for the first time provided statistical material about the deep intellectual changes taking place among Chinese intellectuals.[2] While the influence of the philosophy of Marx and Engels declined since the 1980s, according to these findings, that of non-Marxist German philosophy is on the increase. Though around 5,700 books and essays still appeared on Marx and Engels in the period from 1970 to 1984, in the 1980s the figures for publications of non-Marxist German philosophy suddenly exploded. To give only an idea of the quantities:

Up to 1984, around 1700 books and essays were published in Chinese on German idealism, mainly on Kant, Hegel and Fichte. These figures include translations of works by German philosophers, translations of works by Western authors on German philosophy and works by Chinese authors on German philosophy. About 900 titles alone came from the years 1985/86. In 1986 about 300 titles were published on Hegel.[3]

New research studies indicate the following development: From 1987 to 1992 the number of translations and related Chinese publications about Western philosophy lay between 3500 and 3800 covering all systems of thought in Western philosophy (Marxism, Leninism not included), including Greek philosophy as well as French existentialism and modern American pragmatists. Half of these publications focused on German idealistic philosophy, mainly the idealism of Kant, Hegel and Fichte.[4] This was due in part to the fact that after 1949 German idealism, in particular the philosophy of Hegel, could survive in the shadow of Marxism-Leninism. Many manuscripts on German idealism which could not be published before 1978 were suddenly available for printing at the beginning of the eighties and flooded the book shops.

Still on top between 1987 and 1992 was Hegel with 292 titles, followed by Kant with 233, Nietzsche (87), Heidegger (66), Popper (64),

Wittgenstein (47), Schopenhauer (39), Husserl (35), Feuerbach (35), Gadamer (29), Fichte (27), Einstein (26), Leibniz (18), Habermas (18), Cassirer (18), Mach (17), Jaspers (15), Frege (8), Gödel (8), Schelling (8), Dilthey (7), Adorno (6), Carnap (6) and others.

Furthermore, about 240 studies on Sigmund Freud, Ernst Fromm, C.G. Jung and Alfred Adler were published during the same period. Although not philosophers in the narrow sense, these authors contributed greatly to a 'philosophy of life' with their psychoanalytical approach. Freud accounted for 146 publications (incl. 16 translations of Freud's books), Fromm for 67 (24 translations of Fromm's books) and Jung 29 (11 translations of Jung's books).

Among the other Western philosophers Sartre (72), Plato (34), Aristotle (33) and Hume (33) seem to be the most prominent thinkers. They are followed by Russell (28), Spinoza (25), Descartes (22), Rousseau (21), Locke (20), Piaget (16), Francis Bacon (15), Gramsci (14), Comte (14), Bergson (13), Derrida (13), Berkeley (12), Heraclitus (11), Quine (11), Rorty (11), Dewey (10), Montesquieu (10), Parmenides (9), Ayer (8), Foucault (8), Kuhn (8), Rawls (8), Diderot (7), Socrates (7), Hobbes (6) among others.

In addition, the number of publications covering more than one philosopher or specific aspects of philosophy came to about 850, among them 180 comprehensive surveys, multi-subject biographies, numerous textbooks and fourteen dictionaries of philosophy.

Besides the many general introductions to Western philosophy in general and to German, French, English and American philosophy in particular, several fields of greater interest could be identified: Three major focuses of interest were the fields of aesthetics, philosophy of language and logic. Besides some general introductions (among them six volumes on the history of Western aesthetics containing more than 5000 pages), there are 50 studies on aesthetics, including one dictionary. Philosophy of language accounts for more than 40 studies, and philosophical logic for 23 titles.

Another main field was comparative studies. 54 studies alone discussed the differences between Western and Chinese philosophy. Some focused on the general differences between the two philosophies and cultures, others compared Chinese and Western philosophers: Confucius and Mencius with Protagoras, Socrates, Plato, Aristotle and Kant; Zhuangzi with Sartre; Xun Zi with Hegel; Lu Jiuyuan with Berkeley; Zhang Zai with Spinoza; Wang Fuzhi and Yan Yu with Kant, Yan Yuan with William James, Hu Shi with Gadamer; Zhuangzi with Nietzsche. Three studies investigated the differences between Heidegger and Zhuangzi. Of course, the question regarding the depths of these comparative studies cannot be answered here, but the figures and titles show a rising tendency to investigate the differences between Chinese and Western philosophy.[5]

Besides these general currents in modern Chinese philosophy we can observe a very interesting one which is of some political relevance: the rising popularity of Karl Popper and his philosophy. Popper as well as logical positivism has become more and more influential among Chinese intellectuals. A seminar on Karl Popper was held in Wuhan as early as 1987. At that time, the basic interpretation of his philosophy was given by Fan Dainien from the Chinese Academy of Social Sciences: the modernisation of China, the build-up of 'socialism with Chinese characteristics', should follow the theoretical approaches of Popper, in particular his piecemeal social engineering, as opposed to the former utopian social engineering of the party.[6] More than 100 translations of and studies on Popper and his ideas have already been published. The book which is regarded as very important among the philosophical departments of the universities of China is his 'The open society and its enemies', in which Popper sharply criticises the philosophy of Marxism as a closed system of thought.

Besides Popper, the philosophy of the Vienna Circle recently experienced a comeback in China. Tscha Hung (Hong Qian), the Chinese representative of the Vienna Circle, was rehabilitated in the late eighties. In 1994, an international conference was organised by the Chinese Academy of Social Sciences in memory of Tscha Hung, who died in 1992. This conference focused not only on Tscha Hung and his contribution to modern Chinese philosophy, but covered all aspects of modern Western, in particular analytic philosophy, with the exception of Marxism.[7]

If it is true that Popper as well as the ideas of the Vienna Circle are becoming more and more popular among Chinese intellectuals, then there is reason to hope that these methods of thought will balance the influence of the more conservative and traditionalist currents in the future.

In all Leninist one-party-systems, philosophy (*zhexue*) is a politically highly sensitive matter. Because communist parties do not legitimise their rule by elections but by the pretension to an allegedly true world view, Marxism-Leninism, philosophical discourses on this world view tend to be a reflection of differences within the party and/or between the party and the intellectuals. The development of philosophy in the People's Republic of China thus affords an insight into the development of the political system. Philosophical controversies can serve as an indication of ongoing conflicts within the political leadership. In this respect articles and books on philosophy published in Hong Kong or Taiwan have to be treated differently from those published on the mainland.

Since Chinese intellectuals have always had a strong alignment with the state, in the past as well as in the present, the question arises: is there a possible political implication of this adoption of Western thought? I believe, there is.

In general, the huge number of publications on Western philosophy as well as on Western political science (see below) clearly indicates that the political movements against the government in 1986, which took tens of thousands of students on to the streets, as well as in 1989 were also *outward* manifestations of the deep changes *within* the consciousness of many Chinese intellectuals. While Marxism-Leninism and Maoism still prevailed on the surface, the foundations of other systems of thought had already been laid down and had started to exert their long-lasting influence. This is the general political importance of the study of Western modes of thinking since the 1980s.

Besides these long-lasting effects there was also one aspect that was tied to the specific political situation in the 1980s. The general adoption of Western philosophy was linked with certain political motives and thus utilized for political purposes. This can be demonstrated by the debates since the beginning of the 1980s when certain ideas were picked up by Chinese scholars who, after the death of Mao, tried to develop orthodox Marxism-Leninism into a more liberal form.

One debate which should serve as an example was the debate on Kant's philosophy. After the basic writings of this German philosopher had been translated, scholars such as He Lin, Wang Ruowang and Li Zehou picked up in particular on Kant's idea of *humanism (rendaozhuyi)* and discussed *the value of man in socialism*. According to Kant, man is an end in itself, he is the aim *(ren shi mudi)*, he has an independent value and cannot be used for any purpose. The discussion on Kant's idea of humanism was a sharp criticism of the party and its politics towards the intellectuals, their rights and role in the society. The political character of the debate became obvious when Zhou Yang, a former orthodox Marxist and the President of the All Chinese Writer's Union since 1978, published an article on Kant in the *People's Daily* in which he supported the arguments of the intellectuals.[8] What was the political core of the debate? While picking up Kant's idea of humanity, the intellectuals questioned the class character of Marxist ethics and thus established the idea of independent human rights and individualism.

The party's answer was the campaign against the so-called *spiritual pollution (chingshen wuran)* in 1983 to bring the intellectuals back on the right track. It attacked mainly the theory of Kant's humanism and bourgeois liberal ideas such as love, liberty, democracy and individualism.[9]

In the context of the debates in the 1980s the ideas taken from German idealistic philosophy for example, were utilized in three ways:

(1) Many intellectuals at the philosophical institutes aimed at a gradual reform of Marxism without risking a break with the party. Kant's, Hegel's and Fichte's ideas about the freedom of thought served to legitimise the claims of many intellectuals. By referring to the ideas of the German idealists they demanded more freedom for the intellectuals. At the same time, they emphasized their traditional role as scholars, whose main function was to educate the people and to serve the state. They thus presented a moderate non-Marxist position which offered ideological support for the reform faction within the party.

(2) The demand for more freedom did not necessarily mean that these intellectuals were adherents of Western liberalism: on the contrary, the articles by the Hegel specialist He Lin and the Fichte specialist Liang Zhixue in the 1980s indicated that the discussion of the concepts of state and nation in Hegel and Fichte served to underline a traditionalist position among more conservative Chinese intellectuals against the threat of 'complete Westernisation' and Western liberalism. As far as Chinese foreign policy was concerned, Fichte, because of his role in German history, served as an example for Chinese nationalism and 'anti-hegemonism' (Germany against France at the beginning of the nineteenth century, now China against the US).[10]

By emphasizing the importance of the ideas of state and nation as documented in Hegel and Fichte the intellectuals indicated their allegiance towards the party and the central state probably to placate the conservative faction. It is in this political context that the impressive preoccupation with German idealistic philosophy was given its special political meaning.

(3) After 1989, the traditionalist and anti-Western interpretation of German idealism, in particular of Hegel, seemed to become even more important. Hegel's basic ideas of 'world reason' and the 'absolute' were compared with the Neo-Confucianist's Zhu Xi main ideas: with *li* (the principle of order) and *taiji* (the ultimate),[11] and similar to the discussions in the 1930s, Hegel was again used as a witness for the values of Neo-Confucian, traditional philosophy.[12]

(2) The renaissance of political science

One of the most interesting intellectual developments in the 1980s was the emergence or, better, the comeback of political science in China. This comeback contributed much to the theoretical foundation of the new currents of thought.

Political science was first introduced in China in 1903, when this discipline was taught at the later Beijing University. In 1932 there already existed a political scientists association which in 1946 had about 140 members, and in 1948 more than 40 departments of political science were counted at Chinese universities.[13]

This situation changed dramatically in 1952. When the communists restructured the educational system, political science was eliminated and Marxism-Leninism and Mao Zedong Thought were introduced in its place. Independent political research thus ceased to exist. It was only in the wake of the 'Four Modernizations' that the party rediscovered the value of this discipline and hoped that it could serve the modernization of China like Western investments and know-how.

In 1979 the Political Science Research Institute was established at the Chinese Academy of Social Sciences (CASS), and in 1986 the association of Chinese political scientists joined the International Political Scientists Association (IPSA). Western political science departments and their Chinese counterparts set up large exchange programmes in which numerous Western political scientists went to China as visiting scholars and their Chinese counterparts were invited to Western universities. On the American side we find the names of David Apter, David Easton, Samuel Huntington, Robert Salisbury, Robert Scalapino, Marc Petracca, and on the German side Klaus von Beyme. Compared with other countries the relations between Chinese and American political scientists were the most intensive.[14]

Until 4 June 1989 the discipline played an important role in adopting Western political ideas and methods of political science and in formulating the fundamental ideas for the political modernization in the 1980. On the one hand political science was still based on official ideology as one can see from the numerous handbooks,[15] on the other hand the new academic freedom made it possible for Western ideas of multi-party system, constitutional state, and parliamentarianism to spread among the scholars and students. However, with the suppression of the Democracy Movement in 1989 many political scientists went abroad, among them Yan Jiaqi, director of the Institute of Political Science at the Chinese Academy of Social Sciences and adviser to former CCP general secretary Zhao Ziyang. Students at the departments of political science were re-educated, and the number of students at the departments was cut down by half. In addition, syllabuses were redrafted, ideological control was tightened, and the publication of journals and magazines like *Political Science in Foreign Countries (Guowai zhengzhixue)* and *Political Studies (Zhengzhi yanjiu)* was stopped. All these measures led to a more or less complete suspension of teaching of and research into Western political science in China.

According to recent research findings a large number of books and articles on Western politics was translated in the 1980s and an even greater number of Chinese studies in Western politics was published.

Between 1987 and 1992 about 500 books and articles on Western domestic politics were translated from Western languages. In addition more than 900 Chinese studies were published.[16] One can proceed from the assumption that this development started in the early 1980s and accelerated in the following years.

In July 1989 there was a sharp drop in the number of publications due to the political development. While in the first six months of 1989, 227 books and articles were published, the figure fell to only 60 between July and December 1989, due to the political events on July 4. Surprisingly, the years 1991 and 1992 showed a recovery with respect to publications on Western domestic politics: In 1991 the figure went up to 132 and in 1992 it was 164.[17]

The origins of the translated books and articles published between 1987 and 1992 reveal the main areas of interest:

USA	221	(books: 48; articles 173)
Germany	68	(books: 8; articles 60)
Great Britain	54	(books: 14; articles: 40)
France	27	(books: 6; articles 21)
Italy	13	(books: 2; articles: 11)
Others[18]	111	(books: 10; articles: 101)

A further breakup of the translations together with the about 900 Chinese independent studies shows the key areas of interest:

Western political philosophy, political theory, political science (Marxism-Leninism not included)	571
State and government	503

Western political parties	185
Western social systems (including social security system, labour unions etc.)	115[19]

The main interest during the period 1987-92 was on American political science and the government system of the USA – 135 books and articles were published on the government system of the USA alone. With respect to Western political parties, the main focus was on the Socialist and Social-Democratic parties of Western Europe, in particular the German Social Democrats, the Swedish Social Democrats and the French Socialist Party. Regarding the social system, the Chinese scholars looked mainly at the German and Swedish models of social security and the welfare state.

The areas of interests, which appeared in the translations as well as in the independent Chinese studies, reflected certain directions in the thoughts of the Chinese scholars. Looking for foreign models which could help to modernize the political system of the PRC, the government system and the state structure of the USA seemed to be most important. On the other hand, with respect to the political parties, the Western Social Democrats appeared as an orientation, probably because they had a Marxist background and finally managed to convert themselves into democratic parties which were able to form the government, as for example the Swedish and German Social Democrats and the French Socialists.

(3) The revival of political liberalism and the idea of 'complete Westernization'

Counted among the currents of the twenties that have returned in the eighties are, first, Chinese liberalism in the tradition of Hu Shi but also the ideas of federalism. In the 1980s these are associated with the astrophysicist and dissident Fang Lizhi, whose pragmatic political - statements on the merits of the parliamentary multi-party system could also have come from the mouth of Hu Shi.[20]

Fang's demand for 'complete Westernization' in his famous speech in November 1986 and his remarks on multi-party-system and Western democracy as a model also for China are very similar to the ideas of Hu Shi. Fang did not only challenge one-party-rule, he went even further and called for a complete abolition of Marxism.

Furthermore Fang, as did the liberal intellectuals in the 1920s and 1930s, called for a 'complete Westernization'. Political liberalism, the ideas of parliamentarianism, of the state founded on the rule of law and of human rights achieved in the 1920s and 1930s a first, though very limited effectiveness. At that time, the liberal intellectuals already understood the modernisation of China, the adoption of the Western sciences and the dissemination of liberal ideas as a uniform and interrelated process.

In an official criticism of Fang's book *Philosophy is an Instrument of Physics*,[21] which appeared in 1985, it became clear that the orthodoxies in the Communist Party of China unwaveringly hold on to the leading role of (Marxist) philosophy in the sciences, whereas Fang wished to see philosophy only in a service function towards the latter. Hiding behind that however was nothing other than the question about the claim to leadership of Marxist philosophy or of the ruling state ideology and thus also about the party's exclusive claim to leadership.

Comparable structures of philosophical discourse could already be found in the 'Controversy on Science and Metaphysics' in the twenties, at least it was a question at that time of the opposition between idealistic philosophy and science, and in the thirties in the controversy about dialectic materialism. Here, too, the discussion on the leading role of philosophy with regard to the sciences was a reflection of the conflict about the leading role of the Communist Party of China in Chinese society in general and in the united fronts with the Guomindang (Kuomintang) in particular.[22] But it can also be said in general that the emphasis on the supremacy of (Marxist) philosophy over the sciences is only the communist variation of the classical *ti-yong* concept from the end of the nineteenth century.

A further current of the 1920s and 1930s was the 'New Enlightenment Movement' (*xinqimeng yundong*), in which both liberals and leftist intellectuals took part at that time. It was born out of the 'May Fourth Movement' and felt itself especially indebted to the ideas of the French enlightenment. In the eighties, the enlightening potential crystallized in Beijing around the 'Salon New Enlightenment' (*xinqimeng shalong*), whose members are said to have included, alongside Fang Lizhi, Zhao Ziyang's adviser Yan Jiaqi.[23]

The discussions about federalism also represented a resumption of a theme from the twenties.[24] Federalist ideas in China had their roots in the debates in the Qing Dynasty and in the conceptions discussed in the sixteenth and seventeenth centuries in Gu Yuanwu (Ku Yen-wu), Huang Zongxi (Huang Tsung-hsi) and others on the advantages of regional autonomy over military centralism *(junxian zhidu)*. They were taken up again at the beginning of the twenties when Hu Shi came out in favour of a federation of self-governing provinces (*liansheng zizhi*).[25] The renewed discussion about federalist structures showed, just as the return of philosophical ideas from the twenties, that not only the rule of the Communist Party of China but also the political system of the Chinese central state in its form up to now was being called fundamentally into question.

The discussions concerning liberalism, enlightenment, federalism and even about human rights were all connected with the similarly discussed question of 'complete Westernization' (*quanpan xihua*). The dispute about the supposed necessity of China's Westernization, or about the similarly asserted necessity of going one's own path independently of the West, was not limited to the twenties, but was also continued in the 1930s.

From 1933 to 1935 there took place among Chinese sociologists an up to now little considered controversy on 'complete westernization.'[26] As in the twenties in Zhang Junmai, the well-known argument could be found here among the opponents that the duty was to connect the Chinese (special) path (*dao*) with Western instruments (*qi*), preserve the national characteristics (*guoqing*), and shape Chinese culture on a Chinese foundation (*zhongguo benwei wenhua*).[27]

The arguments strike one as familiar not only from Chinese history; the fear of 'Westernization' – of liberalism, capitalism and generally of 'Americanization' – is obviously a basic pattern in many traditional societies' behaviour in response to modernization.

(4) The ideology of neo-authoritarianism (*xin quanwei zhuyi*)

Neo-authoritarianism developed from 1986 to 1989 and was probably influenced by the theories of Samuel Huntington, Guillermo O'Donnel and others on the transformation of developing countries into market economies.[28]

The main points of 'neo-authoritarianism' can be summarized as follows:[29]

(1) The modernization of the economy and of the political system cannot be carried out at the same time and at the same pace. Before political modernization can take place, economic modernization has to be realized.

(2) Economic as well as political modernization is possible only through authoritarian rule. In this the neo-authoritarians looked at

the successful modernization in Taiwan, South Korea and even Hong Kong. They thought neo-authoritarianism as some kind of 'tutelary democracy', developed by the American sociologist, Edward Shils.[30]

(3) China needed in the eyes of the neo-authoritarians political stability and order. Without political stability and order, modernization was not possible. Therefore they advocated the strengthening of the central political power as long as market economy was introduced. Their favoured 'strong man', who should serve as an 'enlightened leader', was Zhao Ziyang, the then party general secretary.

Some of the neo-authoritarians saw the development of the PR China in the following political perspective shown below:

Tradition	*Transition*	*The future*
Planned economy	Crisis (inflation)	Market economy
Autocracy	Corruption	Democratization
Cultural uniformity	Crisis in faith	Pluralism
Rule by man (Mao)	Disorder	Rule of law[31]

From this table it becomes clear that the neo-authoritarians, though belonging originally to the Marxist camp, were at least in favour of Western style democracy. They advocated a strong and efficient bureaucracy and military. In terms of ideology, they promoted traditional culture as the foundation of national spirit. In addition, they would foster capitalism and science in China and adopt an open-door policy to the West. From these economic, political, social and cultural policies a middle class would emerge in China as a precondition for the establishment of a multi-party system, of political pluralism, the rule of law and finally democracy.

However, the neo-authoritarians were never able to answer the questions: What will happen if the new powerful leader were to degenerate into a cruel dictator? And what could be done to ensure that the new-authoritarian government does not turn into a new dictatorship? They proceeded from the wrong assumption that economic development would necessarily lead to political democracy. They did not realize that there is no necessary contradiction between economic growth and political autocracy. And finally, Western democracy was not possible without the enlightenment movement and the strong commitment of the Western bourgeoisie to democratic ideas. Thus the emergence of democracy was a product of the integration of economic development and democratic ideas.[32]

(5) The renaissance of Chinese traditional philosophy and the emergence of neo-conservatism

In most post-Leninist countries we can observe a strong renaissance of traditionalist thought. Frequently this is linked to nationalistic and ethnic or even racist tendencies. Furthermore, strong tendencies towards re-traditionalization can be observed in non-communist countries too, in particular in the Islamic world, where anti-western movements are on the advance.

The renaissance of traditional political thought in China started around 1986 under the guidance of the Communist Party. The member of the state council, Gu Mu, became the chairman of the newly founded Confucian society. Since 1986 an uncountable number of studies on Confucianism and Taoism have been published. A further indication of the traditional current were three international symposia on Confucianism in the beginning of October 1989, only three months after the crackdown on the Democracy-movement, where more than 300 scientists and adherents of Confucianism came together, some even from Taiwan.

The speeches delivered by high cadres, Jiang Zemin, Gu Mu and others, at the symposiums revealed that the political leadership clearly functionalized traditional concepts in order to broaden its dwindling political legitimization. Confucianism became an instrument to counter Western influence. It was now part of a traditionalist cultural nationalism.[33] The ideas of Confucianism were not regarded as an objective but as an instrument.

Furthermore, between 1986 and 1989 more then 300 articles were published on the modern Neo-Confucianism, represented by Feng Youlan (Feng Yu-lan), Tang Junyi (T'ang Chün-yi), Mou Zongsan (Mou Tsung-san) and Du Weiming (Tu Wei-ming). This renaissance of Confucian thought can contribute to solving the problems of cultural identity, which necessarily arise during rapid modernization. On the other hand, similar to the intellectual situation in the twenties and thirties, modern Neo-Confucianism of the 1980s also shows a clear tendency opposed to Western political liberalism. For the Chinese Communist Party, Neo-Confucianism thus has a clear function: Its authoritarian aspects can be used to build the 'socialist spiritual civilization' and to defend Chinese culture against the so-called threat of 'Westernization'.[34] And since its centralist doctrines, mainly the *Li* formulated by Zhu Xi, the founder of traditional Neo-Confucianism in the twelvth century, had served to legitimize the centralist and bureaucratic rule of the Ming – as well as of the Qing-dynasty in the past – why shouldn't they in the present? At an international congress in November 1990 in Beijing, Zhu Xi, once an ideological archenemy of the Chinese Communists, thus was finally rehabilitated. And the international symposium in Xi'an, also in November 1990, on China's modernization and Chinese traditional culture, not only re-established Confucianism as a means to check the social and political effects of modernization, but as a national ideology.[35]

The rehabilitation of traditional culture, in particular Confucianism, served a dual purpose: Confucianism means order and obedience to one's superior, the devotion to the state, and the protection of the family. It puts the interests of the group above the interests of the individual and thus helps to promote the desperately needed social order and stability. And secondly, Confucianism as a Chinese ideology could help to provide the people with some sort of national identity. National-Confucianism could serve as a bulwark against the ideological impacts from the West following the rapid modernization.[36]

The latest ideological current is neo-conservatism. There are three reasons for the rise of neo-conservatism in China: the collapse of the Soviet Union, the emergence of a new class of government or cadre capitalists, and the rise of nationalism.

Due to the political developments in the former Soviet Union many intellectuals who originally belonged to the neo-authoritarians dissociated themselves from the ideas of Western democracy. They were disappointed with the results of the Democracy Movement and seemed to have started cooperating with policy-makers in the government. These intellectuals had no reservations about the current regime or any criticism of it. They are called the neo-conservatives or neo-realists.[37] They support the government in its efforts to strengthen the power of the centre. To this group belong the professors like Hu Angang and Wang Shaoguang, who studied in the USA, and who are working on how to tackle the problems of regionalization in the country.[38] Xiao Gongqing, in the past a leading theorist of neo-authoritarianism already mentioned above, turned to this neo-conservatism too. Although the Neo-Conservatives seem to follow the mainstream of Western economic and sociological theory, advocate gradualism and oppose any sudden changes, they seem to belong to the general stream of nationalist thinking in China, that has started to dominate Chinese intellectual life.

CONCLUSION

After more than forty years of communist rule, we can now observe the build-up of two basic political positions, which might be the dominating political movements in the future. Both of these can to a certain extent refer to traditions in Chinese thought.

At any rate we have to note that in the 1980s there was not only an extremely disputed and officially combated tendency towards 'Westernization' in the People's Republic of China in the sense of liberalism and federalism, but, as previously in the 1920s and 1930s, there was at the same time a counter-tendency in the form of a revival of idealistic and conservative ideologies.

What do these 'new' currents of thought represent? Are they indicators of a desirable pluralization and democratization of Chinese society in all areas? As desirable as this is, scepticism is yet called for. The Democracy Movement and its ideological foundations revealed strong deficiencies regarding socio-political preconditions, as far as the path to a more democratically, federalistically and pluralistically structured state in future was concerned. The *partial* modernization conducted at the moment by the government with the simultaneous exclusion of any political modernization leads us to anticipate in the long run rather the opposite: It also favours negative developments, and no independent political institutions are being created for their control. At the same time the erection of a counter-ideology, of a 'bulwark' against the political liberalism and pluralism of the West is being conducted. One cannot rule out the emergence of a strong traditionalist anti-Western ideology in China, an amalgam which consists of Confucian elements, combined with set pieces of party ideology and of western, non-liberal philosophy, backed by neo-conservative intellectuals in close cooperation with the party. Under the slogan of 'patriotism' and 'Chineseness' such a nationalistic ideology could be used by the leadership to preserve its political power and privileges.

The renaissance of Western political thought in China, especially of German idealism, and the simultaneous renaissance of traditional Chinese political thought, especially of neo-Confucianism, thus lead to the conclusion that these two developments seem to support a rising nationalism, and not political liberalism and democracy. (In this there is some similarity with the *partial* modernization of Germany as a 'delayed nation' (Plessner) in the second part of the nineteenth and the first part of the twentieth century, and its anti-Western and anti-liberal ideologies.)

The attempts to apply some modes of Western thought (Popper, market economy) do not necessarily imply the rapprochement between China and the West where, in the long run the fundamental political values of Western democracy and parliamentarianism will be adopted in something like a 'democracy with Chinese characteristics'. In my view, Chinese scholars are looking for foreign models in order to make the existing political system more effective, not necessarily more democratic in a Western sense.

Whether the next phase of development threatens to become a modernization with Chinese characteristics, not this time of national-communist but nationalistic-conservative, neo-Confucian and anti-Western characteristics, should in future be the subject of very careful observation.

Notes and references

1. Socialism, Socialist Ownership, Leading Role of the CCP, Marxism-Leninism and Mao Zedong-Thought. Compare *Deng Xiaoping tongzhi guanyu jianchi sixiang jiben yuanze fandui zichanjiechi ziyuhua de lunshu (Comrade Deng Xiaoping on the Four Basic Principles and against bourgeois liberalization)* (Beijing, 1989), p. 1. For a detailed explanation of the 'Four Basic Principles' see *Sixiang jiben yuanze dacidian (Dictionary of the Four Basic Principles)* (Chengdu: jungong yinshuachang, 1992).
2. Cf. Wolfgang Bauer, 'Aspekte deutscher Philosophie im modernen China', *Deutsch-chinesische Beziehungen vom 19. Jahrhundert bis zur Gegenwart*, ed. by Kuo Heng-y and Mechthild Leutner (München: Minerva 1991), pp. 23–42, as well as the bibliography by Wolfgang Bauer, Peng Chang and Michael Lackner, *Das chinesische Deutschlandbild der Gegenwart: A. Deutsche Kultur, Politik und Wirtschaft im chinesischen Schrifttum 1970–1984: Eine Bibliographie* (Stuttgart: Steiner, 1989), and Wolfgang Bauer, Peng Chang and Stephan von Minden, *Das chinesische Deutschlandbild der Gegenwart. Eine Bibliographie 1985–86* (Stuttgart: Steiner 1991).
3. Cf. Wolfgang Bauer, *Aspekte deutscher Philosophie im modernen China.* In: *Deutsch-chinesische Beziehungen vom 19. Jahrhundert bis zur Gegenwart*, Ed. by Kuo Heng-y and Mechthild Leutner (München: Minerva Publikation, 1991), S. 23–42.
4. Werner Meissner, *Die Rezeption der westlichen Philosophie in der VR China, 1887–1992. Eine Bibliographie* (Münster: Lit Verlag, 1996).
5. All figures from ibid.
6. *Popper in China*, edited by W. H. Newton-Smith and Jiang Tianji (London and New York, 1992), p. 11ff.
7. *International Conference on the Vienna Circle and Contemporary Science and Philosophy: In Memory of Tscha Hung* (Beijing, 21–24 Oct. 1994). During the last ten years, the main books of the Vienna Circle have been translated into Chinese.

8. Zhou Yang, 'Guanyu Makesizhuyi yixie lilun wenti de tantao' (An investigation into several theoretical questions of Marxism), in: *Renminribao (People's Daily)* (16 March, 1983), p. 4–5.
9. For further details compare Kelly in Merle Goldman, Timothy Cheek and Carol Lee Hamrin (eds), *China's Intellectuals and the State* (Cambridge/Mass, 1987), pp. 159–82.
10. Cf. He Lin, 'Feixite de aiguozhuyi he minzhuzhuyi (Fichte's patriotism and democratism), *Zhexue yanjiu* (1979), no. 5, pp 42–48; same: *The patriotism of the three great German philosophers - Goethe, Hegel, Fichte* (Beijing, 1989). Liang Zhixue, 'Fichte in China', *Dialektik* (1987), no. 14, pp. 339–344.
11. Cf. Chen Shaoming, 'Heige'er zhexue yu xiandai xinrujia (Hegel's philosophy and contemporary Neo-Confucianism', *Zhexue yanjiu* (1992), no. 2, pp. 60–6.
12. Cf. Werner Meissner, *China zwischen nationalem 'Sonderweg' und universaler Modernisierung – Zur Rezeption westlichen Denkens in China* (München: Wilhelm Fink Verlag, 1994), pp. 147ff.
13. See Zhao Baoxu, 'The Revival of Political Science in China', *PS* (Autumn 1984), vol. 17, no. 4 pp. 745–57.
14. Cf. Kenneth Lieberthal, 'China and Political Science', *PS*, vol. 14, no. 1 (Winter 1986), p. 70/78, FN 28.
15. Cf. *Zhongguo shehuizhuyi zhengzhixue (China's socialist political science)*, ed. Tu Chin *et al.* (Chengdu: Academy of Social Sciences Sichuan, 1986), and *Shehui zhuyi zhengzhixue (Socialist political science)*, ed. Yun Guang (Beijing 1985).
16. For further details see Werner Meissner, *Die Rezeption der westlichen Politikwissenschaft in der VR China, 1987–1992. Eine Bibliographie* (Münster: Lit Verlag, 1996).
17. Ibid, p. XV ff.
18. Sweden, Austria, Canada, The Netherlands, Spain, Belgium, Greece, Denmark, Switzerland.
19. All figures taken from Meissner, *ibid.*
20. Cf. Perry Link, 'The Thought and Spirit of Fang Lizhi', *The Broken Mirror. China after Tiananmen,* ed. by George Hicks (Chicago: St James Press, 1990), pp. 100–14.
21. Fang, Lizhi, *Zhexue shi wulixue di gongju* (Shanghai: Renmin 1985). Cf. the article by Cao, Xinlu, 'Kexue neng baituo zhexue ma? Ping Fang Lizhi fandui Makesi zhuyi zhexue di niulun (Can the sciences get rid of philosophy? Criticism of Fang Lizhi's distortions directed against Marxist philosophy)', *Renminribao* (26 November 1989), pp. 1, 3.
22. Cf. Meissner, *Philosophy and Politics in China* (Stanford: Stanford University Press, 1990).
23. Cf. on this the good overview in Brunhild Staiger, 'Für und wider den aufklärerischen Geist. Zur geistigen Situation Chinas vor und nach dem 4. Juni', *China aktuell* (November 1989), pp. 870–8.
24. Cf. the contribution by Arthur Waldron, 'Warlordism Versus Federalism: The Revival of a Debate?', *China Quarterly* (March 1990), vol. 121, pp. 116–28. The theme was also touched on by Zhao Ziyang's adviser Yan Jiaqi in his speech 'Weilai Zhongguo sibu qu (The four

stages of the future China)' at the *First Congress of Chinese Students and scholars in the United States* (Chicago: 29 July 1989).

25. Hu Shi, 'Liansheng zizhi yu junfa gejuda Chen Duxiu (Ch'en Tu-hsiu) (The self-government of united provinces and the particularism of the warlords)', *Hu Shi zuopin* (Taipei, 1986), pp. 75–82.

26. The most important arguments of the 'Westernizers' at that time were: The uniformity of a culture and the interdependence of all of its aspects (politics, philosophy, economy and social institutions); the superiority of Western culture – the old Chinese culture on the other hand is not suited for the modern world; Westernization is a general, world-embracing trend – if China wants to take an influential place in the world, then it must westernize itself; certain parts of Chinese culture are already Westernized, but only externally (system of government, traffic system, industry), yet this Westernization is not only insufficient but dangerous because it concentrates only on the material achievements of the West and neglects the spiritual foundations of Western society which are the basis of these achievements. A short but excellent overview of the controversy is provided by Petra Kolonko, 'The Challenged National Identity. When Chinese Wanted to Become Westerners. The 'Debate on Total Westernization' in China 1934–35', *East Asian Civilizations* (1983), no. 2, pp. 168–174.

27. Cf. ibid., p. 171.

28. See Samuel Huntington, *Political order in changing societies* (New Haven and London, 1968), in Chinese, *Biandong shehuizhong di zhengzhi zhixu* (Shanghai 1987). Guillermo O'Donnel, *Modernization and Bureaucratic Authoritarianism: Studies in South American Politics* (Berkeley 1973).

29. Cf. Ting Gong and Feng Chen, 'Neo-Authoritarian Theory in Mainland China', *Issues and Studies* (January 1991), vol. 27, no.1, pp. 84–98; Harold Waterman, 'Which Way to Go? Four Strategies for Democratization in Intellectual Circles', *China Information* (Summer 1990), vol. 5, no. 1, pp. 14–33; Marc Petracca and Mong Xiong, 'The Concept of Neo-Authoritarianism', *Asian Survey* (November 1990), vol. 30, no. 11; Yue Linzhang and Zheng Yongnian, 'The New Authoritarianism and Political Democratization', *Chinese Sociology and Anthroplogy* (Summer 1991), pp. 31–43.

30. Edward Shihls, *Political Development in the New States* (The Hague, 1962).

31. Cf. *Xin quanweizhuyi (Neo-Authoritarianism),* ed. by Liu Ling, Liu Jun (Beijing 1989), p. 173, quote from Petracca, Mong Xiong, 'Concept of New Authoritarianism', p. 1103.

32. Cf. Yue Lingzhang and Zheng Yongnian, 'The New Authoritarianism', pp. 33–4.

33. Cf. *Renminribao* (October 8 and 9, 1989), *Guangmingribao* (October 8 and 9, 1989), and XNA, (October 8 and 9, 1989).

34. So Chen Zhengfu and He Zhiqing explicitly in their book *Kongzi, Ruxue yu Zhongguo xiandaihua (Confucius, Confucianism and Chinese Modernization*) (Fujian: xinhua 1992), page 238ff: 'Xiandai xinrujia yu Zhongguo xiandaihua'.

35. Cf. Brunhild Staiger 'Chinas Modernisierung und die traditionelle Kultur', *China aktuell* (January 1991), p. 31–39.
36. The term 'National Confucianism' was firstly used by Jan Philippe Beja in his article 'The Rise of National-Confucianism', *China Perspectives* (Nov./Dec. 1995), pp. 6–11.
37. Cf. Jin Dabai, 'A Neo-Conservative's Thought on Neo-Conservatives', *China Focus* (1 March 1995), vol. 3, no. 3, p. 1,5. Drew Liu, 'The Rise of Neo-Conservatism in China', *China Focus* (January 1, 1995), vol. 3, no. 1, pp. 1–2.
38. Ibid.

2 Grassroots Political Participation in Rural China

Herbert S. Yee and Wang Jinhong

Since 1978 the Chinese Communist Party (CCP) has been pursuing a reform and open-door policy. The movement of restructuring heralded by reforms in the countryside brings China into a historical transformational period of economic development and social changes. What changes, then, have taken place in the socio-economic structure of rural China's grassroots units? What are the structures and functions of political organizations at the basic level in the countryside? What is the situation of peasants' political participation at the basic level? To what extent will all this influence contemporary China's political stability and development?

This chapter attempts to present a macro analysis of the channels, methods, motives and efficacy of peasants' political participation, against the background of socio-economic changes in rural China. Furthermore, based on this analysis, it tries to highlight the significance of peasants' participation to political development in China. It should be pointed out, however, that the political participation this chapter discusses is limited to the rural areas dominated by the Han nationality; participation which relates to minority nationalities is beyond the scope of this chapter.

BACKGROUND OF PEASANTS' POLITICAL PARTICIPATION AT THE GRASSROOTS LEVEL

As in many other developing countries, the political participation of Chinese peasants at the grassroots level is an inevitable outcome of the socio-economic changes in the modernization process. Since 1978 there have been remarkable changes in the countryside's economic and political structure and in peasants' ideology. Furthermore, with the increase in mobility, peasants have come into contact with modernity. The traditional obedient type of peasant has turned into a new type of peasant with consciousness of rights, independence and participation. These factors facilitate the development of political participation at the basic level in the countryside.[1]

Changes in the socio-economic structure in the countryside

The economic reform, which centres on the production-related household contracting responsibility system, stabilizes the rural economy that is based on individual households. The increase in peasants' income creates favourable conditions for the development of industrialization and the readjustment of industrial structure in the countryside. On the one hand, with better cultivation and greater incentive to produce, there appears a surplus in the work force in the countryside, thus providing workers for industrial development; on the other hand, additional rural capital is accumulated to provide the necessary investment for industrialization. Since the eighties, in the provinces of Jiangsu, Zhejiang and Guangdong, township and village enterprises have been rapidly on the rise (see also Chapter 8). The development of township and village enterprises proves to be a feasible way towards industrialization and urbanization. It also changes the economic structure, social outlook, and social stratification in the countryside. The unitary agricultural working class, which concentrates on farming under the traditional economic system, has gradually evolved into modern farmers who specialize, respectively, in farming, industry and trade. Thus, in the basic units in the countryside, there appears a pluralistic pattern of economic interests, which breaks free from the past conformity of economic practices and makes complex the socio-economic structure at the basic level in the countryside.

Changes of political structure at the basic level in the countryside

Before 1978, the system of merging government administration with commune management was practiced in people's communes in the Chinese countryside. The people's communes had both rural government authority at the grassroots level and collective economic management, practising centralized management. Under this system, the social structure at the basic level in the countryside was highly politicized. This system confused the functions of organizations of political power with those of organizations of economic power and deprived peasants of their initiative in economic management. Peasants' enthusiasm in production was quenched and they were made passive and obedient. Moreover, under this system, cadres in people's communes made a living by receiving state salaries; their personal interests did not relate directly to collective interests. Thus they lacked the attitude of being highly responsible to peasants, and their major concerns were to please the higher-level authority.

Because of the shortcomings in this all-in-one system, since 1979 reforms have been carried out to reorganize the political structure at the basic level in rural China. In 1985, according to the arrangements of the Central Committee of the Communist Party and the State Department, township governments and people's congresses were established throughout the whole nation. The system of people's communes was discontinued. Since then, fundamental changes have taken place in the structure of political organizations at the basic level in rural China.

According to the stipulations of the 'Law of Organizations of Local Political Authority in People's Republic of China', the people's congress is set up in a township (*xiang*) or town as a basic unit of political power. Its members, whose tenure is three years, are directly elected by voters. The congress meets at least once every year. The people's congress of a town or township elects its own presidium to preside over the congress. When the people's congress meets, deputies to the people's congress can address inquiries to the town or township administration and its attached departments. The units addressed must respond to the enquiries. When the people's congress is not in session, work is divided among deputies to maintain ties with voters.

In order to keep abreast of the political restructing of establishing township government, the villagers' committees at the village level in rural China have been set up one after another since 1982. According to the stipulation of the Constitution of 1982, the villagers' committees are autonomous organizations of the masses at the basic level. In 1987, the 'Law of Organizations of the Villagers' Committees in the People's Republic of China (trial version)' was passed in the 23rd session of the Standing Committee of the Sixth National People's Congress. This law provides for the organizational system of the villagers' committees and thus the autonomy of villagers is legalized. According to stipulations of this law, the basic functions of a villagers' committee are as follows: First, it takes care of social affairs. Specifically this includes: (1) taking care of public affairs and public welfare in the village, such as education, culture, medical care and hygiene, providing relief and special care to disabled servicemen, and to family members of revolutionary martyrs and servicemen; taking care of widows, orphans and those who need help, and taking charge of building roads, bridges and irrigation works; (2) mediating between civil conflicts; (3) ensuring social stability and security; and (4) keeping the government informed of villagers' opinions and suggestions. Secondly, it manages the collectively owned land and other properties in the village, and supports villagers in developing various forms of cooperative economy. Thirdly, it launches an education movement for raising cultural and moral standards and strengthening the construction of spiritual enlightenment in the countryside, instructing peasants to support the Communist Party and socialism.

Changes in villagers' way of thinking

The development of the rural economy has brought about changes in the peasants' way of life. In the past two decades, centring on the goal of obtaining enough food and clothing, moderate well-being and wealth, the way of thinking typical of Chinese peasants has dramatically changed. The changes mainly involve the following three aspects. First, the mentality of striving for wealth gradually replaces that of traditional peasants, who were content with things as they were. The yearning for and pursuit of wealth has greatly aroused peasants' enthusiasm for reforms. In Mao Zedong's times, because wealth was viewed as a bourgeois way of life, everyone was afraid to raise this topic. In Deng Xiaoping's times, wealth was positively considered as an inexorable demand of socialism instead of a bourgeois way of life. Deng points out, 'we should allow some people in some areas to become wealthy first through honest work'. The viewpoint greatly encourages Chinese peasants. Fuelled by the desire to become wealthy, the peasants' enthusiasm for reforms is aroused and they become a source of support for reforms.

Secondly, with the increase in peasants' mobility, the conservative mentality of leaving the land but not the village is gradually changed. From the latter half of the 1980s, with the emergence of a surplus in the rural workforce, peasants swarmed into cities, particularly into the prosperous areas around the coast. According to the statistics in 1994, every year there were in total about 40 to 80 millions of transient peasants temporarily residing in big and middle-sized cities throughout the nation.[2] For peasants, this experience was an eye-opener and made them aware of the different levels of socio-economic development in various areas; on the other hand, while working in cities, they were influenced by some more open-minded and better-educated urban workmates, and gradually they developed consciousness of rights, equality and independence. For example, since 1993 organized strikes and negotiations with the management in some enterprises in Shenzhen have been commonplace because of delayed salary payments and excessive working hours.[3] This shows that, nurtured in urban civilization, peasants are no longer obedient and passive as they used to be.

Thirdly, peasants' consciousness of independence is strengthened and the traditional mentality of credulity and blind following gradually disappears. On the one hand, the production-related household contracting responsibility system makes peasants acquire initiative in their management; on the other hand, the exchange of commodities and the establishment of the market system gives peasants the initiative in the exchange process. The experience of initiative in both production and exchange in turn arouses peasants' initiative in social and political activities. Since the establishment of the villagers' committees, the election of a village head is the responsibility of the peasants themselves. Peasants elect as branch secretaries of the Party, directors of villagers' committees or heads of village-run collective enterprises, those who are better-educated and who are able to lead them towards prosperity. Before long, in every wealthy and prosperous village, there are a group of 'able persons' (*nengren*) who are familiar with the market economy and good at management.[4] They are able to lead the peasants towards the goals of wealth and rural industrialization. At the same time, the peasants' sense of democracy is strengthened and they are able to elect good leadership or a good cadre, for example, Pan Qiangen in Wan Feng village in Guangdong, Wu Renbao in Huaxi village in Jiangsu, Shi Laihe in Liuzhuang in Henen and Zhou Zuoliang in Happiness (*Xingfu*) village in Hubei. The system of management by able persons is the outcome of peasants' free choice. It should be pointed out, however, that although able persons play a positive role in the development of many villages, they have limitations. For example, their role is not stable and sustained. And as individuals change, everything else can easily change.[5]

The above-mentioned changes taking place in the basic units in rural China closely bear on and directly affect peasants' political participation. If we adopt Samuel Huntington's conception that political participation is a citizen's attempt to influence government policies,[6] changes in economic and social structure in rural China and changes in the peasants' way of thinking are all conducive to political participation. It can be concluded that the increase in peasants' political participation is an inevitable outcome of China's economic development and social changes. There is a striking difference between the present self-motivated political participation and the passive, mobilized participation during the periods of the Great Leap Forward, 1958–60, and the people's communes.

THE CHANNELS AND METHODS OF CHINESE PEASANTS' POLITICAL PARTICIPATION AT THE GRASSROOTS LEVEL

Channels of political participation

By channels of political participation we mean all the possible avenues a political system provides for its citizens to participate in politics. These avenues link up the government with the people who, adopting different methods, can keep the government informed of their opinions. As far as Chinese peasants are concerned, there are both formal and informal channels of political participation. The formal channels refer to various officially designated Party and political organizations whose purpose is to bring peasants' political participation into the operational orbit of the political system. The organizations mainly include: (1) the Party's organizations in the countryside; (2) the people's congresses; (3) offices for the people's letters and appeals for help; and (4) the villagers' committees. According to the law of organizations of local political authority, law of organizations of villagers' committees and 'The Central Committee's Resolution on Strengthening the Party's Ties with the Masses', the above-mentioned four organizations are important avenues for the masses to voice their opinions and express their wishes. Hence, they are formal channels of peasants' political participation. The informal channels refer to various organizations established spontaneously by peasants in order to express their wishes and to influence government policies. These mainly include clan organizations, guild organizations, religious organizations, and joint-households organizations.

Theoretically speaking, there are various official organizations with which Chinese peasants can be involved politically. But in reality, the power of the people's congresses and their deputies is nominal. The bureaucratic practices, low efficiency and complex working procedures block the formal channels and make it difficult for peasants to express their wishes and claims of interests through them. Under these circumstances, the informal organizations are usually very active. In some areas, the formal organizations must even enlist the support of informal ones in order to carry out policies. For example, the policy of birth control at the village level could not be really effective without the cooperation of clan organizations; in order to levy taxes and apportion charges among peasants, the unanimous support of the guild organizations and joint-households organizations is needed. If the informal organizations are in conflict with the government, the Party branch of the village and the villagers' committee, then many problems will be difficult to solve.

Since the family contracting responsibility system was introduced in the countryside, peasants have taken into their own hands greater initiative in economic management. The role of the formal party and political organizations in determining peasants' interests and fate, or in production and management, has weakened. Therefore, generally speaking, peasants' reliance on and identity with the formal organizations decrease, whereas their reliance on and identity with the informal organizations increase. Thus, the peasants are more likely to participate in politics through informal channels than through formal channels. How then do peasants participate in politics at the grassroots level through informal organizations? According to our field work in the rural areas in the provinces of Hunan, Hubei and Guangdong, we find that the main ways through which the informal organizations participate in grassroots politics are as follows:

(1) By electing a clan member as branch secretary of the Party or head of the village; this directly combines clan power with political power and thus legalizes clan power. Take for instance the situation in Beiyan village in Kaiping county, Guangdong. The total population of the village is 3115 and about 80 per cent of the villagers carry the family name Yu. Therefore, in elections at the village level, it is very easy for a member of the Yu clan to be elected head of the village.[7] In Wanfeng village in Shenzhen, Guangdong, people with the family name Pan comprise 95 per cent of the total population of the village. Invariably the posts of branch secretary and head of the village are held by members of the Pan clan. What is different is that the Pan clan has three family branches and there is competition between these branches for the posts of branch secretary of the Party or head of the village.[8] As Qian Hang points out, in many areas the clan mentality has been accepted as a social mentality by local societies.[9] Some re-established clans are trying to find a suitable form of

organization so as to link up with the existing social order. In particular clan organizations are making an effort to cooperate and coordinate with basic level political authorities. Cadres at the grassroots level join quite a few clan organizations and even hold some important positions.

(2) By establishing ties with Party and government officials whose birth place or ancestral home is their village, through activities such as worshipping ancestors and informal talks. Since the open-door policy in 1978, building of ancestral temples, worshipping ancestors, informal gatherings of clan members and the like have been very frequent in rural China. Through these activities, peasants invite those fellow villagers or clan members who have already gained leading positions in the Party or government of the county, the city or the province to return to the village and establish emotional ties, which will facilitate informal political exchanges in the future. Generally speaking, influenced by traditional culture, many Communist leaders still have not got rid of the practices of petit peasants. To some extent they still cherish provincialism and the mentality of looking for family roots and worshipping ancestors. Out of considerations of bringing honour to their ancestors and benefiting their fellow villagers, they will usually do what they can, within what is permitted by policies, to take care of and bring some benefits to their fellow villagers. All this is difficult to settle through formal channels. Sometimes, some high-ranking Communist leaders prefer to engage in small talk of the old days in order to familiarize themselves with the common practices and political situation in the basic units in the countryside. They believe that information gathered this way is more reliable than reports from basic-level officials.

Methods of political participation

By methods of political participation we mean the specific behavioural patterns of citizens participating in politics and attempting to influence government policies. Chinese peasants' political participation involves both conventional and unconventional methods. Conventional methods refer to ways of exerting pressure on the government within the confines of law and according to normal political procedures. Chinese peasants have four main conventional methods: voting, formal contact with officials, submitting a written statement to a higher authority and lodging complaints, and administrative lawsuits.[10]

(i) Voting

Voting is the most important conventional method in which Chinese peasants participate in basic-level politics. Voting is mainly employed in the elections of deputies of the People's Congress of the town or township, heads of villages and representatives of villagers. In the elections of deputies of the People's Congress, the attitude of peasants depends on the competition between clan forces in the countryside. Unless there is keen competition between clan forces, peasants are not interested in electing deputies because deputies have no power to solve practical problems in the countryside. Basic-level problems are up to secretaries of Party committees and heads of towns or townships to resolve. The power of the People's Congress and deputies is only nominal. Therefore, in electing deputies, peasants muddle through rather than considering it as an important right by which they can participate in local grassroots political life. For example, in two elections of the People's Congress at the levels of town or townships in 1978 and 1990, some peasants in the rural areas in Hubei province were unwilling to vote. On the day of voting, village leaders had no choice but to carry a voting-box from door to door to persuade peasants into voting. In some rural areas in Xiaogan, peasants bargained with village leaders when voting. They thought voting interfered with their work and asked for a compensation of 3 to 5 yuan each.[11] In the elections in the countryside of Hunan, such small favours as towels and soap were used to attract peasants to vote.[12]

However, in areas where there is keen competition between clan forces, peasants have a strikingly different attitude towards the elections of deputies of the People's Congress. Because the election of a clan member as deputy will heighten the political prestige of the clan, members of the same clan are united as one and try their best to ensure the successful election of the candidate of their clan.

Comparatively, Chinese peasants in various rural areas pay more attention to the election of the director of the village committee (conventionally called head of the village). This is because the election of the head of the village relates directly to peasants' immediate interests and to the interests of the various clans in the countryside. Although since the family contracting system has been practised the power of the head of the village is not what it used to be in the period of the people's communes, the village head has decisive power in such matters as employing workers in township and village enterprises, changing from rural residence into urban residence, young people joining the army, and contracting of land and forest. Besides, the villagers are familiar with the candidates for village leaders and can easily make decisions. In the election of village heads in some provinces, villagers hold public campaigns and go canvassing. This wins the support of county Party committees and county governments instead of, as formerly, being suppressed.[13]

(ii) Formal contact with government officials

Formal contact with officials refers to peasants' getting in touch with county or township officials individually or collectively, or direct contact with leaders in provincial or central governments. In the face-to-face talks, opinions, suggestions and criticisms are expressed in order to change some unreasonable policies and any situations of mal-treatment. Although peasants' formal contact with government officials meets with many obstacles, sometimes even retaliation,[14] peasants' wishes can be expressed accurately, thoroughly and truly. This avoids the one-sidedness of evading the important and dwelling on the trivial, and holding back any unpleasant information, when local officials report to higher-level authorities. When they are in formal contact with officials, peasants focus on the problems of economic hardship, financial management, contracting, land planning for housing and birth control, as well as problems of embezzlement and corruption by basic-level cadres who acquire personal gains through their abuse of power.

Besides the above-mentioned formal contact, there is informal contact in which advantage is taken of connections with fellow villagers or of blood relationships. Furthermore, peasants individually or in an organized way offer bribes to officials in order to ask for favours or win their support.

(iii) Submitting written statements and lodging complaints

This method refers to the sending of letters to the mass media and some related government organs by peasants to report their situation and to express their suggestions and opinions. Compared with the formal contact with officials, it is rather moderate in character and has less political influence. Unless problems are publicized in the *People's Daily*, *Guangming Daily* or by the Central TV Station, it is generally not very effective. The peasants mainly complain about economic problems, peasants' tax burden, the style of work of basic-level cadres, and implementation of policies. From 1992 to 1995, peasants' complaints focused on local officials' three 'irresponsibles', that is, irresponsible apportioning, irresponsible pooling of funds, and irresponsible charging.[15]

(iv) Administrative lawsuit

In April 1989, the Law of Administrative Litigation was issued in China, which is the first law in Chinese history to permit citizens to bring lawsuits against officials. This is an important milestone in legal construction and democratic politics. In 1994, the Law of State Compensation was published, which is very significant in preventing government organs from damaging citizens' interests. In recent years, incidents of some local departments of agricultural resources selling false pesticides and false chemical fertilizers to peasants have been of common occurrence, and this incurs great popular indignation by peasants.[16] In order to safeguard their own interests, the incensed peasants bring administrative lawsuits against the departments concerned. In the first half of 1993, 207 peasants in Lezhi county in Sichuang province filed a lawsuit against the township government for forcing on them unreasonable apportioned charges. After carrying out investigations, the court ruled that the township government should return all the extra charges to the peasants.[17] The existence of administrative lawsuits indicates that contemporary Chinese peasants have begun to employ legal procedures in political participation to express their claims and exert influence and pressure on the government.

Besides conventional methods, Chinese peasants also adopt some unconventional methods in order to exert pressure on the government. The so-called unconventional methods refer to the behavioural patterns which employ coercive measures which are beyond the accepted norms of the political system. Some scholars think that these unconventional and illegal behavioural patterns should not be included as activities of political participation and that they are anti-governmental activities.[18] Here we employ the concept of political participation in a broader sense, which includes illegal political activities. Generally speaking, there are two unconventional methods in peasants' political participation: destruction, and protests and uprisings.

(i) Destruction. When a government policy or measure is detrimental to peasants' interests and peasants are in no position to change it, they will take destructive measures to give vent to their dissatisfaction. For instance, from 1988 to 1994, the government purchasing price of cotton was relatively low yet the prices of chemical fertilizers and pesticides rose year by year. This reduced the peasants' actual profits from planting cotton year after year. Therefore, in Hubei, a province in which cotton is an important crop, peasants chose to abandon

many of the cotton fields rather than to plant cotton. In 1993, the phenomenon of adulterated cotton, which spread in the cotton-planting provinces of Hubei, Hunan, Anhui and Shandong, was an indication of peasants' dissatisfaction with the policy on the cotton price. Another instance is also very typical. From 1993 to 1995, in some mulberry-planting and silkworm-raising areas in Jiangsu and Zhejiang, the prices of cocoons and raw silk were fixed by the government. Because the low fixed prices reduced the silkworm raisers' earnings, and even made some raisers lose money, peasants destroyed mulberry fields to give expression to their grievances. According to a report on Central TV, from 1994 to 1995, the area of mulberry fields destroyed by peasants in Zhejiang exceeded 8000 mu (1 mu is equal to 1/6 acre).

(ii) Protests and uprisings. Since 1990, the situation of local governments' irresponsible apportioning of charges, irresponsible pooling of funds and irresponsible charging has been increasingly serious. In addition to this, some departments of local governments have for long fallen into arrears in the payment of peasants for grain and cotton purchased by the government, and with peasants' postal remittances.[19] All this adds greatly to peasants' discontent. In some places, the attitude of basic-level cadres and law-enforcing personnel towards peasants is very rude and arbitrary, which intensifies the conflict between peasants and government organs. Peasants gather together in front of township government buildings to protest and demonstrate. In some places the conflict between peasants and the government reaches a hostile state. In recent years, several large peasant uprisings have taken place which have been very influential; the most notable of these was the uprising by peasants in Renshou county, Sichuang province, in June 1993. Because peasants could no longer bear the heavy burden of multifarious taxes, thousands of peasants, led by Zhang Dean and Xiang Wenqing, swarmed to the county seat to protest. This was viewed as a rebellion by the local government. Regular troops were sent to suppress it and eight leaders of this uprising, including Zhang Dean, were arrested. But the peasants refused to back down and the situation deteriorated. Peasants in Bazhong, Wanyuan, Nanjiang, Santai and Gaoxian, which are far from Renshou county, voiced their support for the peasants in Renshou. In order to defuse the tension and prevent the turmoil from spreading, the Central government intervened. The local government eventually gave way and set free the arrested peasant

leaders, declaring the relief of the unreasonable burden which had been forced on the peasants.[20] In addition, from the end of August to the middle of September in 1996, in several townships in Qidong county, Hunan province, thousands of peasants successively went to the township governments to present petitions, demanding a reduction in their multifarious taxes. Peasants clashed with township cadres and broke into the offices of township governments, breaking the glass and destroying office equipment. The police were forced to fire tear-gas shells to disperse the rioters.[21]

THE MOTIVES AND EFFICACY OF CHINESE PEASANTS' POLITICAL PARTICIPATION

An analysis of the basic channels and methods of Chinese peasants' political participation indicates that, since 1978, a lot has been achieved in the way of political participation at the basic level in rural China. The diversification of the channels and the methods of political participation at the basic level suggest that contemporary Chinese peasants' sense of initiative has awakened. The traditional obedient type of peasant has transformed into a modern type of participant. In order to gain a deeper understanding of this transformation, we need to go further into the motives and efficacy of peasants' political participation.

Motives of political participation

(i) Economic motives

Since the production-related household contracting responsibility system was introduced, peasants' economic interests have been affirmed. Therefore, they show great enthusiasm in taking part in reforms. From 1979 to 1985, the rural economy prospered. Peasants' annual per capita income rose from 160 yuan to 397 yuan. The average annual rate of increase was more than 10 per cent, peaking at 20.9 per cent in the year 1982. Besides, during this period, the inflation rate was low, from which peasants benefited a lot. But since 1986, peasants' relative income has been decreasing. From 1986 to 1995, the peasants' annual per capita income increased at a rate below 10 per cent,[22] yet during this same period, prices and the inflation rate have each year been at a high level. The prices of industrial products like chemical fertilizers and pesticides increased year by year, but the prices of agricultural and side-line products were relatively low. The decrease in peasants' real earnings made them feel discouraged and deprived. Motivated by this sense of setback and deprivation, they wanted to express their wishes in order to influence the government's pricing policies for industrial products as well as policies on purchasing prices for agricultural and side-line products.

On the other hand, the peasants' economic burden (taxation and related charges) has been aggravated year by year, seriously damaging their economic interests. According to official statistics from China's Department of Agriculture, the peasants' various items of social burden averaged 16 yuan in 1990 plus various charges at the two levels of township and village, totalling 57 yuan, or about 11 per cent of the past year's annual per capita net income. Investigations in a township in Hubei indicate that in 1989, as compared with the previous year, the peasants' per capita income increased by 2.1 per cent, but the average burden increased by 18 per cent, with an average total of 100 yuan.[23] In the district of Linyi in Shandong peasants' average burden reached 160 yuan in 1992, or about 65 to 80 per cent of their annual per capita net income.[24] Peasants are overburdened with various unreasonable apportioned charges, and they are not understood or sympathized with by officials at the grassroots level. When it is not effective to submit written statements to higher level authorities or lodge complaints, they have no choice but to resort to various unconventional ways to resist taxes or charges. Some even become very hostile and retaliate against basic-level cadres.

(ii) Political motives

With the disintegration of the people's communes and the establishment of the system of villagers' autonomy, the authority of grassroots organizations in the countryside has been concomitantly weakened. Party branches, which used to be the strongholds at the basic level, have been in a slack state in recent years. According to official statistics, there were 800 000 organizations at the village level in the countryside in 1994. About 10 per cent were classified as 'weak and slack' (*ruan ruo huan san*) villages where the Party branch and the villagers' committee lacked cohesive power.[25] Investigations in Beiyan village in Kaiping, Guangdong, show that there were 55 Communist Party members in this village in the 1980s, which should have resulted in a powerful Party organization. But throughout the late eighties and the nineties, the Party organization of this village has always been in a slack state. It has no regular Party activities, has not admitted new members into the Party, and the organization of the Communist Youth League exists only in name.[26]

Since the disintegration of the people's communes in the mid-1980s, social problems in the countryside have become increasingly serious. Burglary, robbery, gambling, clan fighting and superstition are rampant, with local ruffians and hooligans running amuck. Besides, underground societies and gangs have been on the rise. Faced with all these problems, basic-level governments are at a loss as to what to do and at the same time feel that the problems are beyond the reach of their authority. The ability of basic-level organizations to achieve social integration in the countryside has been weakened, which intensifies the disorderly situation. Evidently, the increase of peasants' political participation is aimed at urging basic-level organizations to strengthen their own function of safeguarding justice and social order and ensuring social stability in the countryside. On the other hand, because the ability of Party and government organizations to achieve social integration has been weakened, those clan and religious organizations, which have integrative power, take advantage of this situation and mobilize peasants to participate in local elections and other political activities in order to expand their spheres of political influence. This explains why there has been a general increase in political participation among peasants in recent years.

Political supervision is also implicit in the political motives of peasants' participation. In various political activities which involve peasants, at least one-fifth of their grievances relate to problems of corruption of basic-level officials, public security, agricultural policies and unequal distribution.[27] This indicates that Chinese peasants are no longer confined to caring only about their personal interests: they begin to pay attention to social issues as well as to problems of the Party members' styles of work and discipline. This breaks free from the narrow-mindedness of traditional peasants and shows that peasants begin to develop consciousness of democratic supervision. This is an important indicator of change among the Chinese peasants, from the obedient type to that of participant.

The efficacy of political participation

The efficacy of political participation refers to the actual extent and effect of the citizens' influence on the government's policies or actions. The efficacy of Chinese peasants' participation depends upon the following four factors. First, it depends on the peasants' organizational level. No matter through what channels and methods, if peasants participate in politics individually, the efficacy is very low. Unless they are considered exemplary and worthy of publicizing by the government authorities, peasants' individual suggestions and demands have little influence on government policies. On the other hand, peasants' organized actions can easily draw the attention of the authorities and are very efficacious. The protest of thousands of peasants in Renshou, Sichuan, is a case in point. But the fact is that at present Chinese peasants' organizational level is rather low and their freedom of association is restricted. Except for the Communist Party, which is officially publicized as a representative of the working class in China, there does not exist a peasants' party or a political organization which specifically stands for peasants' interests. After the founding of the People's Republic of China, the Peasants' Union, a national organization representing peasants, was disbanded. And Chinese peasants have been in a scattered and disorganized state ever since.

At present, the various organizations in rural China can roughly be divided into two categories: formal and informal. Formal organizations are the various political, economic and social organizations which are recognized and supported by the government. They include the Party branches, villagers' committees, the branches of the Communist Youth League, women's committees, the militia, township and village enterprises, cooperative foundations, credit cooperatives, and senior citizens' associations. Informal organizations are those which are set up by peasants themselves. They include clan organizations, religious organizations, and joint-households organizations through which different households help each other in economic production.

The Party branches, villagers' committees, women's committees, branches of the Communist Youth League and the militia belong to political organizations. Their main function is to carry out orders from higher level authorities and manage rural affairs. The leaders and main members of these organizations are elites in the countryside rather than ordinary peasants. Township and village enterprises, cooperative foundations, credit cooperatives, supply and marketing cooperatives and associations of science and technology are basically economic organizations. Their main function is to be engaged in professional services rather than organizing peasants' political participation. They do not express their opinions even about local public affairs. Senior citizens' associations are basically welfare organizations, which are responsible for the support of widows and lonely senior citizens. In many rural areas, these organizations are but empty shells. Only the various religious and clan organizations are set up and controlled by peasants themselves. Sometimes they organize peasants to take part in local public affairs and even attempt to influence local governments. But these organizations are usually viewed as the opposites of basic-level political authorities and Party organizations, and therefore as an unstable factor in the countryside.[28] Their activities are restricted, lack legality, are informal and unstable.

Secondly, the peasants' choice of channels and methods for political participation affects the latter's efficacy. There are formal and informal channels, and conventional and unconventional methods. The extent and effect of their influence on the government varies. Through formal channels, peasants are mobilized by Party organizations to take part in political activities. The effect is lasting, stable, and with strong influence. But the trouble is, this mobilized participation does not actually stand for peasants' interests. More often than not, it represents the will of the Party and higher-level authorities. Peasants participate in politics in an indirect way by keeping deputies of the People's Congress informed of their opinions and interests. But because deputies do not have real power, the effect is not lasting and has little influence on the government. For peasants to express their opinions through letters and appeals is a moderate method of political participation. It avoids direct contact with related departments and officials, thus mitigating the intensity of participation. The influence on the government is therefore relatively weak. It is not uncommon for peasants to express opinions through villagers' committees. Because the villagers' committees are relatively autonomous organizations and channels of peasants' management of local public affairs, and because they are helpful in mitigating the pressure of peasants' participation on higher-level authorities, their influence is strong. In informal channels of participation, both the clan and religious organizations have strong cohesive and mobilization power. Both their organizational structure and function are quite lasting and stable. Under certain situations, they have strong influence on local government authorities when they mobilize their members to participate in politics. The guild and joint-households organizations set up by peasants themselves are always in a state of flux and therefore are not stable. They also occasionally take part in local public affairs, but with weak influence.

With regard to conventional methods of participation, peasants' voting has a direct and strong influence on politics. But this method is not often employed. The method which has a direct and strong influence and which peasants usually resort to is contact with officials.

The influence on politics of peasants' written statements and complaints is indirect, mainly depending on how the statements or complaints relate to government policies. This is also a method peasants often employ. Lastly, although the method of filing administrative lawsuits against the government has strong political influence, usually it is not used because peasants generally are not legally minded and are not familiar with legal procedures and provisions.

In regard to unconventional methods of participation, peasants express their dissatisfactions by deserting fields and destroying crops and low-priced agricultural and side-line products. The effect of this on politics is indirect and weak and peasants usually do not resort to this method. Peasants' protests and rebellions exert direct and strong political influence on the government's policies but this is when peasants have no alternative and it too is not often employed.

Thirdly, peasants' educational level and skills of political participation affect the efficacy of their political participation. In the countryside, well-educated peasants have good skills of political participation. They are able to express their interests accurately and develop systematic rational thinking. They can choose proper channels and methods at the right moment. Besides, they can influence and mobilize other people and play a leading role in political participation. On the other hand, poorly educated peasants do not possess the necessary skills of political participation. They are not able to express their interests clearly and do not know how to choose effective methods. Some even do not know how the government is run. Therefore, their political participation is blind and sporadic. According to statistics at the end of 1994, China has a rural population of 855 million, making up 71 per cent of the total population.[29] Of the rural population, illiterates and semi-illiterates make up 22 per cent, those with primary school education 39 per cent, junior middle school 31 per cent, senior middle school 7 per cent, specialized middle school 0.45 per cent and colleges and technical institutes 0.08 per cent.[30] This indicates that illiterates, semi-illiterates and those with only primary school education account for the majority, and those with junior middle school education and above the minority. According to Almond and Powel, educational level relates positively to political participation.[31] Well-educated people are more inclined to participate in politics. Thus it can be concluded that Chinese peasants likely to have a relatively high level of political participation account for less than 40 per cent (those with junior middle school education and above) of the rural population. This partly explains the generally low efficacy of political participation.

Fourthly, the efficacy of peasants' political participation depends on the extent to which participation relates to government policies. Government policies are an external factor influencing the efficacy of peasants' political participation, but they are rather important. For instance, when the central government pursues a policy of lightening peasants' financial burden, whatever channels and methods peasants employ to express their wishes and interests, they can effectively influence the government and receive attention. But when the government policies change, the same methods will no longer be effective. Therefore, in order to be efficacious, peasants' participation must relate closely to government policies. That is to say, peasants should be able to grasp the crux of the government policies at every stage and realize how the government is being run. Certainly, this involves the problem of political transparency as well as problems of political exchange between the government and the masses, which are yet to be solved in China.

CONCLUSION

A systematic analysis of political participation at the grassroots level in rural China indicates that, since the reform and open-door policy, with changes in economy and social structure, the peasants' way of life and way of thinking has dramatically changed. The traditionally conservative and narrow-minded petit peasants have been transformed into a new type of peasant, with consciousness of participation and independence. Although the pace of transformation has been slow, Chinese peasants have been awakened after all. This is an important milestone of political development in twentieth-century Chinese society.

Judging from the channels and methods of political participation in the countryside, the scope of peasants' participation has been growing. Peasants' political participation involves not only affairs in their own communities, that is, attempts to influence government policies in order to safeguard their personal interests and the interests of their communities, but they also begin to pay attention to social and political problems of a general nature.

With regard to the efficacy of peasants' political participation, because it is restricted by peasants' organizational level, their choice of channels and methods, their educational level, skills of participation, and the relation between their participation and government policies, it is impossible for their political participation to be very effective. Besides, the bureaucracy of government organs constrains peasants' enthusiasm for political participation. Whether in the management of rural affairs, or in policy-making, the governments at the basic level are only interested in pleasing the higher-level authorities and turn a deaf ear to peasants' interests and requests. They often run everything without consulting peasants. This bureaucratic style of work quenches peasants' enthusiasm for political participation and makes some peasants feel they are in no position to participate in grassroots and state affairs. Thus they develop a sense of indifference to politics.[32] This situation is detrimental to the development of political participation in the villages.

Since the disintegration of the people's communes (which merged political power into economic management), the function of the Party and government organizations has begun to weaken, partially or wholly losing the capacity of social management and integration. As a result, clan organizations, associations of fellow villagers, and guild and religious organizations which have strong cohesive force and the power of social integration, have been flourishing. Besides, with the rise of economically minded able persons, the traditional class of 'gentles' who manage local affairs appears once more in various forms in rural China, becoming a main force for integrating the countryside. Furthermore, clan power is merged into political power as prestigious heads of clans are elected as secretaries of the Party branches or heads of villages. Some clan organizations even get in touch with high-ranking local and central government officials who have blood ties or are fellow villagers, forming an influential network of connections between government officials and local 'gentles'.

The challenge facing the government is how to keep abreast of the actual situation of political development in the villages and lead the clan and other informal organizations in the right direction of development. The government should strengthen their positive functions, such as social integration, maintaining normal social and political order in the countryside, and setting up new moral norms and village regulations. On the other hand, the government should minimize and eliminate the negative functions of informal organizations, such as clan fighting, practices of superstition, the rise of underground societies and gang forces, and bribery in elections at the village level. If the government only suppresses peasants' aspirations to participate in politics and does not mediate between itself and the peasants, there is the danger of driving the peasants to rebel. In Lishu county, Jilin province, a cadre in the Bureau of Civil Affairs, which is in charge of elections of villagers' committees, candidly pointed out: 'Villagers' autonomy is inevitable. If there were still no democratic elections, a Li Zicheng[33] would emerge. Because only through elections can villagers express their wishes and give vent to their grievances and have ease of mind.'[34]

Notes and references

1. Samuel Huntington, *Political Order in Changing Societies* (New Haven: Yale University Press, 1968).
2. See Jiang Liu *et al.* (eds), *An Analysis and Prediction of Chinese Social Situation in 1995–1996* (Beijing: The China Social Science Society Press, 1996), p. 78.
3. Personal interviews conducted in Shenzhen in August 1994 and December 1995.
4. See Xu Yong, 'From Able Man Management to Rule by Law: the Transformation of Management Model in Villages', paper presented at the Annual Meeting of Chinese Political Science Society, Wuhan, May 1995.
5. Zhang Houan and Xu Yong, *Political Stability and Development in Chinese Villages* (Wuhan University Press, 1995), p. 956.
6. Samuel Huntington, *Political Order in Changing Societies*.
7. Personal interviews conducted in Kaiping in January 1996.
8. Field work in Wanfeng Village in March 1995.
9. See Qian Hang, 'Several Questions About Clan and Kinship Research in Contemporary Chinese Villages', *Village Economy and Society* (*Nongcun Jingji Yu Shehui*), no. 5, 1993, pp. 9–14.
10. See Cheng Tongshun, 'Contemporary Chinese Peasants' Political Participation', *Jianghai Xuehan* (Nanjing), no. 1, 1995, pp. 37–9.
11. Personal interviews with members of the Standing Committee of Hubei's Provincial People's Congress in March 1990.
12. Personal interviews with university students from Hunan province in May 1996.
13. See Zhang Houan and Xu Yong, *Political Stability and Development in Chinese Villages*, pp. 1083–99.
14. Typical is the case of Yu Zuomin of Daqiuzhuang, Jinghai county, Tianjin. Yu was the Party secretary of Daqiuzhuang. He retaliated and tortured those peasants who dared to reveal his corrupt activities to higher-level authorities. Some were even beaten to death. See Yu Hongfeng, *The Secret Story of China's Prosperous Village Daqiuzhuang* (Beijing: Police Officers Education Press, 1993).
15. Jiang Liu *et al.* (eds), *An Analysis and Prediction of Chinese Social Situation in 1994–1995*, p. 264.
16. Ibid., 1996, p. 293.
17. Zhang Houan and Xu Yong, *Political Stability and Development in Chinese Villages*, p. 285.

18. See Lianjiang Li and Kevin J. O'Brien, 'Villagers and Popular Resistance in Contemporary China', *Modern China*, vol. 22, no. 1 (January 1996), pp. 28–61.
19. In China, people can send cash via post offices. The receiver will then be notified by the post office to pick up the cash. However, some post offices in the countryside withhold the money from the designated receiver.
20. He Pin, *Post-Deng Xiaoping China* (Canada: Mingjing, 1994), pp. 474–5.
21. *Ming Pao* (Hong Kong), 8 November 1996.
22. Statistics from China's Statistics Bureau.
23. The Office of Social Education of Hubei Province (ed.), *Selected Documents of Socialist Ideology Education*, 1994.
24. He Pin, *Post-Deng Xiaoping China*, pp. 467–8.
25. See Jiang Liu *et al.* (eds), 1995, pp. 167–70, 316.
26. Personal interviews in Kaiping in January 1996.
27. *The 1996 Society Blue Book*, published by the China Social Science Press, 1996, p. 38.
28. Xiao Tangbiao, 'The Developing Clan Organizations and their Impact on Social and Political Stability in Chinese Villages,' in *Socialist Studies* (*Shehui zhuyi Yanjiu*), edited by Centre of Village Studies, Central China Normal University, Wuhan, 1995, pp. 91–3.
29. Fan Ping and Wang Xiaoyi, 'The Basic Situation of Peasants in 1995,' in *The 1996 Society Blue Book*, p. 287.
30. Jiang Liu *et al.* (eds), *An Analysis and Prediction of Chinese Social Situation in 1994–1995*, p. 317.
31. Gabriel A. Almond and Bingham Powel Jr., *Comparative Politics : System, Process, and Policy* (Boston: Little, Brown, 1978).
32. Min Qi, *Chinese Political Culture* (*Zhongguo zhengzhi wenhua*) (Kunming: Yunan People's Press, 1989), p. 233.
33. Li Zicheng was a noted peasant rebel in the late Ming dynasty.
34. Zhang Houan and Xu Yong, *Political Stability and Development in Chinese Villages*, p. 1097.

3 Public Maladministration and Bureaucratic Corruption

Sonny S. H. Lo

Public maladministration and bureaucratic corruption are serious problems that, it can be argued, are undermining the legitimacy of the Chinese Communist Party (CCP) in the People's Republic of China (PRC). While much attention has been focused on the development of public administration in the PRC, especially the recent attempts to implement civil service reforms, little research has been conducted on public maladministration, a thorny problem that requires urgent remedies and yet reveals a multitude of obstacles to solutions. Although there are numerous studies on corruption in the PRC, few attempts have been made to discuss corruption in the context of public maladministration. This chapter seeks to adopt a new perspective, analyzing the major features of public maladministration in China, discussing the remedies for maladministration and bureaucratic corruption, and examining the obstacles to such remedies.

Public maladministration can be defined broadly as 'administrative action or inaction' resulting from 'improper considerations or conduct'.[1] It embraces all the features of poor governance, such as injustice, failure to carry out legislative intent, unreasonable delay, administrative error, negligence, inadequate investigation, unfair policy, partiality, arbitrariness, inefficiency, violation of law or regulation, abuse of authority, discrimination, and other acts that are frequently inflicted upon the governed, intentionally or unintentionally, by those who govern.[2]

To put it succinctly, public maladministration is characterized by three major categories of administrative impropriety: (1) managerial incompetence; (2) abuse of power; and (3) bureaucratic corruption. Bureaucratic corruption refers to unclean acts committed by government officials, such as 'bending the law, discarding morality, dishonesty, venality, nepotism, appointment of jobs and contracts to unqualified persons, awarding decisions and services in exchange of bribes and kickbacks, and government by favour'.[3] Bureaucratic corruption brings about fraud, waste and abuse, thus exacerbating the extent of public maladministration.

There are three types of remedy for public maladministration: managerial, legal and political.[4] The managerial approach to public maladministration entails management-oriented reforms and aims at maximizing 'effectiveness, efficiency and economy'.[5] Modern techniques of scientific management in the areas of recruitment, promotion and functional specialization can be utilized to tackle the managerial roots of maladministration. From a legal perspective, administrative laws can be enacted to check the power of bureaucrats particularly those 'street-level' bureaucrats who have frequent and direct interaction with citizens at the grassroots level and who enjoy a considerable degree of discretion in their work. Examples of these 'street-level' bureaucrats are the police officers patrolling on the street and, in the context of China, cadres and CCP members who deal with livelihood issues concerning citizens at the provincial, county and village levels of the government. The legal approach to public maladministration is contingent upon the judiciary's ability to check the executive power and to protect individual rights. Finally, the political approach to public maladministration emphasizes governmental openness and responsiveness, the legislature's assertiveness in checking any arbitrary action committed by the state, and citizen participation in selecting their representatives who can transfer their complaints and views to the governing authorities.

This analytical framework does not necessarily mean that remedies for public maladministration must proceed toward the separation of power between the judiciary, the executive and the legislature – a Western model implicit in the three approaches mentioned above. Maladministration is a fact of life that exists in varying degrees in all countries. Solutions to public maladministration can be explored creatively by political leaders in the non-Western world. In other words, the content of the three approaches to maladministration can be very different from the West. In practice, during the Maoist era, the PRC adopted an ideologically oriented political approach to curbing bureaucratization, an approach that was at one time successful but which has been substantially abandoned in the reform decades since the mid-1970s.

THE MAOIST APPROACH TO PUBLIC MALADMINISTRATION AND BUREAUCRATIC CORRUPTION

The Maoist approach to public maladministration and bureaucratic corruption was highly political. Ideology became an instrument through which CCP members and cadres were expected to become the servants of the public. Small study groups and political campaigns were launched to mobilize citizens, party members, cadres and government officials to engage in criticisms and self-criticisms. The concept of 'mass line' (that cadres should meet the masses and listen to the opinions of the masses) was practised. The Maoist style of mass participation and politicization was not aimed at tackling the problem of maladministration, a concept non-existent in Mao's China, but was intended to direct the PRC toward the path of 'permanent revolution'.[6] But so long as the Maoists tended to distrust the bureaucracy and believe that the bureaucratic mentality should be wiped out by using political campaigns and implementing the mass line, a Maoist approach to public maladministration and bureaucratic corruption arguably did exist.

An unintended consequence of politicizing the public in Mao's China was to elevate Marxism–Leninism–Maoism to a level which contained some ingredients of a 'public service ideology'. Caiden elucidates that a public service ideology emphasizes the implementation of the 'general will'; the role of government officials as the 'servants of the public'; the subordination of 'personal interests'; the performance of official duties efficiently and economically; the appointment of officials on the basis of merit rather than on other criteria; and a legal constraint on public officials.[7] The Maoists recruited party members and government officials on the basis of their ideology (redness) rather than on merit (expertise), and they regarded law as a tool of the socialist state to penalize class enemies instead of a check on bureaucratic power (see Chapter 4 on China's legal reform). Nonetheless, CCP members and cadres were urged to implement the 'general will' – being 'good' socialists who served citizens wholeheartedly. Ideology in Mao's China was the most powerful weapon to restrain any arbitrary behaviour of street-level cadres and CCP members. As a result, bureaucratic corruption was checked and public maladministration was curbed to some extent.

Since the 1970s, however, China has de-ideologized and de-politicized the masses and elites to such an extent that public maladministration and corruption have become uncontrollable diseases. By virtually abandoning Maoism, political leaders in Deng's and post-Deng China have generated an ideological vacuum that has as yet not been filled by any effective political approach to tackle public maladministration. By publicizing the slogan that 'getting rich is glorious', citizens have been encouraged to pursue materialistic gains in the process of market reforms. Stimulated by numerous opportunities to get rich, government officials, CCP members and cadres are extremely vulnerable to materialism. As one scholar notes: '[M]any bureaucratic–comprador companies have thrived in coastal provinces in the period of "reform". These companies have made many members of the ruling class millionaires, or even billionaires'.[8]

Another observer who analyzed the income differentials in Deng's China argues that there was a 'bureaucratic bourgeoisie'; that cadres 'at all levels had indulged in bribe-taking, reselling state property for their own profits'; and that some units were 'forced to enter the market in order to pay their running expenses and boost their employees' salaries'.[9] Cadres, CCP members and officials cannot resist the temptation to 'get rich quick' and become corrupt easily. This has exacerbated the degree of public maladministration which, if not arrested, could sooner or later plunge the CCP into a crisis of legitimacy – as with Romania under the rule of Ceausescu.

THE CHARACTERISTICS OF PUBLIC MALADMINISTRATION IN DENG'S AND POST-DENG CHINA

Managerial incompetence

Examples of public maladministration in Deng's China abounded and proliferated in all three dimensions of public administration: managerial, legal and political. Managerially, many government departments failed to deliver the services to satisfy public needs. In Guangzhou city, for example, after 30 public toilets were dismantled due to urban redevelopment, there were insufficient toilets for citizens, particularly when there were concerts and soccer matches in the city.[10] The problem was that government departments lacked any long-term plan prior to the dismantling of public toilets.

Public maladministration reached crisis proportions in some cases where citizens resorted to desperate measures to make their views heard. In March 1995, an eighty-year-old woman in Shanghai committed suicide by setting herself on fire in protest against the municipal government's policy of evacuating her from her home, which would be demolished and replaced by a high-rise building.[11] The tragedy came to the attention of the central government and the Vice-Premier, Li Nanqing, asked why the Shanghai municipal government disobeyed Beijing's order not to replace old buildings with skyscrapers. The root of the managerial malaise in Shanghai was that when the municipal government redeveloped old districts into new commercial ones, it failed to formulate a policy of relocating citizens, who were forced to look for accommodation themselves and who eventually suffered from having to reside in temporary shelters where hygiene was undesirable and the supply of water or electricity insufficient.

Managerial incompetence was commonplace in all of the coastal cities, like the Shenzhen Special Economic Zone (SEZ). The scramble for application forms for stock shares in August 1992; the sudden explosion of a warehouse filled with explosives in Qingshuihe zone in August 1993; and the occurrence of numerous accidental fires causing workers' deaths in factories – all these illustrated the seriousness of managerial impotence in Shenzhen. Beijing was infuriated by Shenzhen's maladministration. One report published by the Central Discipline Inspection Commission (CDIC) in December 1993 found that Shenzhen's top cadres 'possessed properties which were incommensurate with their income'.[12] In response, Beijing ordered the Guangdong provincial government to reshuffle the Shenzhen leadership, sent work teams to inspect the Shenzhen administration, and warned that Shenzhen officials who violated party discipline would be penalized.

Street-level bureaucrats in Deng's China often took advantage of their administrative 'discretion' to enrich themselves. In Shanghai, a storage keeper conspired with a 32-member crime syndicate to steal 350 tons of meat from 1988 to 1991, causing the government to lose 200 000 yuan.[13] In 1995, some Hong Kong citizens complained to the mass media in Hong Kong that Shenzhen hospitals refused to provide treatment to patients in emergency situations, the hospital authorities demanding cash payment prior to any treatment being given. In Shenzhen, some Public Security Bureau (PSB) officers were notorious for conspiring with prostitutes, 'catching' Hong Kong people and imposing heavy fines on them.[14] In the Lowu checkpoint where Hong Kong people's luggage is inspected by the mainland's disciplinary officers, one Hong Kong citizen, who was annoyed by a People's Armed Police (PAP) officer who kept on talking with another officer, angrily asked the officer to stop talking.[15] The officer was infuriated and he confiscated the travel document of the complainant. The angry Hongkonger lodged a complaint to the officer's superior, but the Hong Kong citizen was reprimanded and urged by the superior to stop complaining. At the same time, the talkative officer shouted at the Hongkonger. If public servants in Shenzhen did not reflect upon their arbitrary behaviour, it would be difficult for the SEZ to improve its regional image in the long run.

Abuse of power

The phenomenon of officials abusing their power was extensive in Deng's China. One example was a county Party secretary in Guangdong province: she reportedly had an affair with her driver, who was eventually promoted to became head of the Transport Police and later chief of the county's PSB.[16] The behaviour of the married Party secretary and her 'boyfriend' aroused the anger of citizens, who complained to the Anti-Corruption Bureau of the Guangdong provincial government. To pre-empt an investigation by the authorities, the Party secretary surrendered 1 million yuan to the authorities and claimed that this huge amount of money originated from the gifts she had received. Yet, the Anti-Corruption Bureau discovered that her move was initiated to block an attempt to look into her moral and administrative impropriety and that she still possessed 370 000 yuan amassed from bribes.

Other cases of official abuse of power included using public vehicles for personal use; unnecessarily buying expensive cars in violation of the existing rules on car use by cadres; allowing relatives to occupy apartments exceeding the official size limits; utilizing public expenditure to host lavish dinners, organize tours, and buy expensive gifts for guests; and cultivating *guanxi* (personal ties) to subsidize sons and daughters to study overseas.[17] One confidential document of the CCP reported that 90 per cent of the relatives of high-ranking retired cadres had used public funds to study in the United States, Canada, Western Europe, Australia and Japan; and that 48 per cent finally resided in foreign countries after their graduation.[18] The document called for a control upon the 'special privileges' of retired high-ranking cadres and their relatives, and influential patrons within the government, whose opportunities of going abroad were much higher than those of ordinary citizens without *guanxi*.

The pervasive abuse of power by CCP members can be illustrated by the case of Ouyang De, a Party secretary of Donggan city in Guangdong province. He conspired with two of his assistants to ask for bribes from enterprises; exercised his discretion to allow relatives of other subordinates to acquire one-way visas to visit Hong Kong; permitted his son to invest in prostitution businesses; struggled against those cadres who had moral integrity and who were keen to fight corruption; and formed cliques or patron–client networks so as to enrich those involved.[19] Although Ouyang was removed from his post and returned the bribes he had received to the authorities, his case exposed the rapid degeneration of party discipline at the local level. Under the protective umbrella of localism, Ouyang's subordinates became millionaires. Localism provided a breeding ground for public maladministration, personal gain and bureaucratic corruption.

Bureaucratic corruption

Another case parallel to Ouyang De's abuse of power and bureaucratic corruption was the scandal involving Chen Xitong, the former Beijing mayor. In April 1995, Wang Baosen, who was Chen's associate and the deputy mayor of Beijing, committed suicide. Wang was investigated by the central government for his corrupt activities, and it was found that he and Chen had cooperated together to enrich themselves. Chen had reportedly formed a private army, employing his security guards to spy on the activities of some Beijing leaders so that material detrimental to the top leaders' images could, if necessary, be used to protect Chen's 'independent empire' in Beijing.[20] One government report on the Chen case, prepared by the CDIC and numbered 950 135, revealed that he had resisted the CDIC's attempt to look into Wang's corrupt activities; held dinners and dance meetings with prostitutes; assisted 29 relatives to secure job positions in the government; permitted relatives to obtain one-way visas to settle in Hong Kong; received bribes and gifts amounting to 2 800 000 yuan; and privately possessed machine-guns in his home.[21] The case of Chen showed how a top CCP member could degenerate from a 'revolutionary' in former times to a decadent and power-hungry official in the materialistic Deng era.

Disciplinary forces in Deng's China were pursuing money-making activities which not only undermined their administrative ethics but also brought about maladministration. For example, the People's Armed Police (PAP) was underpaid and lacked funds. Consequently, its members tried to get rich by illegal means. The central government could provide only 70 per cent of the total expenditure of the PAP, which also relied on local governments for subsidies. In addition, units of the People's Liberation Army (PLA) used their military vehicles for 'speculation, profiteering or smuggling'; and these commercial activities, in the words of a foreign military attaché in China, were 'against the very ethics a soldier is trained in [because] he is supposed to serve the country, not himself or his unit'.[22] One report prepared by the CCP disclosed that triads penetrated the disciplinary forces, including the PLA, police and customs, and that some triad members even paid bribes to become government officials in villages.[23]

The most notorious agency plagued with bureaucratic corruption was the PSB. In Guangxi province's Yinzhou city, one PSB chief requested his subordinates to release some people who had operated a casino illegally and who had been arrested and later he was found to be the casino's boss.[24] A Chinese cliché describing public distrust toward the police says, 'cops and robbers are of the same tribe'.[25] Many corrupt police officers are the product of materialism and an ideological vacuum in Deng's and post-Deng China. As one observer put it accurately:

> While they subsisted on a basic salary and led an arduous life serving the people, some 'people' were spending [Reminbi] 360 000 on a dog or paying good money for a smile from a movie star. This was different from the days when the police and the military were idolized by the youth.[26]

Bureaucratic corruption of the PSB showed that there was a serious 'management gap' in Deng's China where public administration was underdeveloped. As one scholar argues:

> Deng's reform reveals a management gap in the process of modernization wherein the spectacular success in agriculture and the emphasis on economic development have led to the rapid growth of business management but inadequate attention to public administration. Methods which have been proven effective in the profit-oriented business sector are blindly applied to the public sector, which concerns itself principally with providing services.[27]

More alarmingly, bureaucratic corruption has already penetrated deep into China's legal system, where some court judges abuse their power and receive bribes. One former judge of the Shenzhen Intermediate People's Court (SIPC), Zhang Xin, wrote an article critical of the SIPC's chief judge, Wang Changying.[28] According to Zhang, Wang accepted bribes twice, used his power to retaliate against enemies and illegally arrested opponents. Zhang wrote letters of complaint to Jiang Zemin, Premier Li Peng, the CDIC head Wei Jianxing and the mass media. But there was no reply. Even worse, Wang ordered the arrest of Zhang, who was asked by the SIPC's judicial officials not to complain again about Wang. Zhang eventually suffered from police brutality in a re-education camp. Beijing's leaders were reportedly shocked by the extent of public maladministration and particularly bureaucratic corruption, like the case of Beijing's mayor Chen Zitong and deputy-mayor Wang Baosen in 1995. Some leaders said that 'if this situation continues, our party will collapse'.[29]

REMEDIES FOR PUBLIC MALADMINISTRATION AND BUREAUCRATIC CORRUPTION

Managerial remedies

From a managerial perspective, civil service reform has been implemented since 1993, the year in which the Provisional Civil Service Regulations were enacted. Recruitment of civil servants by merit was piloted in the State Council and some 'test points' (*shi dian*) in provinces, special economic zones and autonomous regions. However, the Personnel Department said that major problems were that public management was over-centralized and its managerial techniques were outdated. Still, there was an increase in the number of applicants for civil service positions. In Xian city, 1439 peasants applied for the posts and 79 of them were eventually recruited in 1996.[30]

Another managerial remedy was to eliminate sinecures in various government departments. In 1993 there were 34 millions cadres in the PRC, and over 60 per cent of them were employed by county governments.[31] The Personnel Department decided to cut 25 per cent of cadres in the CCP, 20 per cent in the central government, and 25 per cent in regions and cities. Yet, trimming the size of the bureaucracy encountered problems of (1) resistance from the dismissed cadres, who complained that the government did not care about their well-being; (2) opposition from enterprise managers; and (3) the use of *guanxi* and nepotism by cadres to maintain their own positions or protect the interests of their relatives.[32] Managerial remedies clearly encountered political hindrance.

Although managerial reforms were implemented, the salaries of civil servants remained relatively low. Raising the salaries of civil servants is crucial to curbing public maladministration. In July 1993, the CCP postponed a plan to reform the pay system of civil servants, for the 'basic pre-requisites' of such reforms were nonexistent.[33] These 'prerequisites' included, for example, a strong fiscal condition in central government, trimming the size of the party-bureaucracy, and some progress in the reform of state enterprises. Financially, raising the salaries of civil servants would necessitate not only an annual increase of 3.2 to 3.5 billion yuan in the central government's expenditure, but also a total expenditure of 220 to 230 billion yuan in the PRC.[34] In 1993, however, the number of staff members in government agencies was only reduced by 7500 – a figure that achieved 15 per cent of Beijing's target. In the final analysis, the CCP was concerned about the negative reaction of state enterprises to the civil service's pay reform. Due to all of these factors, reforming the salary of civil servants has been postponed indefinitely.

The managerial remedy required political sensitivity and finesse. In November 1994, the CCP's Propaganda Department publicized those party members willing to return the luxurious cars they possessed. Yet, there were 280 complaint letters from CCP members and citizens to the newspapers, the New China News Agency and the Propaganda Department, saying that this publicity had an undesirable public impact and reflected badly upon the CCP.[35] In response to public opinion, Ding Guanjin – the Propaganda Department's chief – went into damage control, ordering the subordinate organs to 'correct' the publicity praising the questionable officials.[36] The CCP had failed to anticipate the possibility of negative public reaction to its publicity of officials who had actually violated party discipline.

Managerial remedies have so far not been accompanied by the political will to penalize corrupt and incompetent public servants, regardless of their ranks and status. One researcher observes:

> The party's traditional approach to some chronic problems, such as corruption, is untouched by the [civil service] reforms. The CCP's reliance on persuasion and inner-party discipline, on the one hand, and harsh treatment, including death, for corrupt low ranking officials, on the other, has apparently failed to stem the problem. The system continues to allow officials to short-circuit official corruption investigations by appealing to powerful patrons further up the political hierarchy. The attraction of mutual benefits is apparently too strong to bring the problem under control.[37]

As a matter of fact, the persistence of patron–client networks in the PRC constitutes a political stumbling-block for any attempt to curb public maladministration and bureaucratic corruption.

Ultimately, managerial solutions to maladministration and corruption encounter a traditional problem: the widespread use of *guanxi*. Some cadres utilized their personal relations with CCP leaders and superiors to block the process of recruiting and promoting civil servants on the basis of merit.[38] This was by no means a new phenomenon, for in the past most cadres who had their performance appraised by superiors tended to 'disregard their work and spend time and energy to cultivate good *guanxi* with leading cadres'.[39] The managerial approach to tackling maladministration was destined to face a cultural hurdle because cadres and party members skilfully used *guanxi* as a means to achieve their personal interests, and to render attempts at establishing a Western-type bureaucracy abortive.

Legal remedies

Apart from the managerial approach, legal remedies have been employed to cope with public maladministration in Deng's and post-Deng China. The judiciary set up telephone hot-lines for the masses to file complaints against lawyers, some of whom overcharged the clients, and some accepted the clients' payment but failed to provide services. The Administrative Procedure Law (APL, also known as Administrative Litigation Law), which was enacted by the National People's Congress (NPC) in April 1989 and came into effect in October 1990, can be viewed as a 'street-level management law' trying to curb the administrative discretion of bureaucrats.[40] The APL was applied successfully in some cases involving the abuse of power by officials, offering a channel for the redress of grievances to citizens. In 1996, some Hong Kong citizens also used the APL to sue the mainland developers, who collaborated with corrupt government officials but failed to build apartments in accordance with the schedule stated on the contracts with Hong Kong buyers. It seems that the APL provides a useful means by which citizens can check the arbitrary behaviour of officials.

Unfortunately, political hindrance limits the ability of the courts to implement the APL. 'Party immunity', according to a legal expert, was apparent. CCP leaders could exercise their power to infringe civil liberties, in cases such as (1) the confiscation of all 300 000 copies of the independent-minded *World Economic Herald* in 1989, and (2) the abortive attempt by dissident Han Dongfang to file a lawsuit against the Ministry of Public Security for cancelling his passport in September 1993. While cases involving political dissidents critical of the government tend to be 'high-level' political issues that cannot be tackled by the APL, those 'low-level' ones involving the exploitation of peasants by local cadres sometimes cannot be legally dealt with by the court. For instance, in Shanxi province, although peasants wrote a complaint letter about the exploitative behaviour of local cadres, they failed to get any response from the court.[41] Ideally, judicial officials require a certain degree of political autonomy from any influence from the CCP elites who have a vested interest in opposing the APL's implementation.

Another legal remedy was to implement the Administrative Penalty Law in October 1996, which restricted the period of detention by the PSB. The Law was endorsed by the National People's Congress (NPC) in March 1996, requiring the PSB to apply for arrest warrants in order to continue imprisoning any suspects after 30 days of detention. Yet, this law did not really limit the state's ability to arrest political dissidents at will. As shown in the cases of Wang Dan and Liu Xiaobo, who were arrested by the authorities in October 1996 for participating in 'counter-revolutionary' activities,[42] the law appeared to be a cosmetic measure which did not impose a genuine constraint on the PSB's powers.

Laws have been utilized to control the administrative impropriety of government officials – a small step in the remedies for maladministration and corruption. Under the cadres' disciplinary regulations, they are required to hand in gifts they receive from citizens. Some cadres follow such regulations and their gifts include computers, video cameras, jewellery, cognac, Swiss watches and audio-visual equipment. Meanwhile, the quality of many police officers is so questionable that the Personnel Department and the PSB decided to have two pieces of legislation enacted. One is concerned with recruitment and the other with dismissal, both being aimed at hiring good quality officers and eliminating those who 'seriously undermine the image of the police'.[43]

Although legal means are employed to prevent cadres and officials from doing business, the distinction between public and private sectors remains unclear. As long as such distinction is vague and not defined precisely, government and business can forge an unholy and symbiotic alliance. In these circumstances, members of the bureaucratic bourgeoisie can act more as entrepreneurs enriching themselves than as public officials serving the citizens. In many cases, cadres and business people have a vested interest in monopolizing a particular business sector. While cadres utilize their political power and *guanxi* to help business people secure licences, the latter help the former who are dissatisfied with their low salaries to get rich swiftly.[44] The PRC government is using legal means to react to problems of maladministration, rather than anticipating and addressing them beforehand.

Problems associated with this incremental approach to legal remedies are compounded by the questionable quality of judicial officials. The government of Guangdong province has enacted a law banning corruption in the courts, where some officials accept bribes from litigants and pervert the course of justice.[45] On the other hand, corrupt officials utilize legal loopholes to defend their cases and it becomes difficult for the courts to prosecute them. For example, one director responsible for sports affairs in Fujian province was prosecuted for receiving 57 000 yuan in bribes from a company in return for facilitating the process of issuing lottery tickets.[46] Due to insufficient evidence, the court failed to prosecute the director and it subsequently released him. If officials involved in maladministration and corruption make use of legal means to protect themselves, the tasks of anti-corruption and anti-maladministration require far more sophisticated investigatory skills on the part of judicial officials than ever before.

Another obstacle to legal remedies is that the target of punishment has been restricted to low-ranking officials, not high-ranking cadres. Occasionally some top CCP members, like Chen Xitong, are purged. But the punishment tends to be mild. As long as penalties are not severe, the temptation for CCP members to receive bribes is high. The moderate level of punishment perpetuates a vicious circle in which bureaucratic corruption becomes a 'low-risk' but 'highly rewarding' activity.[47] A drastic increase in the penalties on both low-ranking and high-ranking officials can render bureaucratic corruption a high-risk and low-rewarding act, which will reduce the pervasiveness of maladministration.

Political remedies

The CCP relies on purges to eliminate corrupt and incompetent officials. But this is a stop-gap measure that cannot effectively uproot the problem of maladministration in the long run. It was reported that the CCP feared that, if Chen Xitong were required to appear in the court, he might expose in public the identity of other high-ranking corrupt officials.[48] Thus, his case has been frozen and is handled in a low-key manner that will not undermine the CCP's legitimacy.

Politically, the CCP since the 1970s has implemented policies designed to encourage citizen participation and thus hopefully consolidate its legitimacy (for grassroots political participation, see Chapter 2). Some complaint channels have been established to deal with citizens' grievances. For example, in view of the fact that some primary and secondary schools collected from parents all kinds of illegal fees, such as 'fees for inspecting the hair of children', the Guangdong government set up telephone hot-lines for complaints at the provincial, county and municipal levels.[49]

Yet, channels for citizen participation in checking the arbitrary action of officials remain insufficient. Some angry citizens who are victimized by public maladministration become so desperate that they resort to petitions to top CCP leaders. In 1996 Jiang Zemin was twice intercepted by peasants who complained that local cadres were corrupt and exploited them.[50] In the 1990s, violent confrontations between villagers and urban residents on the one hand and PSB and PLA officers on the other became a commonplace in South China, especially in Guangdong province, where such conflicts are extensively covered by the news media in Hong Kong. In fact, conflicts at the grassroots level reflect the seriousness of public maladministration in China. Apart from inadequate participatory channels, there are political stumbling blocks for the Central Discipline Inspection Commission (CDIC) in its fight against bureaucratic corruption and in its attempt to curb public maladministration. First and foremost, the CCP elites oppose the CDIC's work. In December 1994, 12 members of the Commission tendered their resignation to the central government on the grounds that their work had been 'interfered with abnormally by the party'.[51] In January 1995, 19 of the 103 members of the Commission abstained from voting for the CDIC report, because they believed the report, which said anti-corruption work was 'fruitful', should have revealed that the CDIC's operation was resisted by the party and government leaders.[52]

Political elites who have vested interests resist any attempt to disclose their assets and family background to Commission members. The CDIC's document, No. 94043, asserted that provincial party leaders had reservations about disclosing their personal matters pertaining to the Commission's investigation.[53] Horizontally, the CDIC's power is checked by the provincial party committees. Vertically, it is under the influence of the top leaders and party committees, some of whom provide a protective umbrella for corrupt and incompetent subordinates.

Furthermore, the quality of some CDIC investigators is low and they lack authority in the minds of the populace, partly due to the Commission's limited powers.[54] Even worse, the CDIC's work has been internally undermined to a considerable degree by patron–client politics. The 13 executive members of CDIC are actually split into three loosely organized groupings. One is determined to fight corruption and maladministration, whereas another grouping loyally supports Li Peng, who actually wishes to monitor the Commission's work.[55] The third grouping, to the CDIC's embarrassment, comprises a minority of executive members who were Chen Xitong's subordinates. For example, CDIC executive member Wang Gang was the former deputy Party secretary in Beijing from 1988 to 1992, when Chen Xitong was Beijing's mayor and deputy Party secretary.[56] Wang is the CDIC member responsible for managing confidential matters, but his credibility and the Commission's image were undermined to some extent by the Chen Zitong scandal.

Arguably, an alternative political means to curb maladministration could be a reactivation of the Maoist approach, politicizing the masses and elites through ideologization. This does not imply that class struggle, a political weapon that plunged Maoist China into chaos and anarchy during the Cultural Revolution, should be adopted. Rather it can be argued that the concept of mass line could be applied to indoctrinate government officials and cadres with a sense of some public service ethos. Having said that, nevertheless, it would probably be difficult to politicize the peasants, who are generally suspicious of the 'policy wind' which ideologized and radicalized them in the past.[57] In Jiangsu province, peasants resisted any effort made by the CCP to inculcate socialism through work teams sent to the countryside.[58] Some peasants demonstrated outside the office of the work teams, whereas others petitioned the county government and maintained that work teams should be dismantled. As the victims of radical Maoist policies, peasants are afraid of government policy that aims at re-indoctrinating them – an obstacle to an ideological approach to maladministration.

Political reforms in Deng's and post-Deng China could be a panacea to public maladministration. There have been calls for changes in the one-party system in China, albeit such demands were infrequent and weak. In October 1996, the CCP's think-tanks studied a number of models for political liberalization, including a proposal for the election of the CCP's 200-odd Central Committee members by the PRC's 57 million Party members.[59] Village elections were actually held in 1996, but many non-Party members who were elected as village leaders were eventually asked to join the CCP. This cooption of the newly elected village leaders, however, is by no means conducive to a political solution for public maladministration, because they become part of the ruling class and will sooner or later be vulnerable to corruption and patron–client relations.

Nonetheless, since the Deng era, China has been envisaging a gradual increase in the assertiveness of the legislature, which could emerge as an alternative to counter the problem of maladministration. Some provincial people's congress members are increasingly critical of the government. In 1992–3, for example, deputies of provincial congresses in Zhejiang, Jiangsu, Ningxia, and Hunan criticized the lack of power of their assemblies, saying that they should have more power to supervise the performance of government officials.[60] Ten members of the provincial congress at Jiangsu province maintained that direct elections should be introduced at the county and village levels.[61] Hence, some of the people's representatives in the PRC wish to adopt a political approach to tackle maladministration, checking the executive power through the introduction of village elections and the increased power of provincial legislatures.

The political approach to public maladministration appears to be increasingly supported by elites in post-Deng China. Since the 1990s, the NPC has become more assertive, with more capable legislators questioning the central government's policies.[62] In addition, more NPC members cast their votes against the government budget law in 1994 than ever before – a symbol that legislators did not want to act as a 'rubber-stamp' endorsing government policies.[63] Although the process of reforming the legislature remains relatively slow, some representatives of Hong Kong to the NPC adopt an independent outlook, occasionally criticizing corruption and maladministration in the mainland.[64] The Hong Kong deputies to the NPC, some of whom have rich experience in the Hong Kong Legislative Council, can provide a momentum for the gradual political modernization of the Congress. After the death of Deng in early 1997, an unprecedented number of NPC deputies voted in March against the anti-corruption and anti-crime report prepared by the Supreme People's Court,[65] a further indication that post-Deng China is witnessing progress in using a political approach to tackling public maladministration.

Political reforms, however, are so far not allowed to proceed in a direction that will undermine the CCP's legitimacy and governance. For the time being, the NPC's checks and balances upon public maladministration are still insufficient. The Chinese People's Political Consultative Conference (CPPCC), moreover, remains a discussion forum without any significant impact on, or effective input into, government policy-making. In October 1994, 22 members of the CPPCC wrote a letter to the central government, hoping that the CPPCC would have its functions reformed and expanded. Yet, top Chinese leaders such as Jiang Zemin, Qiao Shi and Li Ruihuan said that their demand had a 'wrong tendency' of using the CPPCC to supervise the CCP's work.[66]

After all, 'bureaucratic accountability' is an alien concept to PRC officials and CCP leaders. Bureaucratic accountability requires that formal and informal measures be adopted to make the civil service more responsive, transparent and accountable for its actions to the public.[67] This is a Western practice that, if implemented in the PRC, would necessitate a transformation of Chinese political and administrative culture – a gigantic task in a non-Western setting. Even so, it can be argued that some elements of bureaucratic accountability in the West could be selectively applied in the PRC. For example, improving the 'personal ethics', 'professionalism', and 'commitment' of public officials, tightening the rules governing the bureaucracy, and reforming the criteria of performance evaluation are arguably cross-cultural managerial techniques.[68] In fact, Deng's China in the 1990s gradually implemented some of these reforms. Yet, a further acceleration and deepening of managerial reforms are necessary to keep maladministration under control in post-Deng China.

Politically, the relatively weak, government-controlled and uncritical mass media in China cannot serve as an effective deterrent to public maladministration. However, some citizens utilize the available political space provided by the mass media to attack maladministration. In Shandong province, for example, some peasants were exploited by village cadres who sold the farmland for profits but who refused to reduce taxes.[69] As a result, the alienated peasants hired actors to perform the corrupt behaviour of cadres, producing a programme that was eventually shown on the television. The programme aroused the concern of top CCP leaders, who feared that if the mass media continued to expose the corruption of village cadres, this would provide a catalyst for further mass alienation. It is ironic that, while the media can occasionally expose cases of maladministration, the CCP is over-sensitive toward the reverberating impact of a more independent media on its legitimacy and political dominance.

CONCLUSION

Since the Deng era, the PRC leaders have been implementing managerial and legal reforms to tackle public maladministration, including bureaucratic corruption. Nonetheless, the alliance between the capitalist class and the bureaucratic bourgeoisie constitutes a political stumbling block for these remedies. The CCP's political preponderance, without sufficient checks and balances from the legislative branch and the mass media, perpetuates a desperate search for effective remedies for public maladministration and bureaucratic corruption. Ideologically, the CCP's 'official adherence to Marxism makes it extremely difficult to either admit the existence of a capitalist class or exploitation'.[70] The difficulty of acknowledging the capitalist and bureaucratic exploitation of the masses in Deng's and post-Deng China means that solutions to public maladministration are bound to be conservative, incremental, piecemeal and limited to managerial and legal measures in the short run.

Any effective strategy to uproot the problem of public maladministration requires the political will of the post-Deng leadership. It requires the will to surrender at least part of the power of the CCP, subjecting the ruling party to the scrutiny of the increasingly assertive legislature, the relatively compliant mass media and the masses. It also requires a certain degree of re-politicization and re-ideologization, despite the fact that there would be opposition to this by the ruling class from above and by the peasants from below. With the benefit of hindsight, one crucial element of the Maoist approach to public maladministration could arguably be reactivated, namely the mass line. Indoctrinating the cadres and civil servants will improve public administration. In the era of market reforms, the ideological vacuum in China is not filled by either political reforms or the expansion and institutionalization of grievance channels. Without sufficient participatory channels through which citizens can check the power of the ruling class, the seeds of political instability and turbulence remain entrenched in post-Deng China. It is politically imperative for the CCP and post-Deng leadership to cultivate a genuine public service ideology among the ruling elites. Otherwise, public maladministration and bureaucratic corruption will result in mass alienation, eventually precipitating a serious crisis of legitimacy that the CCP would sooner or later find it difficult to tackle.

Another option for the CCP to uproot the problem of public maladministration and bureaucratic corruption is to grant an amnesty to corrupt officials when other reforms, legal and managerial, are implemented successfully.[71] Since the date of such an amnesty would constitute a clean break from past practices, harsh penalties would henceforth have to be applied to all officials at both the low-ranking and high-ranking levels. Any move to initiate such an amnesty should ideally be preceded by an acceleration of managerial, legal and some degree of political reforms. At the same time, the triangular relationship between the government, the CCP and the business sector will have to be delineated in a much clearer manner. Otherwise, the political alliance between business and bureaucrats will remain strong and continue to have a corrupting influence on public administration.

Unfortunately, ideals may not conform to the reality. In the meantime, there are no signs that the CCP and post-Deng leaders will implement drastic and innovative measures to cope with maladministration and corruption. If the CCP continues to adopt an incremental approach to reforms, public maladministration will persist. Ultimately, the effective remedy will still be political reform, regardless of whether it includes either the re-application of the mass line concept to inculcate a public service ethos amongst CCP cadres, or the modernization of China's political system toward the separation of powers, as in the West.

Notes and references

1. K. C. Wheare, *Maladministration and Its Remedies* (London: Stevens & Sons, 1973), p. 11. Wheare extracted this definition from an annual report of the Northern Ireland Commissioner for Complaints in 1970.
2. B. Frank, 'The Ombudsman and Human Rights Revisited', *Israel Yearbook on Human Rights,* 6 (1976), p. 134, cited in Gerald E. Caiden, 'Public Maladministration and Bureaucratic Corruption', *Hong Kong Journal of Public Administration*, vol. 3 (1981), p. 56.
3. Gerald Caiden, 'Public Maladministration and Bureaucratic Corruption,' pp. 56–7
4. David H. Rosenbloom, 'Public Administrative Theory and the Separation of Powers', *Public Administrative Review*, vol.43 (May/June 1983), pp. 219–27.
5. Ibid., p. 220.
6. See Maurice Meisner, *Mao's China*: *A History of the People's Republic* (New York: Free Press, 1977), Conclusion, pp. 384–89.
7. Caiden, 'Public Maladministration and Bureaucratic Corruption', p. 57.
8. Li Minqi, 'China: Six Years After Tiananmen', *Monthly Review*, vol. 47, no.8 (January 1996), p. 7.
9. Chang Chen-pang, 'The Resurgence of the Bourgeoisie in Mainland China', *Issues & Studies* (May 1994), p. 43.

10. *Oriental Daily*, 7 October 1996, p. A21.
11. *Frontline* (May 1995), pp. 40–1.
12. *Cheng Ming* (February 1994), p. 17. The son of the former Shenzhen mayor, Li Hao, not only earned a huge profit by speculating in the property market, but also participated in smuggling activities. Li's daughter utilized her father's connections to enrich herself in the stock market. For these stories, see *Open Magazine* (1 December 1995), pp. 16–17.
13. *Frontline* (October 1996), p. 30.
14. *Frontline* (March 1994), p. 32.
15. Ibid.
16. *Oriental Daily*, 1 October 1996, p. A21.
17. *Trend* (November 1994), pp. 14–15.
18. *Trend* (April 1995), pp. 10–11.
19. *Frontline* (August 1995), pp. 6–9; and (October 1995), pp. 26–7. It was said that prostitution in Dongguan under Ouyang De was more serious than that in Shenzhen.
20. *Frontline* (June 1995), p. 23.
21. *Trend* (October 1995), pp. 17–18.
22. Cheung Tai Ming, 'The Army Goes to Business', in Frank Ching (ed.), *China in Transition* (Hong Kong: Review Publishing Company Limited, November 1995), p. 99.
23. *Oriental Daily*, 11 October 1996, p. A22. In fact, the Hong Kong triads are penetrating the mainland areas where they can reap quick profits. A typical example is the Ling Ding island near Zhuhai, a place notorious for widespread prostitution. Four Hong Kong triads established their bases by bribing the mainland disciplinary forces. See *Oriental Daily*, 1 October 1996, p. A17.
24. *Ming Pao*, 3 October 1996, p. A15.
25. Anthony Kuhn, 'Cops and Robbers', *Far Eastern Economic Review*, 9 June 1994, p. 16.
26. Kam C. Wong, 'Public Security Reform in China in the 1990s,' in Maurice Brosseau and Lo Chi Kin (eds), *China Review 1994* (Hong Kong: The Chinese University Press, 1994), p. 58.
27. Stephen K. Ma, 'Reform Corruption: A Discussion on China's Current Development', *Pacific Affairs*, vol. 62, no. 1 (Spring 1989), p. 51.
28. *Frontline* (May 1994), pp. 44–46.
29. *Cheng Ming* (August 1995), pp. 14–15.
30. *Ming Pao,* 8 October 1996, p. A12.
31. *Trend* (October 1993), pp. 32–3.
32. *Trend* (October 1993), pp. 34–5.
33. *Cheng Ming* (September 1993), p. 31.
34. Ibid., p. 32.
35. *Trend* (December 1994), p. 11.
36. Ibid., p. 11.
37. John P. Burns, 'Civil Service Reform in China', *Asian Journal of Political Science*, vol. 2, no. 2 (December 1994), p. 72.
38. When the author taught a course for some mainland-Chinese cadre training programme in Hong Kong in 1993, one cadre told me that it was difficult for him to be transferred to become a civil servant because

he did not have good *guanxi*. For the clash between Chinese traditional values, like *guanxi*, and the Western ideal model of a meritocratic bureaucracy, see Steven E. Aufrecht and Li Siu Bun, 'Reform with Chinese Characteristics: The Context of Chinese Civil Service Reform', *Public Administration Review*, vol. 55, no. 2 (March/April 1995), p. 178.

39. King W. Chow, 'The Management of Chinese Cadre Resources: The Politics of Performance Appraisal (1949–84)', *International Review of Administrative Sciences*, vol. 54 (1988), p. 368.
40. Hon S. Chan, 'Judicial Review and Control over Administrative Discretion in the People's Republic of China', *Review of Central and Eastern European Law*, no. 2 (1992), p. 139.
41. Yang Haikun, 'Market Economy, Administration and Administrative Litigation', paper (in Chinese) presented at the conference on 'The Resolution of Administrative Grievances', University of Hong Kong, 10–11 December 1993, p. 10.
42. Wang was charged with 'subverting' the government by writing articles critical of the CCP, and by his attempt to help those political dissidents who were released but who faced financial problems. See *Oriental Daily*, 13 October 1996, p. A7. Also see Jasper Becker, 'Prisoners of the same old system', *Sunday Morning Post*, 13 October 1996, p. 11.
43. *Ming Pao*, 28 September 1996, p. A13.
44. Li Donghao, 'Cure the Illness of 'Officials–Business' Monopoly,' *National Affairs Review* (Hong Kong Chinese magazine), no. 30 (July 1993), pp. 10–15.
45. *South China Morning Post*, 12 October 1996, p. 7.
46. *Frontline* (November 1995), p. 9.
47. I borrow these two terms from Jon S. T. Quah, 'Corruption in Asia With Special Reference To Singapore: Patterns and Consequences', *Asian Journal of Public Administration*, vol. 10, no. 1 (June 1988), p. 88.
48. *Apple Daily* (13 October 1996), p. A10.
49. *Ming Pao* (11 October 1996), p. A11.
50. *Ming Pao* (11 October 1996), p. A10.
51. *Cheng Ming* (March 1995), pp. 20–1.
52. Ibid., p. 21.
53. *Trend* (November 1994), p. 13.
54. *Trend* (November 1994), p. 15.
55. *Frontline* (February 1996), pp. 28–32.
56. Ibid., p. 30.
57. The Maoists used 'policy winds and class struggle campaigns to generate a radical environment at the local level'. See David Zweig, *Agrarian Radicalism in China, 1968–1981* (Massachusetts: Harvard University Press, 1989), p. 32.
58. *Cheng Ming* (January 1992), pp. 24–5.
59. *South China Morning Post* (2 October 1996), p. 9.
60. *Cheng Ming* (October 1993), p. 29.
61. *Cheng Ming* (October 1993), p. 29.
62. See, for example, Kevin J. O'Brien and Li Lianjiang, 'Chinese Political Reform and the Question of 'Deputy Quality'', *China Information*, vol. 8, no. 3 (Winter 1993–4), pp. 20–31.

63. There were 337 NPC members who voted against the budget; 2110 voted for it; 225 abstained; and there were 40 invalid votes. See *Ming Pao*, 23 March 1994, p. A15.
64. For the role of Hong Kong deputies in the NPC, see Ng Hong-mun, *A Memoir in the NPC* (Hong Kong: Ming Pao, 1990), pp. 169–170.
65. *South China Morning Post*, 15 March 1997, p. 1. Out of 2720 delegates, 515 voted against the report and 331 abstained. The last time deputies expressed opposition to the government was in 1995, when 605 of the 1746 delegates voted against the appointment of Jiang Chunyun as Vice Premier and 401 abstained.
66. *Trend* (February 1995), pp. 14–15.
67. For the various mechanisms that can enhance 'bureaucratic accountability', see Thomas B. Smith, 'The Comparative Analysis of Bureaucratic Accountability', *Asian Journal of Public Administration*, vol. 13, no. 1 (June 1991), pp. 97–9.
68. These terms are derived from ibid., p. 97.
69. *Frontline* (March 1995), pp. 28–9.
70. Richard Levy, 'Corruption, Economic Crime and Social Transformation Since the Reforms: The Debate in China', *Australian Journal of Chinese Affairs*, no. 33 (January 1995), p. 21.
71. In the case of Hong Kong, a partial amnesty was granted by Governor Murray MacLehose in 1977 to those people who committed corrupt offences before 1 January 1977. The amnesty was granted in response to a police protest over the power of the Independent Commission Against Corruption. See Norman Miners, *The Government and Politics of Hong Kong*, Fifth Edition (Hong Kong: Oxford University Press, 1995), p. 97. Arguably, the PRC could imitate the Hong Kong case of granting an amnesty for corrupt offences committed before a particular date.

4 Legal Reform in the Quest for a Socialist Market Economy

Carlos W. H. Lo

The conclusion of the discussion of the 1989 Democratic Movement at the ninth plenary session of the Thirteenth Chinese Communist Party (CCP) Central Committee, on 9 October 1992, cleared the way for Deng Xiaoping to realign the Party on the basis of a liberal economic reform which he had publicized widely since returning from South China in February 1992. The Fourteenth Party Congress in October 1992 saw the revival of his 'cat theory' – to develop productive capacity by introducing a socialist market economy into the socialist system – and gave him a mandate to accomplish this task.[1] This progressive idea of economic reform, which holds public ownership and a market economy as compatible in the socialist planned commodity economy, appeals to creative thinking in the search for working principles.[2] Thus an atmosphere of ideological relaxation in the economic realm was brought about. Deng's political thought was later internalized in the Party Constitution, which led to the amendment of the Constitution of the PRC to legitimize a market economy in socialist China.[3] Following the exodus of conservative figures, the economic reformers have gradually regained dominance in Chinese politics since the Eighth National People's Congress (NPC) in March 1993. With reform inspirations from the CCP's Politburo members such as Zhu Rongji, Qian Qichen, Li Lanqing, Li Ruihuan and later Wu Bangguo and Jiang Chunyun,[4] the reform momentum was further consolidated.

Against the background of political uncertainties as a result of the June-Fourth Incident, the Party's preference in re-shaping China's changing political order was for a strengthened framework of law rather than for Mao's style of nihilistic rule. This preference was demonstrated by resuming the legal reforms. The death of Deng Xiaoping marked the end of the revolutionary era in China. The non-violent political succession under President Jiang Zemin demonstrated that a post-revolutionary society has already taken shape. China has indeed become an 'established one-party system', an authoritarian rule based on a legal foundation.

In studying legal reform in China's quest for a socialist economy, this chapter will start with an outline of the changing political context for the socialist legal reform in the post-crisis era. It will then examine the legislative activities, the legal institutional development, and the promotion of the nation's legal awareness in the communist regime. Finally, it will look at law implementation in both criminal and non-criminal sectors.

CHANGING POLITICAL CONTEXTS FOR SOCIALIST LEGAL REFORM

Li Peng's clean and efficient government

The June-Fourth Incident strengthened Premier Li Peng's belief that a clean and efficient government would serve the people better in the course of socialist modernization than a democratic government. In the wake of Zhao Ziyang's liberal era, his conservative view – that democratization should be a gradual process conditioned by economic development and should only be promoted on the basis of political stability – has governed the political development of China.[5] Throughout the 1990s, in an atmosphere of rampant corruption and economic uncertainty, Li Peng has endeavoured to clean up the government and the Party with a view to exercising stable and able governance in post-crisis China.[6] His legal empire stressed mostly the repressive function of law to maintain social order.[7]

While Deng Xiaoping's redefinition of the policy orientation to pursue a socialist market economy in 1992 did not change fundamentally Li's authoritarian ruling philosophy, it did broaden his scope of legal regulation. For Li, the establishment and development of a socialist market economy should be conducted under state tutelage.[8] In this process, law should play an important part as the chief regulative mechanism, providing a clear definition of, and demarcation between, government and market.[9] In short, he concluded that a clean and able government on the basis of rule by law was needed to administer such an economic transformation.

Deng Xiaoping's anti-bourgeois liberalization

On the ideological front, China has put an end to all the ideological debates which questioned the Marxist rationale to its very foundation.[10] The result has been greater ideological control. From Deng's point of view, Marxism had to remain monolithic on the ideological front in order to legitimize the Party leadership and so ensure a stable communist rule in China. Pluralism was strictly prohibited. While extensive ideological education has been imposed on society, Deng did not return to the Maoist mode of ideological control. His political experience and pragmatic leadership style were incompatible with excessive 'leftism' in the purge of bourgeois liberalization. The intensity of anti-bourgeois liberalization was shown to be limited and non-violent as Deng urged continuous vigilance against 'left' deviation. Hence, a degree of ideological tolerance remained. Subsequently, Deng's pragmatic thinking was revived[11] and calls to an 'emancipation of mind' were heard again.[12] This was particularly the case after Deng's visit to South China in January 1992, when the Party resolved to speed up reform.

Jiang Zemin's socialist market economy

With the mandate from Deng, Jiang Zemin quickly emerged as the chief spokesperson for China's reform and Chinese Marxism. His supreme status in Chinese politics was eventually entrenched in the Fifteenth Party Congress, held in September 1997 following the death of Deng earlier in the year.[13] Taking stability as the baseline for China's advancement to modernization, Jiang has given explicit priority to promoting the rapid development of productive forces by marketizing production relationships. Unlike Zhao Ziyang's aggressive growth-centred economic line, his view of reform emphasized the quality of growth focusing on the efficacy of the reform process.[14] Moreover, marketization had to be conducted within the broader context of a planned economy where market forces were subject to state intervention in the form of macro-control. In this process, the benefits of Western knowledge, experience and technologies were reaffirmed, while 'corruptive' Western ideologies were still banned. Although material progress was used as an indicator of reform success, Jiang made it clear that cultural and ideological purity could not be sacrificed for temporary economic growth, and the authority and validity of Marxism remained beyond challenge.[15]

In the creation of a market economy, Jiang renewed the stress on the regulative functions of law, as a regulative legal regime was urgently needed to run a market economy.[16] New attention was given to improving the socialist legal system with emphasis on providing legal infrastructures, re-enforcing judicial independence, improving the quality of legal personnel, training lawyers and promoting popular legal awareness.[17] In short, with the socialist reform movement gathering momentum in the Eighth National People's Congress and confirmed in the Fifteenth National Party Congress, Jiang geared the legal reform to the development of China into a legally regulated society.

LEGISLATION[18]

Both the NPC and its Standing Committee had been busy with legislation since the communist regime re-affirmed its commitment to legal rule in the wake of the 1989 political crisis. In the period between August 1989 and 1994, the NPC and its Standing Committee passed 67 pieces of legislation and 31 decisions on legal issues, and amended ten existing laws. In the heyday of political purge and anti-bourgeois liberalization, the focus of legislation was on enacting laws for the government to tighten its grip over society. The decline of political fever had brought rampant corruption and soaring crime rates to the government's attention and laws were made to restore public order. With economic reform back at the top of the Party's agenda, the communist regime had geared its legislation to the introduction and development of a socialist market economy.

Legislation on constitutional issues

Two constitutional documents, both widely known as mini-constitutions, adopted by the NPC in April 1990 and March 1993 respectively, provided the constitutional schemes for China to integrate Hong Kong and Macau into the people's republic. The Basic Law of the Hong Kong Special Administrative Region of the People's Republic of China prescribes the constitutional framework for operationalizing the principle of 'one country two systems' after Hong Kong was returned to China from the United Kingdom in July 1997. Likewise, the Basic Law of the Macau Special Administrative Region of the People's Republic of China lays down the constitutional principles for Macau to establish and run a highly autonomous government after its reversion to China from Portugal in December 1999.

The amendment of the 1982 Constitution in May 1993 changed substantially the course of building socialism in China. In recognising that China is at the preliminary stage of socialism, the amended bill constitutionally legitimized a socialist market economy in the communist regime, putting an end to the chronic debates on the compatibility between market and socialism. The public ownership structure was modified to allow the state enterprises to run their businesses free from the state's direct intervention.

Legislation for tightening control over society

The 1989 political crisis highlighted the inadequacies of the existing system of law which had prevented the regime from exercising effective control over society, particularly in times of crisis.[19] The Party quickly filled the vacuum.

The Law on Mass Rallies and Demonstrations, adopted in October 1989, defines a legal scheme for people to conduct mass rallies and demonstrations. The Law on State Security of the PRC was enacted in 1993 to allow the state security organ to tighten state security. The long-awaited Martial Law of the PRC was passed in March 1996 to provide a set of procedures for employing martial law to restore law and order in any situation of political disturbance. This law prescribes that the NPC Standing Committee and the State Council are vested with the authority to declare martial law.

Legislation for improving and maintaining public order

To improve the deteriorating public order, laws have been passed to combat crimes. 'The Decision on Strengthening the Integrative Control of Social Order' asked government authorities at all levels to mobilize the masses and give strong support to both public security and judicial organs to combat and prevent crimes. Specific legislation was enacted to ban drugs, to prohibit prostitution, and to punish those who hijack aircraft, trade in pornographic articles, and steal cultural relics. Additionally, decisions were adopted to impose severe punishment on those engaging in economic crimes, and those abducting and kidnapping women and children. Finally, the 'Regulation of the People's Republic of China on Administrative Penalties for Public

Security' was revised in May 1994 to broaden the jurisdiction of the public security organs over disruptive misdemeanours.

Legislation for reforming criminal justice

In an attempt to accord greater protection to the rights of defendants and to align with international practice, the regime has amended the two criminal codes to improve the criminal justice system. By adding 61 articles to the original 164, the revised criminal procedural law has rectified some of the former unfair arrangements. First of all, the principle of presumption of innocence is adopted. Second, the status of defence counsels is improved, with the prosecution-dominated trial being replaced by a more balanced representation of both the prosecution and the defence. Third, early involvement of defence counsels in criminal cases is arranged to provide them with more time to collect evidence and prepare the defence. Fourth, cross examination of evidence is allowed, which opens the way for courtroom debates. Fifth, more protection is given to defendants, particularly during the investigation stage. For example, the length of time that a public security organ can detain a suspect for interrogation is now explicitly limited to twelve hours and the practice of detaining a defendant by means of issuing summons to him consecutively is prohibited. In short, the revision was a major step to rationalize the criminal procedure and guarantee a fairer trial. As for the re-codified criminal law, some major improvements were made, apart from adding 260 more articles in order to provide a clearer and more concrete yardstick for adjudication. These included the abandonment of the notorious principle of crime by analogy, the replacement of 'counter-revolutionary crimes' by 'crimes endangering state security', and the re-definition of criminal economic activities to put the criminal law within the context of a socialist market economy.[20]

Legislation for introducing and regulating the socialist market economy

Economic laws adopted in this period can be classified into four sets. The first set of laws is for the government to regulate and control the market. This includes laws for carrying out the government's fiscal and monetary policies such as the Budget Law, the Auditing Law, and the Law on the People's Bank of China. The second set is for establishing the boundary of the market economy and maintaining its order. This includes laws which define the relationship between state and market. Among those adopted are the Urban Real Estate Management Law, the State Compensation Law and the Arbitration Law. The third set is for the operation of the free market. Most of these laws are concerned with financial and commercial matters, and they include the Advertisement Law, the Corporation Law and the Law on Commercial Banks, and the Insurance Law. The fourth set is for attracting foreign investment and facilitating the growth of foreign trade. Most laws governing foreign investment and trade fall into this category, including the Law on the Protection of Taiwan Investment and the Foreign Trade Law. Taken as a whole, a legal system appropriate to a socialist market economy has gradually emerged.

Legislation for improving public and social administration

The system of administrative law has been strengthened to improve the government's public and social administration.[21] In the realm of public administration, the administration of environmental protection received a boost with the adoption of the Environmental Protection Law in December 1989; this replaced a provisional law in this field after a decade of trial and error. Other major administrative laws adopted included the City Planning Law, the Civil Aviation Law, and the Law on the Collection and Management of Tax. As for social administration, the Law on Maternal and Infant Health Care was passed in 1994; the Food Hygiene Law was revised in 1995 to improve public health administration; and the Education Law and the Sports Law were adopted in 1995 for the government to promote social well-being. Additionally, the Law of Administrative Penalties, passed in March 1996, standardizes the procedure for imposing administrative sanctions on citizens, legal entities, and other organizations which may have violated administrative rules and regulations.

Legislation for institutionalizing the legal system

The legislation boom of the 1990s had put tremendous pressure on the implementation mechanism, and a number of laws were also enacted to promote the well-being of the legal system. Among them, the laws of judges, procurators and people's policemen, adopted in February 1995, aimed to institutionalize the personnel management systems of judges, procurators and people's policemen; to improve their professional quality in order to raise the standard of judicial practices and that of law enforcement; and to ensure that they perform their duties according to law.[22] With similar orientation, the Lawyers' Law was adopted in May 1996. This specifies the conditions for legal practice, the rights and obligations of practising lawyers, and their legal responsibilities. The Prison Law was enacted in December 1994 to rationalize the heavily criticized prisons administrative system by formally putting the prisons management under the supervision of the people's procuratorates.

LEGAL INSTITUTIONAL DEVELOPMENT[23]

In 1990 and 1991, political considerations dominated the institutional development of the judicial system. During this period the Party reasserted its leadership over the judicial organs.[24] Since the beginning of 1992 economic considerations have dominated the reforms. These found expression in the rapid expansion of the regulative functions of judicial organs. Since then, the orientation of judicial reform has been to align the Chinese judicial practices with those of the West.[25]

Tightening Party control over the judicial system

In reviving the instrumental notion of law, the Party brought the judiciary under its tight control. Political departments were established in both the court and procuratorate structures to take charge of political aspects. Education in ideology was widely conducted among judicial personnel, and political redness was used as the chief criterion for appointing cadres into the leading positions in judicial organs.[26] Although the Party had kept on stressing its leadership over the judicial system, such an ideological enthusiasm had gradually subsided in the whirlwind of Deng's market economic reform.

Building a clean and honest image of the judicial system

Much effort had been committed to cleaning up the judicial system through tightening the discipline of judicial personnel. Comprehensive disciplinary checks and law enforcement examination were conducted annually and legal cadres who violated the laws were severely punished. In the court system, between 1990 and 1994, 414 judicial personnel were criminally sanctioned, among them 207 judges. In the procuratorate system, leading cadres who were found guilty of corruption included the former Chief Procurator of the Wushi Municipal Procuratorate of Jiangsu province. In addition, the supervision of legal proceedings was strengthened to ensure that cases were handled strictly according to prescribed procedures. To facilitate external supervision, both the courts and the procuratorate made their operations more transparent by releasing more information on their activities to the public. More positively, the latter had invited non-Communists as honorary procurators to take part in procuratorate work. Finally, the judicial organs and their personnel were banned from involvement in any profit-making economic activities.

Upgrading the professional competence of judicial personnel

As judicial activities became more specialized, upgrading the professional competence of judicial personnel became urgent. A cadre training system was gradually established in both the court and procuratorate systems to provide specialized and high-level on-the-job training programmes for judicial personnel. In the court system, the Senior Judges Training Centre and other judges' training centres at both municipal and provincial levels were set up to improve the quality of judges at different levels. In addition, a large number of short-term training courses were organized by courts at all levels every year. Similar developments also took place in the procuratorate system. The Senior Procurator Training Institute was set up in 1989, followed by the establishment of local ones, to organize training for procurators. The training of procuratorate cadres was organized by the procuratorate cadre training schools. Some success was noted as the percentage of judges with post-secondary qualifications increased from 17 per cent in 1987 to 70 per cent in 1994.

To ensure the professional quality of new recruits, the principle of 'openness, equality, competition and merit' was adopted, which prescribed that all applicants had to be formally examined and assessed. This merit principle was also applied to promotions, and more young legal personnel with higher professional qualifications were appointed to leading positions. The founding of the judges and procurators associations in 1994 were milestone events in the professionalization of the judicial system. With the promulgation of the Law of Judges and the Law of Procurators in 1995, both the courts and the procuratorate have taken steps to institutionalize the personnel systems for judges and procurators.

Strengthening judicial structures

As the scope of the socialist legal system expanded, corresponding adjustments in the judicial structures to accommodate these functional expansions were being made. The trend of functional differentiation was particularly pronounced in the court system, where one could witness the proliferation of specialized courts, both in types and in numbers. The administrative courts were set up in people's courts to dispense administrative justice according to the Procedure Law, which became effective in 1990. The intellectual property rights courts were introduced in 1995 to enforce laws and regulations related to the protection of intellectual property rights.[27] Due to the rapid growth of economic activities, the number of economic courts was significantly increased; by 1995, each of the nation's 3488 people's courts had already established an economic court.[28] Other specialized tribunals which were set up or increased in number in the people's courts included maritime courts, real estate courts, foreign economic courts, and juvenile courts. In the procuratorate system, most procuratorates had set up a separate anti-corruption bureau to handle cases of graft and bribery.

As the number of judicial activities at the basic levels had increased rapidly, strengthening the judicial structures at the basic levels emerged as an urgent task. Both higher and intermediate people's courts increasingly played an active role in improving the infrastructure of basic people's courts. The people's tribunals (*renmin fating*), which were agencies of basic people's courts mostly established in rural areas, were the main focus in this reform drive, as they handled a large number of civil and economic disputes cases and were severely under-resourced. The arbitration system which resolved a majority of civil disputes at basic levels was also targeted. For the procuratorate, the county procuratorates were entrusted with the responsibility for strengthening procuratorate structures at basic levels. Since 1990, procuratorate offices have been set up in most of the major towns and villages throughout the country.

Improving logistic support

Inadequate logistic support for the operation of the judicial system had hampered the quality of judicial practice and the efficiency of judicial administration. For example, because of a shortage of funds, about 20 per cent of people's courts were without trial chambers and over 30 per cent of people's tribunals were without proper administrative offices in 1993. Resources have been committed to build more trial chambers (*shenpian fating*), to upgrade technological facilities, to modernize information technologies, and to improve the communication networks and the legal medical services. In particular, special efforts have been made to tackle the resource problems of judicial organs in remote and disadvantaged areas.

Developing the lawyers' system

Despite the fact that the Communist regime had brought the lawyers' system back under its control after a decade of relaxation, the reform of the lawyers' system has proceeded steadily. Most effort has gone into structural reform. A licensing system was adopted to govern who might practise as a lawyer, a partnership structure for private provision of legal services was introduced, and a uniform fee schedule was formulated. Furthermore, a penal regulation was announced in 1992 to discipline lawyers' who are found guilty of misconduct, while a code of conduct was issued in 1993 for lawyers to follow. In 1992, China's lawyers' system was internationalized as foreign law firms were allowed to set up their offices in major cities in China, while China's law firms were permitted to begin their operations in other countries. The newly enacted Lawyers' Law has put China's lawyers' system within the context of a socialist market economy, fundamentally altering the nature of the legal profession from public service to private practice.

Other major endeavours included improving the quality of lawyers and enlarging the work force to serve the socialist market economy. In the former case, a greater degree of specialization in different aspects of legal work was introduced, and training programmes for lawyers were organized by the Ministry of Justice. In the latter case, the qualifying examination system was reformed to allow more people to acquire the lawyers' qualification. The schedule of national examinations was revised in 1994 to make it an annual event. In addition, a number of provinces and municipalities were allowed to lower the national qualification standard.[29] Because of a severe shortage of lawyers, lawyers' licences could be granted to people with solid legal experience including those working in judicial bodies and legal research institutions.[30] Finally, legal services at the basic levels were consolidated. County and district justice authorities were given responsibility for the development of legal service offices, both at street level and in rural areas, to assure the quality of legal workers and their services.

PROMOTING NATIONAL LEGAL CONSCIOUSNESS[31]

In resuming her progress towards a legal society, China launched a second five-year extensive programme of popularizing law in 1991. Legal education was incorporated as a core component into education programmes from primary to tertiary levels to sustain the development of a legal tradition in China. Special arrangements, such as conducting classes in farmers' homes by local officials, were made to raise the legal consciousness of people in rural areas.[32] This socializing process gathered momentum when the regime started a campaign to familiarize the population with laws related to a socialist market economy.

The development of legal studies in academic institutions, legal periodicals, and law presses was normalized when the regime resolved to regulate the socialist market economy by means of law in late 1992. Since 1990, the trend towards specialization in technical legal research has been particularly noteworthy. For example, the Centre of Judicial Authentication was established in the Politics and Law University of China in 1992, and the Research Centre for Laws of Technology was set up in the University of Beijing in 1990. The number of law societies and research associations in specialized areas has also increased significantly. Among them is the Chinese Public Health Law Society and the Chinese Criminology Research Association.

China's inauguration of a legally regulated economy in 1993 had made the study of economic law very popular. Between 1993 and 1994, some 64 tertiary institutions introduced the study of economic law in their curricula while 25 started to offer degree programmes in international economic law. Unprecedentedly, self-financing legal institutions were allowed to offer law study programmes. For example, Dehang Lawyers College, established jointly by Jilin University and the Chinese Lawyers Affairs Centre in December 1993, admits both undergraduate and postgraduate self-funded law students.

Specialization also took place in legal periodicals and newspapers. A majority of the 24 new legal periodicals recorded between 1991 and 1994 dealt with specialized areas such as justice administration, military law, intellectual property rights, juvenile delinquency, and legal medical issues. Likewise, four out of six newspapers which began publication in this same period were run by judicial organs reporting the activities of lawyers, procuratorates, and courts.

JUDICIAL ACTIVITIES IN POST-CRISIS CHINA[33]

After more than a decade of active legislation, China had created a relatively complete system of law to govern and regulate almost every aspect of social life. However, law implementation remained a weak link in the judicial sector, due to the slow pace of development of the legal infrastructure, the low level of legal awareness of all parties concerned and, most important of all, the rapid increase in workload for the judicial organs because of rapid social and economic development.

Handling crimes of counter-revolution

The anti-bourgeois liberalization campaign and the political purge launched by the regime generated a large number of political charges in the wake of the June-Fourth Incident. Leading figures in the 1989 democratic movement, such as Chen Ziming, Wang Juntao, Chen Xiaoping, Wang Dan and Bao Tong, were all found guilty of conducting counter-revolutionary activities.[34] People who exercised democratic rights and freedoms outside the parameters set by the Party were severely punished. For example, Gao Yu, former Deputy Chief Editor of *Economic Weekly*, was convicted of 'leaking state secrets' in 1994 and sentenced to six years' imprisonment.[35] Hong Dongfang, leading mainland labour activist, was denied a home passage by China's public security organs for allegedly engaging in subversive activities while receiving medical treatment in the United States in 1993.[36] Celebrated dissidents such as Wang Dan, Wang Xizhe and Wei Jingsheng were placed under the surveillance of public security organs and their activities were heavily circumscribed. Wei was later arrested, accused of attempting to overthrow the government and sentenced to 14 years' imprisonment.[37] On the whole, despite the persistence of the Communist regime's tough stance against political activists and dissidents, there has been a rapid decrease in the volume of counter-revolutionary cases handled by the courts since 1990.

Combating the crimes of graft, bribe-taking and embezzlement

Some organized efforts have been made by judicial authorities to deal with the crimes of graft, bribe-taking and embezzlement. Anti-corruption units were set up by most procuratorates at all levels to conduct investigations and to arrest in corruption cases. The reporting system was strengthened to encourage the public to bring corruption cases to the notice of judicial organs by guaranteeing that the identities of those reporting information would be kept confidential to prevent possible acts of reprisal. Actions have also been taken to raise public awareness of corruption and to publicize the government's anti-corruption policies by conducting anti-corruption exhibitions and by publicising typical corruption cases.

In the period 1990 to 1995, both the courts and the procuratorates handled a large number of corruption cases. The former concluded an average of 27 000 cases every year, while the latter filed and investigated more than 48 000 cases each year. Some notable trends can be observed. First was the increasing involvement of leading cadres in corruption activities, particularly those at departmental/bureau levels or above. Second was the increasing amount of ill-gotten gains involved, from 810 million yuan in 1990 to 4.9 billion in 1995. Third was the rapid increase in the number of both 'big' and 'serious' cases. Even 'super-big' cases involving more than one million yuan were no longer uncommon, and more than a hundred of such cases were recorded in 1995.[38] Fourth was the further intensification of corruptive practices among Party cadres and state personnel, reportedly those in charge of financial and economic activities, as indicated by the sudden and significant increase in the number of corruption cases since 1995.

The judicial authorities had achieved some success by punishing a number of high-ranking cadres and government officials engaging in corruption. Among those penalized were Shen Taifu, former president of the Beijing Changcheng (Great Wall) Machinery and Electronics Group (death penalty), and Ouyang De, Vice-Chairman of the People's Congress of Guangdong Province (15 years' imprisonment). These cases, to a considerable extent, have had a demonstration effect.

After years of efforts against corruption, China is still regarded as one of the most corrupt countries in the world.[39] For most observers, the Party has yet to show its determination to hit the 'big tigers', as cadres at ministerial-provincial levels or above have remained untouchable. The case of Chen Xitong, the former secretary of the CCP Beijing Municipal Committee, the highest level of government official committed for crimes of corruption to date, has been recently referred by the Party to the judiciary for formal prosecution and trial after months of consideration.[40] The way this case is resolved will demonstrate how free a hand judicial authorities will be given to handle other corruption cases. Considering current institutional strengths, China lacks an effective anti-corruption mechanism. The anti-corruption network in the procuratorate system, headed by the Anti-Corruption and Bribery Administration of the Supreme People's Procuratorate established in November 1995, has yet to prove its competence.[41] One cannot be optimistic in the absence of a supposedly powerful weapon to combat corruption – the 'Law on Punishing Graft and Bribery' – which is still not yet ready for the NPC's consideration after five years' preparation!

Dealing with general criminal activities

In the suppression of crimes, the regime has adopted a 'strike hard' policy against violent and hard-core crimes. This allows the police and the procuratorate to speed up investigation and prosecution, and the courts to speed up trials and to punish criminals severely. To make the voice of 'strike hard' heard, trials have been conducted in public, sentences have been given much publicity, capital punishment has been vigorously applied,[42] and public executions have been commonly practiced.

Cracking down on violent crimes has been the core activity of the judicial organs. Under such a rubric were the crimes of murder, robbery, rape and theft. Most efforts have been directed to areas and localities with high crime rates, for example, Shenzhen and Weizhou in Guangdong Province. Other major crimes targeted included the abduction and selling of women and children, and pornography-related crimes.

Drug smuggling, trafficking and transportation increased markedly in the 1990s, as indicated by the number of cases cracked. Between 1991 and 1993, there was an increase of over 77 per cent while the figure in 1994 was more than four times that of 1991. Under a nation-wide anti-drug campaign, the National Narcotics Control Commission was established in November 1991 to take full responsibility for drug control[43] and anti-drug organs were set up by governments in localities in provinces such as Yunnan, Sichuan, Guangxi and Guangdong, where drug problems were particularly acute. In order to fight drug crimes in a timely manner, the higher people's courts of Yunnan and Guangdong Provinces were empowered to examine and approve death sentences accorded to drug smugglers and traffickers.[44]

Juvenile delinquency has been a disturbing problem that called for special judicial attention. Between 1990 and 1994, more than 32 000 youths under 18 years of age were convicted every year, accounting for 6 to 7 per cent of total defendants convicted. Although there was no sign of rapid deterioration, there was a worrying trend, in that those committing major crimes had increased from 57 per cent of the total in 1990–1 to above 63 per cent in 1992–4. Most people's courts set up a juvenile court to hear juvenile criminal cases, with a separate set of legal proceedings tailored to the trials of young defendants. In dispensing justice to young defendants, the stress was on correcting them through education rather than giving heavy penalties.

Punishing economic crimes became more urgent as the pace of market reform quickened. There was a significant increase, of 33 per cent, of such cases from 1993 to 1994 and the number of cases increased to 13 452 in 1995. On the hit list were criminal activities related to swindling, tax evasion, smuggling and trafficking in smuggled goods, manufacturing and marketing counterfeit and shoddy products, counterfeiting state currency, and various cases which led to serious disruptions of the country's economic order. In handling economic crimes amidst China's transition to a socialist market economy, the judicial authorities have been very uncertain in demarcating criminal from non-criminal economic activities, as some market operations were previously unknown to most legal personnel.

Major non-criminal judicial activities

Apart from handling criminal cases, the judicial organs have been active in settling non-criminal judicial problems. Among the major non-criminal sectors were administrative, civil and economic.

1. Settling administrative disputes

The implementation of the Administrative Procedure Law in October 1990 provided people and legal entities with a set of formal procedures by which to sue government departments and state personnel in order to compensate for losses which they had incurred as a result of maladministration. The number of cases handled in 1991 was 90 per cent greater than that in 1990, and in 1995 the volume of cases soared to four times that of 1990.

To ensure that administrative cases can be effectively settled, administrative courts have been set up in people's courts to handle administrative disputes. It was found that the major obstacles for effective settlement of administrative cases were the conservative attitudes amongst three concerned parties: *citizens* feared to engage in lawsuits with the government; the *government authorities* found it difficult to accept the role of accused party; and the *courts* were reluctant to deal with the government. Five categories of administrative cases have received greatest judicial attention, namely, public security administration, city construction administration, industrial and commercial administration, land administration, and taxation administration.

2. Settling civil disputes

Settling civil disputes has been consistently the heaviest non-criminal assignment for judicial organs. There has been a noticeable increase in the number of cases since 1993, coinciding with China's market reform. In 1995, more than 2.7 million cases were handled and concluded, almost 50 per cent more than the figure for 1990. Over half of the cases were resolved by arbitration. For effective and timely resolution of civil disputes, the majority of cases were handled by the people's courts at basic levels.

There were altogether six major categories of civil cases. First were cases on divorce, marriage and family disputes, which received the top priority. Second came debt disputes, which had increased significantly under the regime's liberal economic policies. Third were cases related to real estate and housing, the result of drastic land and housing reforms which occurred between 1993 and 1995. Fourth were those on labour disputes, concerning wages, insurance, and labour welfare, which proliferated under the regime's maketization of the labour system. Fifth were disputes concerning indemnity for injuries or losses of property arising out of accidents and negligence. Sixth were cases related to the infringement of the rights of the person, such as defamation, and unauthorized use of one's portrait and name. There has been an increasing involvement of parties outside mainland China – including Hong Kong, Macau and Taiwan – in civil disputes.

3. Settling economic disputes

In regulating the economy by means of law, the Party has provided a legal mechanism for settling economic disputes, something alien to the communist regime for almost three decades. The inauguration of a socialist market economy has increased economic activities and hence has generated a large volume of economic cases that needed adjudication. The total number of economic cases that the people's courts handled in 1995 was 1.27 million, twice that of 1990.

Settling disputes over economic contracts was by far the most important function of the courts in handling economic cases. As China's economy became more marketized, special attention was given to cases related to finance and banking, including disputes over loan contracts and disputes concerning the raising of capital. Perhaps, the cases on the bankruptcy of enterprises have received the biggest public attention, as the adoption of the Law of Bankruptcy was a milestone event in China's economic reform. There has been a rapid increase in the number of cases on the bankruptcy of state enterprises, and a total of 904 such cases was recorded in 1993–4. Settling disputes over intellectual property rights, although remaining small in number, has emerged as one of the courts' most urgent tasks under external pressure for an effective protection of foreign trademarks, patents and copyrights in China.[45] Finally, economic activities in the rural areas have also been brought under the legal umbrella, and resolving economic disputes among rural enterprises, mostly concerning production contracts, was the chief responsibility of basic-level courts. In handling economic disputes, the courts have lacked an effective mechanism to enforce court decisions, and hence the non-compliance rate in this area is exceptionally high.

CONCLUSION

Deng Xiaoping's pragmatic policy line stressing the paramount importance of political stability has enabled China to break away from the former pattern of cyclical political development characterized by successive alternations between periods of order and chaos in the post-crisis era.[46] Law and order with emphasis on the state's authoritarian control was quickly resumed under Li Peng's vision of clean and able government. The scale of ideological retreats proved to be limited due to Deng's apprehension of excessive leftism. Once political stability was restored in the legal conclusion of the June-Fourth Incident, Deng quickly revived the reform drive and Jiang Zemin took up the task of inaugurating a socialist market economy. Political dictatorship was quickly eroded under this renewed stress on economic liberalization. In the new climate, the regulatory role of law in economic reform has been stressed. Once again, law is regarded as essential for securing political order and promoting socialist construction – a consensus shared by both Jiang Zemin and Li Peng.

In the reform of the socialist legal system, China has recorded significant advances in legislation, legal institution building and raising the legal awareness of the population. Legislative endeavours have centred mostly on developing a system of economic law for introducing and operating a socialist market economy. Other major areas of legislation have included criminal justice, public and social administration, and institutional reform. Institution building has a wide coverage, with efforts on tightening Party control over the judicial system, building a clean and honest image, upgrading the quality of legal personnel, strengthening judicial structures, improving logistic supports and institutionalizing the lawyers' system. The nation-wide campaign for developing a national legal culture has been intensified with the objective of educating both cadres and the public to manage their activities by means of the law. In the development of legal research and legal periodicals, the trend towards greater specialization has persisted. As for legal education, economic law and international economic law have emerged as the most popular law programmes.

In the administration of justice, the workload of the judicial organs has increased rapidly since 1990 due to the rapid expansion in the scope of the legal system. The growth of judicial capacity has lagged behind the actual demand for law implementation, which has compromised the effectiveness of the legal system. In criminal justice, combating the crimes of corruption and cracking down on violent crimes were the most urgent priorities of judicial organs, but little success has been recorded, as neither corruption nor criminal activities show any signs of being checked. Handling counter-revolutionary cases has remained an important judicial activity despite the fact that the number of such cases has decreased significantly since 1991. In the non-criminal sector, the judicial organs have been active in settling administrative, civil and economic disputes. Indeed non-criminal cases have constituted more than 60 per cent of the total of judicial work every year.

On the basis of this study, one can observe that the 1989 crisis and the purge afterwards, although they undermined the prestige of law, have not done any permanent damage to legal reform. We may conclude that socialist legal reform in the post-crisis era has basically provided a legal foundation for China to advance its task of introducing a socialist market economy.

Notes and references

This chapter is prepared under the project 'The Administration of Criminal Justice in the People's Republic of China: Case Analysis', departmental general research fund, the Hong Kong Polytechnic University. I would like to thank Keith Forster of the Southern Cross University for his kind assistance in revising this chapter.

1. See Jiang Zemin, 'Accelerating Reform and Opening-Up', *Beijing Review*, No. 43 (26 October–1 November 1992), pp. 9–32. For the discussion of the Fourteenth Party Congress in this respect, see Tony Saich, 'The Fourteenth Party Congress: A Programme for Authoritarian Rule', *The China Quarterly*, No. 132 (December 1992), pp. 1137–48.
2. 'Gist of Speeches Made in Wuchang, Shenzhen, Zuhai and Shanghai by Deng Xiaoping', *Beijing Review*, Nos. 6–7 (7–20 February 1994), p. 10.
3. See 'New State Leaders Elected', *Beijing Review*, No. 14 (5–11 April 1993), pp. 4–5.
4. See 'Profiles of China's New Vice-Premiers', *Beijing Review*, Nos. 14–15, (3–16 April 1995), pp. 20–1.
5. See 'NPC Session Stress Rectification', *Beijing Review*, No. 13 (27 March–2 April 1989), pp. 5–6. Li reiterated his idea of 'clean government' again at the Fifth Session; and Li Peng, 'Report on the Work of the Government', *Beijing Review*, No. 15 (13–19, April 1992), p. xiii.
6. See 'Fighting Corruption by Means of Law', *Beijing Review*, No. 20 (18–24 May 1992), p. 4.
7. See Li Peng, 'Continue to Work for a Stable Political, Economic and Social Development in China', *Beijing Review*, No. 16 (16–22 April 1990), p. XVII.
8. Ibid.
9. See 'Law, Order: Vital for the New Year', *Beijing Review*, No. 2 (9–15 January 1995), p. 5.
10. See Carlos W. H. Lo, *China's Legal Awakening: Legal Theory and Criminal Justice in Deng's Era*, (Hong Kong: Hong Kong University Press, 1995), pp. 17–32.
11. See 'Fresh Impetus from Deng's Message', *Beijing Review*, No. 15 (13–19 April 1992), p. 4.
12. See 'Learn from the West, Party Chiefs Says', *Beijing Review*, No. 22 (1–7 June 1992), p. 4.
13. 'Jiang Unveils New Hierarchy', *South China Morning Post*, 20 September 1997.
14. See Jiang Zemin, 'Principles on Modernization Drive', *Beijing Review*, No. 45 (6–12 November 1995), p. 8.
15. 'Party Stresses Value of Marxist Foundations', *South China Morning Post*, 11 June 1996.
16. Jiang Zemin, 'Accelerating Reform and Opening-Up', p. 23.
17. See Ibid. Also 'Political Reform, Next Target', *Beijing Review*, No. 51 (21–7 December 1992), p. 4.
18. Most of the details of legislation are drawn from the following sources: *Zhongguo faxue nianjian 1990–1995* (*China Law Year Book 1990–1995*), (Beijing: Beijing falu chubanshe 1990–1995); *Zhonghua renmin gongheguo zuigao renmin jianchayuan gongbao* (*The Bulletin of the Supreme People's Procuratorate*), 1990–1996; and *Zhonghua renmin gongheguo zuigao renmin fayuan gongbao* (*The Bulletin of the Supreme People's Court*), *1990–1996*.
19. See Carlos W. H. Lo, 'The Chinese Communist Party's Perspective of Crisis and Methods of Crisis Solving During the 1989 Democratic

Movement: A Legal Perspective', *Asian Affairs*, Vol. 19, No. 2 (Summer 1992), pp. 111–12.
20. 'Amended Criminal Law Contains 260 More Articles', *Beijing Review*, No. 17 (28 April–4 May 1996), pp. 17–19.
21. For discussion on the idea of administration by law, see Carlos W. H. Lo, 'Law and Administration in Deng's China: Legalization of the Administration of Environmental Protection', *Review of Central and East European Law*, No. 5 (1992), pp. 453–73.
22. See 'Continued Improvement in Chinese Legislation', *Beijing Review*, No. 2 (8–14 January 1996), pp. 22–3.
23. Most of the details of legal institutional development are drawn from the following sources: *Zhongguo faxue nianjian 1990–1995* (*China Law Year Book 1990–1995*); *Zhonghua renmin gongheguo zuigao renmin jianchayuan gongbao* (*The Bulletin of the Supreme People's Procuratorate*), 1990–1996; and *Zhonghua renmin gongheguo zuigao renmin fayuan gongbao* (*The Bulletin of the Supreme People's Court*), *1990–1996*.
24. See Liu Fuzhi, 'Zuigao renmin jiancha yuan gongzuo baogao' (Report on the Works of the People's Supreme Procuratorate), *Renmin ribao* (13 April 1991), p. 5. Also Wily Wo-Lap Lam, 'Party Boosts Control Over Judicial System', *South China Morning Post* (4 April 1991), p. 7.
25. See 'Judiciary in Line with International Norms', *Beijing Review*, No. 49 (5–11 December 1994), pp. 5–6.
26. See Ibid.
27. See 'Legal System Construction vs Market Economy', *Beijing Review,* (No. 47) 20–6 November 1995, p. 12.
28. Ibid.
29. Ibid.
30. 'Lawyer System Reform to Match Market Economy', *Beijing Review*, No. 44 (1–7 November 1993), pp. 4–5.
31. Most of the details of national legal consciousness are drawn from the following sources: *Zhongguo faxue nianjian 1990–1995* (*China Law Year Book 1990–1995*); *Zhonghua renmin gongheguo zuigao renmin jianchayuan gongbao* (*The Bulletin of the Supreme People's Procuratorate*), 1990–1996; and *Zhonghua renmin gongheguo zuigao renmin fayuan gongbao* (*The Bulletin of the Supreme People's Court*), 1990–1996.
32. 'Enhancing Public Awareness of Law', *Beijing Review*, No. 11 (18–24 March 1991), p. 6.
33. Most of the details of judicial activities are drawn from the following sources: *Zhongguo faxue nianjian 1990–1995* (*China Law Year Book 1990–1995*); *Zhonghua renmin gongheguo zuigao renmin jianchayuan gongbao* (*The Bulletin of the Supreme People's Procuratorate*), 1990–1996; and *Zhonghua renmin gongheguo zuigao renmin fayuan gongbao* (*The Bulletin of the Supreme People's Court*), 1990–1996.
34. See Carlos W. H. Lo, 'Trials of Dissidents of the 1989 Democracy Movement: The Limits of Criminal Justice Under Tang Hsiao-p'ing', *Issues & Studies*, No. 12 (December 1992), pp. 33–40.
35. 'Plea for release of 16 Journalists', *South China Morning Post* (5 June 1996).

36. To Defy Mainland Expulsion', *South China Morning Post* (16 August 1993).
37. 'Evidence for Wei Jingsheng's Crime Authentic', *Beijing Review*, No. 3 (15–21 January 1996), pp. 14–15.
38. Ren Jianxin, 'Zuigao renmin fayuan gongzou baogao' ('Report on the Work of the Supreme People's Court'), *Renmin Ribao* (*People's Daily*), (22 March 1996), p. 3.
39. See 'China Tops Asia's Graft Graph, Say Businessmen', *South China Morning Post* (8 April 1996).
40. See 'Fallen Party Boss to Go on Trial for Graft', *South China Morning Post* (10 September 1997).
41. See 'Sharpening the Sword Against Corruption', *Beijing Review*, No. 14 (1–7 April 1996), pp. 18–19.
42. For example, it was reported that in the three-month period between April and June 1996, the later wave of an anti-crime crackdown, over a thousand executions had taken place; 'Crime Purge Sees 98 More Executed', *South China Morning Post* (25 July 1996), p. 7; also 'Courts to Step Up Executions', *South China Morning Post* (2 May 1996).
43. See 'The War Against Drugs', *Beijing Review*, No. 50 (11–17 November 1995), pp. 12–14.
44. Ibid., p. 13.
45. See 'Protection of Intellectual Property Rights', *Beijing Review*, No. 35 (29 August–4 September 1994), p. 4.
46. Among scholars who hold this perspective of cyclical development are Meisner and Townsend. See Maurice Meisner, *Mao's China and After* (New York: Free Press, 1986); James R. Townsend and Brantly Womack, *Politics in China*, 3rd edition (London: Scott Foresmen, 1986).

Part II
Foreign Policy Issues

5 Sino–American Relations in the Post-Cold War Era

Ting Wai

The disintegration of the Soviet bloc, as well as the Soviet Union (USSR) itself, removed the strategic rationale that formed the basis for Sino–American relations for almost two decades. When the USSR was a common threat for both powers, *realpolitik* determined that strategic relationship prevailed over other considerations such as ideological conflicts, the nature of political institutions, and mutual economic interests. With the advent of the post-Cold War era, Sino–American relations need to be built on new bases. The vicissitudes of Sino–American relations since 1989 support the diagnosis of Harry Harding, that the two countries are bound by cooperation, competition and conflict in all aspects of their relations.[1] However, the question of the extent to which the opportunities of cooperation between the two countries in a certain area are affected or sacrificed by competition and conflict in other areas remains to be examined. It is obvious that national security issues and economic interests are becoming the prime considerations for the foreign policy decision-makers of both nations, thus further development of Sino–American relations should seek better understanding and common ground on these two basic factors. But the Chinese perception of the hegemonic nature of the only superpower, which seeks to promote its own (Western) values of democracy and human rights, further complicates the difficult relations in the beginning of this post-Cold War period.

It has always been argued, both in Beijing and Washington, that the two nations can never downgrade the importance of the opposing power in their foreign policy world-view. Chinese scholars emphasize two facts. First, both nations are simply super-sized, in terms of land area, population and natural resources. Secondly, the two countries are so different from each other: one is the most advanced capitalist developed country, while the other is the biggest socialist developing country.[2] In some aspects such as economic relations, their natures could be basically complementary, but in other aspects relating to national security and strategic calculations, the difference in values and world-views may become a source of conflict.

In the eyes of the American government and strategic analysts, whether the People's Republic of China (PRC) succeeds or not in her grandiose reform in economic development poses serious problems to American interests, given the fact that political institutions will not be changed in China, and one-party dominance, together with the related problems of the decline of legitimacy of the regime, its loss of authority, leadership succession, and intra-party factional conflicts, will prevail. If China encounters severe difficulties or even fails in her reform programmes, with the state losing control over the society, and the central authority weakening its leadership and coordinating role in face of the local authorities, the potential scenario of heading towards disintegration is a nightmare for all the neighbouring countries. Simply an exodus of refugees from China is considered a destabilizing factor in regional security, let alone any mass protests on a grand scale or internal armed conflicts. In contrast, if China grows healthy and strong, but the reform of economic and financial institutions and legal provisions lags behind, economic imbalances inside China and trade conflicts with the outside world will definitely occur. In addition, the emergence of a more assertive regional power will prompt neighbours to judge China's intentions. The perception of a potential military threat from China would initiate an arms race in East Asia.[3] This would destabilize the precarious balance which is maintained by the American presence in the heterogeneous Asia–Pacific region and the increasing economic interactions within the region.

The makers of Chinese foreign policy have mixed feelings towards the United States (US), the only superpower left in the post-Cold War era. On the one hand, the American market is vital, especially for the livelihood of the people living in the coastal areas of China, and for the rapid increase of China's foreign currency reserves. On the other hand, the US is perceived as the only hegemonic power which seeks to export its own values regarding democracy and human rights through intervention in other countries' internal affairs. Moreover, for the vehemently nationalistic Chinese Communist Party (CCP), at least some Americans are hostile to China. It is alleged that in the eyes of these people, a rich and powerful China would be a serious threat to the US, hence they would like to see a poor, backward, and dormant China.[4] This perception of the Americans' intention leads the Chinese Communists to believe that the essence of the American policy *vis-à-vis* China is 'containment', China being the new belligerent target after the collapse of the USSR and the Soviet bloc.

We would like in this chapter critically to examine how the mutual perceptions of the two countries affect their respective evaluations of Sino–American relations. To what extent do their perceptions influence the foreign policy decision-making processes in the two countries? What kinds of structural constraints arising from the new international political order are imposed on the future development of Sino–American relations? This chapter will start with a brief study of the bilateral relations before 1989 and how the two powers were bound by common interests. While it is difficult to define clearly common interests in the post-Cold War period, we would like to seek the underlying reasons for the difficult relationship by examining the Chinese perception of the US's role in the new international political order, and how public opinion in the US has changed since 1989. A survey of American foreign policy imperatives will help to understand the basic problems and to see the prospects for the future. This will also be useful in clarifying how Sino–American relations could be influential in the future domestic politic-economic changes in China.

SINO-AMERICAN RELATIONS AFTER 1989: THE LOSS OF COMMON INTERESTS

Before 1989, with the reformist leadership and its line of thinking firmly in power, and despite attacks from the conservatives of the CCP who criticized bourgeois liberalization from time to time, the Chinese government appeared assertive and confident. It adopted an open-minded and balanced view of the West. A former US diplomat, Charles Freeman also a close observer and participant of Sino–American relations since Nixon's historical visit to China – claims that the bilateral relationship before the end of the Cold War was quite satisfactory. He says that during the period 1979 to 1989, the US government adopted three principles. First, it sought to avoid ideological debate, but at the same time tried to narrow down the differences step by step, and China did change more than the US. Second, the US tried to integrate China into regional and global institutions and help her become a responsible part of the new order, and this worked. Third, the US sought to promote conditions conducive to finding better solutions to problems left over by history, such as Taiwan and Hong Kong, but the US avoided taking sides. This also worked.

However, since 1989, not only has there been a lack of strategic rationale due to the decline of the USSR, but also American policies towards China have focused on differences instead of common interests. The US government creates or revamps new institutions, such as the Missile Technology Control Regime (MTCR) and World Trade Organisation (WTO), but it tends deliberately to exclude China, thus deferring her conformity to international institutions.[5]

In the eyes of American realist thinkers, it is often argued that in order to transform the bitter relationship into a more fruitful one for both parties, the two should seek to build their relations on new grounds of common interest. But with the elimination of the common enemy, what is the common interest? Henry Kissinger still thinks from the geo-strategic perspective and stresses that the common interest of the two countries is 'preventing hegemony in Asia, and we have remained on friendly terms despite ups and downs'.[6] This realist perspective is suffering from a fundamental paradox: with the disappearance of the USSR, who else will and can replace it to become a hegemonic power in Asia? In fact, both countries are worried primarily by the unilateral actions of the other in extending its influence in the Asia–Pacific region. China is afraid of American hegemony, while the US is worrying about the nationalistic ambitions of China. In the eyes of Chinese leaders, apart from the US, the only power to cause concern over possible hegemonic tendencies in the Asia–Pacific region, owing to its intention to revive militarism, is Japan. Again, paradox emerges in the Chinese foreign policy conception, as the US is needed to check the Japanese ambition. Joseph S. Nye Jr, a former Assistant Secretary of Defense, said that 'the Chinese privately concede that the American military presence has helped keep the peace by restraining the military ambitions of China's old foe, Japan'.[7]

If common strategic interest cannot be established, what common interests can the two countries pursue? Charles Freeman points out many other areas where Sino–American cooperation could produce encouraging results: strategic stability in Asia, global environmental protection, proliferation of arms, organized crime, illegal emigration from China, regional issues such as the Middle East and Korea, and reforming China's institutions to cope with the market economy. However, the American initiatives towards Beijing on most of these issues are considered as intervention in China's domestic affairs. The US is perceived as a superpower which insists on imposing her wishes upon China in fostering changes so as to further Amercan interests. After the June-Fourth incident, China keeps on emphasizing that after the collapse of the Soviet empire, the US needs to look for a new enemy, and that is China, together with other anti-Western nations like North Korea and Cuba. At the same time, the CCP, facing the declining authority of the state and its loss of legitimacy, has been promoting a strong sense of nationalism and using patriotism as an instrument to unify the masses and maintain the necessary political stability and integration. The only superpower left is naturally portrayed as the main potential enemy,[8] so as to foster strong nationalistic feelings among the Chinese public. With the perception of the American intention as 'containment' against China, and the portrayal of the US as a potential enemy which promotes the 'Chinese threat' conundrum, on what bases can the two nations cooperate?

THE ROLE OF THE US IN THE POST–COLD WAR INTERNATIONAL ORDER: CHINESE PERCEPTIONS AND MISPERCEPTIONS

Since the advent of Deng Xiaoping as the paramount leader of China, starting from the late 1970s, Beijing's foreign policy steered away from Mao's aggressive policy of 'world revolution', and remained very consistent thereafter. An 'inward-looking' policy was adopted: development of external relations was promoted only in order to serve the ultimate goal of modernization of the whole country. An independent foreign policy, with non-alignment and equi-distance to all powers as the norms, helps China to normalize her relations with the rest of the world. Economic interests prevail over ideological confrontations and the pragmatic leaders are keen to explore trade and investment links with all countries concerned. Even the export of arms is considered as beneficial to the modernization of national defence in particular and economic development in general. Moreover, China seeks to pursue a balance among the major powers in East Asia (US, Russia and Japan), so that no dominant one could challenge Chinese interests in the region. She is also reluctant to take foreign policy initiatives.[9] She tends to be reactive, rather than to act as in the age of Mao.

The end of the Cold War in 1989–91 led to serious reconsiderations by China's strategic analysts. Their perceptions of the new international political order in the post-Cold War period obviously reflect the dominance of hardliner thinking in domestic politics. They add new substance to the original Chinese foreign policy framework in the open and reform era by emphasizing the long-term strategy of the West, especially the US, in promoting fundamental changes in socialist countries. This is depicted as the famous 'peaceful evolution' strategy – attempting to transform China through various exchanges by peaceful means. It is stressed that the fundamental structure of the new world order is dictated by a multipolar framework, with regional powers of strategic-political, economic, and/or military importance playing vital roles in regional and global affairs. However, the US plays a very peculiar role as she is the only superpower. This scenario is the same as that perceived by Samuel Huntington, who reads it as a 'uni-multipolar' world. In the new world structure, large-scale world conflicts will hardly occur, but regional hegemonism will try to fill in the 'power vacuum' left over by the demise of superpower rivalry. With more potential instabilities due to regional hegemonists, the world tends to become more unstable than was the case with the rigid bipolar structure of the past.[10]

The US plays a dominant role in Chinese leaders' strategic thinking. Washington is still perceived as a hegemony that wants to impose her principles on the Asian powers in order to solve her problems, instead of seeking some common ground through dialogue so as to narrow down the political gap. But US policies are doomed to fail as she continues to 'hurt Asian countries' sentiments'.[11] Although it has great interests in the Asia–Pacific region, the US is not an Asian power. American leaders are considered by China as not having enough understanding of Asia's history, culture and value system. China would like to see the continued presence of American armies in this region to maintain the equilibrium and stability of the region, but she does not want to see too much interference by the US in Asia. It is alleged that the US wants to play a dominant role in regional affairs but does not respect the fact that the Asians are heterogeneous and different in cultural backgrounds and values. Chinese analysts always stress the strong desire of Chinese people to look for independence and disentanglement from foreign intervention, and accuse the US of not being able to comprehend this kind of feeling.

In reality, China's perceptions are grounded in a blend of two elements. First, it is the ideological assessment of the increasingly overwhelming influence of the US in China which is being further opened up, especially in the post-Cold War era. Second, it is the *realpolitik* approach in the evaluation of its internal and external security problems. Internal security, that is, political stability and the integrity of the nation, is not only conceived as resulting from appropriate domestic policies. It is alleged that domestic order is also threatened by the US.[12] So for both external and internal security considerations, the US should be repulsed, and the portrayal of the US as a 'trouble maker' to China is useful in unifying the masses. It is the same ideological–*realpolitik* consideration that puts the US before everything – that blinds Beijing to understanding how others perceive the behaviour and actions of China, including its foreign policies and military build-up.

A Chinese specialist in international relations, Liang Shoude, dean of the School of International Studies in Peking University, insists that the Cold-War mentality of the West should be eliminated. The decline of the USSR and the lack of a common enemy should not necessarily lead to deterioration in Sino–American relations. If the Cold War is over, the relationship can be built on new grounds. China and the US should overcome the differences due to social systems. He maintains that in Chinese official documents the term imperialism is not used anymore to denote US actions. This proves that China is also anxious to get rid of the Cold-War mentality by not commenting on the nature of the superpower.[13] The Five Principles of Coexistence, especially mutual non-intervention, are considered excellent in promoting relationships in the new era. However, what Liang fails to point out is that, if China tends to link up internal threats and external threats, external security being important in affecting the internal stability of the regime, China's neighbours, together with the US, would also consider the interaction of Chinese domestic politics and foreign policies in their evaluation of China's state behaviour. It is not only the military build-up of China that alarms her Asian–Pacific neighbours. Other variables that result from China's domestic development, in combination with the military muscle, are the real factors in arousing serious worries amongst neighbouring countries. If the Chinese communist regime continues to lose its authority and legitimacy, and China goes down the road of disintegration and destabilization, the numerous social problems such as refugees, crime, drugs, triads, and smuggling in such a vast country will create big troubles for the neighbours. If the regime, in order to remedy its loss of legitimacy, adopts an excessive nationalistic or even jingoistic position in order to unify the Chinese people, the strong anti-foreign sentiments that develop thereafter would certainly be detrimental to the interests of neighbouring nations. What will they think when, at the same time, the People's Liberation Army (PLA) increases its defence expenditure? And the PLA gains further financial strength for its modernization through weapons trade and private businesses, activities which are not transparent to the outside world? Potential political instability blending with a stronger military strength is the actual reason for anxiety and suspicion. The missile test in July 1995 and the further missile test and war game exercises in March 1996 to deter the Taiwan people reflect the irredentist principles urging Taiwan to reunify with China. It is apparent that the primary concern of Beijing in the next few years will be reunification problems of Taiwan and Hong Kong; China thus will put aside its conflicts with the neighbours on the South China Sea. But the South-east Asian nations will think about the cross-strait crisis in March 1996 differently: if menaces using missiles can be launched against compatriots in Taiwan, what about the other neighbours who are not compatriots?

All these worries and scepticism about China's behaviour are criticized as groundless by Beijing: they are all reflections of the theory of 'Chinese Threats' instigated by some people in the West, who do not want to see a prosperous, stable and powerful China. What China fails to admit is that a more prosperous and militarily-strong China, but suffering from increasing political and social chaos due to the mismanagement of the great political-economic transition, would be a source of insecurity for all nations in the Asia–Pacific region. By emphasizing external hostile actions, the Party–state hopes to camouflage the domestic problems created as a result of its own flaws and shift the focus of attention of its people to the perceived threat. A fast developing economy can only boost a more assertive and nationalistic attitude of the leaders *vis-à-vis* the West.[14] Modernization of armed forces, together with standing firmly against the alleged pressure from the West, bolsters the dignity of Chinese leaders and helps consolidate national identity in their eyes.

US PERCEPTIONS AND POLICY ORIENTATIONS IN RELATION TO CHINA

'A China that is alienated from the United States could work against American interests...Deterioration in US–China relations could lead Beijing, which is increasing military strength, into a more hostile military posture in Asia and beyond.'[15] The Americans are not convinced that China has no ambition to become a regional power and eventually a global power, which would then assert its influence in world affairs. American foreign policy during the Bush administration sought to maintain good bilateral relationships with all the major regional powers. By making use of these bilateral relations, the US, though her relative national strength is declining, could nevertheless exercise a large degree of influence in the affairs of different regions. The policy of 'beyond containment', proclaimed by Bush in May 1989, emphasized the importance of continual dialogues and exchanges with socialist countries in a world which was becoming more and more interdependent, so as to facilitate their gradual evolution towards political democracy and a market economy. This was denounced as the 'peaceful evolution' strategy by China after the June-Fourth event. The paradox is that the US has further developed its multiple exchanges in all aspects with China since 1989, but in the Chinese press 'peaceful evolution' has not been criticized any more since 1992.

In China American foreign policy is discussed using an analogy of two axes, an interventionist (internationalist)/isolationist one, and the other an idealist/realist one. There are only a few extremist; most analysts identify with more moderate positions around these axes. It is believed that the policy orientations of President Bush can be categorized as inclining towards internationalism and realism. It is in the interest of the US to engage China in helpful dialogue and to maintain high-level contacts. In all parts of the world 'selective intervention' might be needed, and America's leadership in Asia needs the support of Japan and China.

With the advent of the Clinton administration, some might be afraid that because he was chosen as a domestic president, he may focus only on the internal affairs and economic situation of the US. In foreign relations he may tend to become an idealist, as the Democrats are inclined towards promoting the idea of democracy and Western attitudes to human rights. In reality, Clinton does not really perform as an isolationist–idealist. Bush's policy towards China simply continues. With the declaration of 'A National Security Strategy of Engagement and Enlargement' by President Clinton in February 1995, a clearer idea of his policy evolved. The strategy of enlargement was first initiated by Anthony Lake, national security advisor to Clinton, in September 1993; this means enlargement of the world's free community of market democracies.[16] By 'engagement', Clinton means the US must exercise global leadership. Preventive diplomacy is needed, but the US engagement must be selective, based on her long-term national interests, and should act unilaterally, in alliance or even multilaterally.[17] Clinton's policy towards China is characterized by the so-called 'comprehensive engagement' in the words of Winston Lord.[18] Dialogues and high-level contacts, including military exchanges, are promoted, and the basic consideration is to assist China to be better integrated in the world. It is argued that any kind of containment policy aiming to isolate China would not only be ineffective in causing structural change in the country, but would force her to become hostile to the US. Lord stresses that this policy

> assumes neither Chinese agressiveness nor Chinese benevolence. It means neither acquiescence in what we see as inappropriate actions by Beijing, nor attempts to isolate China and frustrate her development. Containment would be a self-fulfilling prophecy of mutual enmity. And it would not be supported by our Asian partners.[19]

Apparently the Clinton administration aims not to sensitize Beijing by provoking her constantly through issues of domestic political problems and human rights, and not to isolate her in the global economic system. On the one hand, this policy reflects a rather common sentiment among American officials and scholars; as described by an American scholar, 'moralistic criticisms of China can actually undermine American interests by engendering a nationalistic reaction that strengthens domestic Chinese political actors who are less friendly to the United States than are other more moderate elements'.[20] On the other hand, in reflecting another public opinion which appears more antagonistic to China, US officials do not forget to remind the Chinese leaders that a very nationalistic posture, armed with a stronger military muscle, would worry the whole Asia–Pacific region. China could then be isolated, a consequence unfavourable to her economic development. It is noted by James Lilley, former ambassador of the US to China, that the strategic relationship built up between the US and India, and Washington's resuming diplomatic relations with Vietnam in 1995, are measures to boost a stronger stance *vis-à-vis* China. Moreover, regarding the South China Sea issue, Washington adopts a strong and clear position: insistence on free passage in the sea lanes of the South China Sea, and that littoral states should not resort to using force in resolving the territorial disputes.[21] This clearly gives a signal to China that while the US would like to consider the perceptions of Chinese leaders, the latter are also urged to consider their neighbours' perceptions.

How to find out the most appropriate role for a superpower, especially in the post-Cold War order, is difficult. Political actions and military involvement abroad may be denounced as intervention by the left, though the same actions may be deemed insufficient or lacking in strength by the right. In the case of the difficult Sino–American relations, the right-wing Republicans such as Patrick Buchanan condemn China for incurring large trade surpluses with the US. By promoting economic protectionism, he even argues for the withdrawal of Most Favoured Nation (MFN) status from China. The left-wing radicals in American public opinion naturally opt for stronger actions against the abuse of human rights in China.

In January 1994, the former Secretary of Defence in Clinton's administration, Les Aspin, had already outlined four broad challenges or dangers to American security:

1. Dangers posed by nuclear weapons and other weapons of mass destruction (WMD).
2. Regional dangers posed primarily by the threat of large-scale aggression by major regional powers.
3. Dangers to democracy and market reform in the former Soviet Union, Eastern Europe, and elsewhere.
4. Economic dangers to national security, which could result if the US failed to restore a strong, competitive, and growing economy.[22]

A careful appraisal of the relative importance of different aspects of US foreign policy imperatives may show that military security and economic exchanges override ideological issues such as democratization and human rights conditions in others nations. In regard to China, the relative importance of the various policies can be placed in the following order:

1. Stability of the Asia–Pacific region. The US does not want to see a militarily strengthened China provoking an arms race among countries in East and South-east Asia. Chinese exports of missiles and strategic materials that help to build WMD are of primary concern. Peaceful means to solve the mainland–Taiwan crisis is a long-term policy.
2. US economic interests. Washington clearly welcomes the further opening up of China, but wants the latter to abide by international norms in its trade and economic behavior, and to establish the necessary financial regulations and legal provisions in coping with fast economic growth (see Chapter 4). Opening up the Chinese market for American products, intellectual property rights, and China's entry into the World Trade Organisation are essential issues.
3. Domestic politics of China and the prospect of democracy. Although the US is high-sounding in hoping to see democratization corresponding to economic and social pluralism, Washington's intention and capability to foster democracy is rather limited.

Engaging China economically and hoping to form a social foundation for democratization is the adopted means.

4. Human rights in China. Despite the constant dispute between the PRC and the West on whether there exists a universal value of human rights, what the US and the West can do for improving human rights conditions in China is very limited.

While the priority of policy imperatives is quite clear, for the American decision-makers some tactical problems remain to be solved. How can the US affect Chinese political and strategic considerations, without being accused of intervention? Are Western ideas of human rights universal? If so, does any international standard exist that can be accepted by third world countries, including China? How do Americans talk with those Chinese who maintain that sovereignty overrides human rights, and national interests prevail over ethics in foreign relations? If ideological differences are likely to persist, on what grounds of common interest can Sino–American relations be built in the future?

PROBLEMS AND PROSPECTS

It has been argued that Sino–American relations are like a pendulum that swings between cooperation and conflict. However, this is a rather vague categorization of the relationship, as all kinds of bilateral relationships can also be described in such a way. Harry Harding adds competition. His other description of the nature of Sino–American relations – that it is a 'not friends, not enemies' relationship – merits attention, as it was also echoed by Stanley Ross, assistant to the Secretary of Defense responsible for Asia–Pacific affairs.[23] Prof Jia Qingguo of Beijing University has a similar observation. He stresses that Sino–American relations can be categorized as 'limited cooperation, limited conflict'.[24] If it is true that external behaviour is determined largely by domestic politics, then it follows that with a relatively weak government in both countries – especially during Clinton's first term and Jiang Zemin under the shadow of Deng Xiaoping – radical amelioration of relations was inconceivable, while indecision and sources of instability became tangible from time to time. However, Clinton in his second term appears to be more self-assertive, and Jiang, after the Fifteenth Party Congress held in September 1997, has successfully consolidated his power. Two leaders with a stronger power base, and who appear to be more confident of themselves, might be helpful in promoting a better relationship.

In 1995, the Clinton administration faced considerable pressure from the Congress, who almost unanimously supported Taiwan's President Lee Teng-Hui's visit to Cornell.[25] Many Congressmen are still adopting a 'confrontation' approach. They see China as an 'emerging authoritarian and nationalistic superpower', which is becoming a threat to global security and the American cause for promoting democracy. A subtle containment policy to pressurize China on issues important to the US is therefore needed.[26] There exists also a minority that prefers a policy to promote political change in China. If China is considered important to the US, strong actions initiated by the American government are deemed necessary. But this in turn requires a clear vision of the role of the US in the new world order, and a strong conviction to implement a well-conceived policy. Unfortunately the Clinton administration is lacking in both vision and conviction.

Jiang Zemin has apparently consolidated his power in the post-Deng era. He attained the climax of his career in 1997. This was illustrated by his high-profile participation in the ceremony for the handover of the sovereignty of Hong Kong on 30 June 1997, his re-election as Party General Secretary in the Fifteenth Party Congress, and his state visit to the US in October 1997. The successful visit, applauded in the Chinese media, symbolized a normalization of relations, in contrast to the difficulties in 1995. According to sources not yet confirmed, the more reconciliatory attitude of the Chinese Foreign Minister, Qian Qichen, towards the US was criticized by the dogmatists and the military, though Qian was supported by Jiang. The very strong posture of Beijing against Washington immediately after Lee Teng-Hui's visit to the US signifies a concession made by Jiang towards the hardliners.[27] No leader in the Chinese regime can afford to accept the responsibility of 'losing' Taiwan, the separation of Taiwan from the mainland being labelled as a 'national crime'. Thus, it is easy to achieve a strong consensus within the leadership. The homogeneous, nationalistic leadership in China contrasts sharply with the more heterogeneous leadership pattern in the US, as can be demonstrated by the decision-making process of inviting Lee to the US.

Regional stability and Taiwan

Although Lee Teng-Hui always declares his opposition to Taiwan independence, he does in fact fight to seek international recognition of his idea of 'one-nation, two-states'. That is to say, the two regimes should be equal and legally recognized by the global community. The eventual re-entry of Taiwan to the United Nations is a natural corollary. Apparently he gains support from certain members of the US Congress, and China considers this as an American intervention in Chinese domestic affairs. China considers the Taiwan question as the core of Sino–American relations. This sensitive issue cannot be easily solved, given the fact that Taiwan's ambition to achieve a better position in the world, as well as America's policy on this issue depends to a large extent on the domestic environments, irrespective of Beijing's world-view.

The reason why Taiwan becomes a vital problem in Sino–American relations is that Beijing is suspicious of the American intention to separate Taiwan definitively from the mainland. The PRC keeps on criticizing rigorously the 'two-China' or 'one-China, one-Taiwan' policy, the ambition of Taiwan and some American politicians. It is always alleged that the Americans consider the separation of China as in the interests of the US. In fact, although the 'two-China' policy has never been officially adopted, the prevention by the US government of any military action launched by either side of the Taiwan Strait testifies a *de facto* policy of 'two-Chinas'. This is lucidly depicted by an American observer of American relations with Taiwan and Hong Kong:

> Having been responsible for salvaging the doomed Nationalist regime, Washington refused to fight to restore its control, making impossible either claimant's final assumption of total power. The United States not only stopped the Communists from crossing the Straits to liberate Taiwan but also refused to help the Nationalists try to return to the mainland. Containment in Asia faced both ways, restricting the 'free' as much as the Communist Chinese. For American leaders, a 'two Chinas' policy made it possible to protect allies and innocents on Taiwan while also accepting the reality of communist domination on the the mainland. It did not matter that neither China welcomed the fragmentation, the loss of territory, political legitimacy, or military security. Washington was not, in the end, much disturbed by the Chinese response and successfully fended off efforts to exact retribution. American policy seemed realistic and practical to each succeeding administration, and so it was sustained.[28]

It is generally believed that the missile tests and war games launched by the PRC in March 1996 against Taiwan were not aimed at deterring the people in Taiwan from voting for Lee Teng-Hui, as Lee would certainly be elected, but rather to send a clear signal to Taiwan officials, as well as to the general public, that, whatever the election results, independence is unequivocally prohibited. Even seeking more 'space for survival in the international society', as always proclaimed by Taiwan leaders, is regarded as action to achieve independence by the nationalistic Chinese leaders. The democratization process in Taiwan, and the first election by universal suffrage of a president who can only exercise his rule on the island but has full sovereign power, certainly complicates the whole issue. Although PRC officials always claim that the military exercises were not directed against democracy in Taiwan,[29] what would they say if the people in Taiwan opted for independence by democratic means? China would definitely send forces in such an eventuality, despite the fact that her capability to invade and occupy Taiwan by military means is doubtful.[30] So it is not exaggerating to say that 'a democratic Taiwan ... engendered a feeling among super-patriots in Beijing that democracy was an unpatriotic idea, a slogan invoked to negate the legitimacy of Beijing's claim that Taiwan ... was still a province of China.'[31] Democracy in Taiwan certainly complicates Sino–American relations. American public opinion is generally sympathetic to a democratic Taiwan, while at the same time the image of China after June Fourth is badly tarnished. A fearful menace on such a grandiose scale against Taiwan not only leads to the sending of two US aircraft carrier battle groups to the South China Sea; it also leads to stronger statements from the US Department of State. The former Assistant Secretary of State for East Asian and Pacific Affairs, Winston Lord, reiterated the significance of the Joint Communique of 17 August 1982, signed between China and the US. He stressed that the intentions of the US of not increasing the quantity and quality of arms supplied to Taiwan, or even gradually reducing the sales, were 'premised on the PRC's continued adherence to a policy of striving for peaceful reunification with Taiwan'.[32] Although Lord maintains that the PRC has not changed this policy, the corollary is simple. If the PRC resorts to force in solving the Taiwan issue, the US government might change its policy, probably by augmenting the quantity and quality of weapons sold to Taiwan, as requested by the latter continuously.[33] Thus, the *de facto* 'two-China' policy is sustained.

In short, two important factors add to the volatility of Sino–American relations in relation to Taiwan. First, it is the US wish to defend the status quo of cross-strait relations by preventing armed invasion launched by either side. Worries about the potential American intervention would deter the PRC from resorting to force. However, the prolonged maintenance of the status quo – division by the US – would lead the Chinese leaders to be doubtful about the real intention of the

US. Second, the democratic government in Taiwan will attract more sympathy towards its goal of expanding its space for survival in the international community. But seeking international recognition is considered by the PRC as action that would lead to ultimate independence. Favourable echoes in the US to Taiwan's actions would only complicate the relationship between Beijing and Washington.

Proliferation of arms

In relation to the stability of the Asia–Pacific region, second to the Taiwan issue is the Chinese transfer of nuclear technology and the proliferation of arms and strategic materials to other countries. This has become a sensitive and difficult issue in Sino–American relations. China's subtle action in convincing North Korea to abandon her nuclear development plan in 1994 and accept the American conditions is highly regarded by Washington. However, in the supply of missiles and nuclear technology to other countries, including Saudi Arabia, Syria, Iran and Pakistan, disputes always happen. Beijing adopts a rather strong stance: why is China not allowed to export weaponry, while the US is the largest exporter of arms in the world? In the first White Paper on defence, published in November 1995, *The Arms Control and Disarmament of China*, it is postulated that, 'they [the great nuclear powers], on the one hand compete to sell their advanced weapons in the international market, or even use the sale of weapons as a means to interfere in the domestic affairs of other countries, but on the other hand forcing discriminatory measures of non-proliferation and arms control towards the developing countries'.[34] China exports arms primarily to promote its regional security interests, and to further its 'great power aspirations and the dynamics of the PRC defence industries'.[35] But apparently China uses the export of arms and technology as a leverage in bargaining with the US. Negotiation on, and the eventual signing of, the agreements on non-proliferation are used to seek favourable terms and substantial returns from the US, in case of difficult negotiations on other issues.

Despite the strong rhetoric against American hegemony in this regard – the US being accused of using multilateral frameworks to constrain the freedom of manoeuvre of other nations – China signed the Nuclear Non-Proliferation Treaty (NPT) in 1992, the Nuclear Test Ban Treaty in 1996, and the Chemical Weapons Convention in January 1993 (but ratified only in 1996). She also promised the US that she would abide by the Missile Technology Control Regime.

Before the visit of Jiang Zemin to the US, China entered the Zangger Group, the export control arm of the NPT, on 16 October 1997. Thereafter, China has to fulfill the requirements imposed by the Group when exporting nuclear technology.

China is also very irritated by the accusation of a potential 'Chinese threat', and always tries to prove that her military expenditure is still very low. Although we believe that China puts heavy emphasis on economic investments and that the precious capital needed for economic development will not be sacrificed for the sake of military needs, it is clear that a rapid growth in GDP would lead to a rapid increase in the absolute defence budget, even if the percentage of GDP used for defence were to remain at a low percentage – 1.3 per cent for the year 1994, according to official figures. What is more, the multiple business activities of the People's Liberation Army (PLA), with more than 20 000 commercial enterprises,[36] has enriched the army. Whether this is a source of corruption within the army, or a force that helps the modernization of the PLA, remains to be studied. But it is not surprising that neighbouring countries are keeping a sceptical eye on the military development of China.

Significance of trade for China and the US

The trade deficits that the US incurs in Sino–American trade has reached an alarming level. The size of deficit, in billions (thousands of millions) of US dollars, is shown in Table 5.1. The central column gives figures from official US sources; the column on the right gives the 'real' deficit, as calculated by Nicholas Lardy, an American economist.[37]

Table 5.1 The US trade deficit with China (in billions of US dollars)

Year	*Official US sources*	*'Real' deficit*
1990	10.4	7.4
1991	12.7	8.4
1992	18.2	11.9
1993	22.8	14.2
1994	29.5	19.7
1995	33.8	22.3
1996	39.5	26.8

China insists that the American method of calculating these trade deficits in the years prior to the return of Hong Kong is not correct. All the products manufactured by Hong Kong industrialists in China and exported through Hong Kong are classified as Chinese products, although the Hong Kong capitalists benefit the most; while all the American products that are eventually exported to China passing through Hong Kong are not counted. In more specific terms, some Chinese exports to the US have value added in Hong Kong. About 25 per cent of the value is added, but this is not reflected in the American figures. US exports to Hong Kong which are then re-exported to the PRC are not counted as American exports to China. Thus, Nicholas Lardy estimates that the trade deficit with China should be cut by almost half, as shown in the column on the right, above.

However, it is clear that in trade transactions the US is very important to China; while the Chinese market, though potentially very big, provides relatively little for American interests, given the sheer size of the US economy. China's exports to the US are about a third of its total, while US exports to China are only about 2 per cent of total US exports.[38] As a result, the US government is keen to force China to open up its market, to protect the patents and copyrights of American products, and to reform China's financial institutions and legal provisions. The two memoranda signed in 1992 on copyright and market access, and the agreement on the Protection of Intellectual Property Rights signed in February 1995, are considered by the Americans as a success, since China has at least agreed in principle to accept the international norms in international economic exchanges. Economic interdependence will be the impetus that facilitates further exchanges between the two. Further financial and monetary reforms in China will pave the way for her eventual entry to the WTO. Nevertheless, the domestic reforms that the US would like to see in China may be a long and painful process, not only for China, but also for others. Despite the obligation imposed by the Agreement of February 1995 that called for a special enforcement year to close down 29 pirate compact disc companies in China, the losses of the American software and music companies increased rather than decreased. China has closed seven companies that produced pirate products, but still one-third of the world's pirate CDs, software, and videos come from China.[39] In the failed negotiation on this matter in April 1996, the US representative presented a detailed 'plan of action' that would require Beijing to take strong measures, but 'the Chinese reaction was extremely negative'.[40] This can be easily understood, as China felt offended when she was 'ordered' by the US to do something, although the request was justified. Following the continuous stream of requests and criticisms made by the US towards China, China is seemingly becoming more intolerant as she is strongly convinced that Washington only wants her to be integrated into a world order of *pax Americana*. A more intransigent and rigid attitude is developing in China and her reactions appear more and more nationalistic in nature.

Human rights in China

Another important factor in Sino–American relations is the human rights condition in China. By de-linking MFN from the human rights conditions in China, the Clinton administration unilaterally abandoned in May 1994 the instrument of MFN as a means to foster the liberation of political prisoners in China – this despite the fact that MFN had been used skilfully and subtly by Bush in ameliorating human rights conditions in China. Facing opposition from the Congress, Bush granted MFN status to China without any conditions, thus saving the face of the octogenarian leaders in China. But he made it very clear to Beijing that if the human rights situation was not improved the next year, the weight of the opposition from the Congress might render his veto ineffective.

Apparently succumbing to increasing pressure from the American business sector, Clinton adopted a straightforward policy of delinking MFN from human rights. This clearly resolved his problem and also upheld the continued prosperity and stability of both Taiwan and Hong Kong, as these two capitalist enclaves under different governments are increasingly relying on China due to their enormous investments in the mainland. Both former Governor of Hong Kong, Chris Patten, and the former representative of Taiwan in the US, Luo Hsiao Chung, were opposed to the elimination of MFN status granted to China.[41] The delinking of human rights from MFN should be seen by China as a friendly action, but paradoxically it cannot help to promote a better relationship. Prominent dissidents who had been released before the decision was made in May 1994 were re-arrested (they were released again after Jiang Zemin's visit to the US in October 1997). What other instruments can be used by Clinton is not clear. Economic sanctions, like freezing credits or imposing tariffs on certain Chinese products, may be considered. However, facing an economically stronger China, which had accumulated more than 140 billion US dollars in foreign currency reserves by the end of 1998, and the increasing interests of American businesses in establishing links with China, economic sanctions are now outdated as a means to bring about changes in China.

The occasional but timely release of political prisoners, a major concern of human rights activists in the West, is still used by China as a kind of political instrument for other ends. The release of Wei Jingsheng, just two weeks after the visit of Jiang Zemin to the US, leads one to suspect that it was the result of a deal that helped to create a better atmosphere to facilitate his visit, and to improve China's international image.

CONCLUSION

In general, it is an exaggeration to say that a new Cold War has developed between the two nations. A cold war is inconceivable, given the multiple exchanges in all aspects. With increasing interdependence flowing from the complex networks formed with the outside world, Beijing needs to carry out further reforms in economic, financial, legal and eventually, political institutions. This is certainly in the interests of the US, which is seeking a comprehensive and constructive engagement with China. The key issue is that China would like to integrate in the global economic system, but she declines to become part of the world order dictated by the US. An increasingly prosperous China, with a regime losing its legitimacy, is becoming more and more self-assertive as it faces challenges and pressures from the West. A more nationalistic stance reflects the Chinese leaders' wish to be treated with dignity. Difficulties will persist, but limited cooperation may also be possible in the future of Sino–American relations. But cooperation is needed only to resolve conflicts, as has been demonstrated by Robert Ross. Based on his study of the history of Sino–American relations from 1969 to 1989 he says: 'US and China interests in cooperation are not common interests. Rather, US–PRC cooperation is primarily required to resolve conflicts of interest. Moreover, the issues at stake in the 1990s are less pressing than the immediate security interests of the Cold War era.'[42] The domestic political ecology of the two countries, whether it be the political succession in China or changing public opinion in the US, will increase uncertainties and will become an important variable in affecting the policy imperatives of the two governments.

Notes and references

1. See Harry Harding, *The Fragile Relationship: Sino–American Relations since 1972* (New York: The Brookings Institution, 1992.)
2. Jia Qingguo, 'Reconsidering Sino–American Relations', *American Studies* (Beijing), No. 1 (1995), p. 38.
3. See especially *United States and China: Relations at a Crossroads, policy paper* (Washington, DC: The Atlantic Council and National Committee on United States–China Relations, February 1993.)
4. Author's interview of scholars in the Institute of Contemporary International Relations, Beijing, July 1995.
5. Ambassador Charles Freeman's seminar on Sino–American Relations, Fairbank Center for East Asian Research, Harvard University, 8 March 1996.
6. See interview of Henry Kissinger in *Far Eastern Economic Review* (16 November 1995), p. 26.
7. See 'A Test of Gunboat Diplomacy, 1996 Model', *New York Times,* Week in Review, 17 March 1996, p. 4.
8. See Patrick E. Tyler, 'China's Campus Model for the 90s: Ernest Patriot', *New York Times*, 23 April 1996, p. A4.
9. See David M. Lampton, 'China and the Strategic Quadrangle: Foreign Policy Continuity in an Age of Discontinuity' in Michael Mandelbaum (ed.), *The Strategic Quadrangle* (New York: Council on Foreign Relations Press, 1995), p. 66.
10. See Ting Wai, 'China and the New International Political Order: Perceptions and Policy Orientations', in K. S. Liao (ed.), *Politics of Economic Cooperation in the Asia–Pacific Region* (Hong Kong: Institute of Asia–Pacific Studies, Chinese University of Hong Kong, 1993), pp. 45–65.
11. See Xi Laiwan, 'New Asia–Pacific Policy of the United States and its Prospects', in Hsueh Chun-tu and Lu Zhongwei (ed), *China and her Neighbours: Prospects for the Twenty-First Century* (Beijing: Current Affairs Publishing Co., 1995), p. 191.
12. David Shambaugh is correct in pointing out that 'Chinese definitions of national security have always included an essential linkage between internal and external security, and have always considered threats to political "stability" to be threats to national security'. See D. Shambaugh, 'The Insecurity of Security: the PLA's Evolving Doctrine and Threat Perceptions towards 2000', *Journal of Northeast Asian Studies*, vol. 13, No. 1 (Spring 1994), p. 6.
13. Seminar of Liang Shoude on Sino–American Relations, Hong Kong Baptist University, 5 October 1995.
14. An American observer may have reason to say that 'economic growth could feed China's nationalism and assertiveness as much as its democracy. The prospect is chilling'. See Robert J. Samuelson, 'Trading with the Enemy', *Newsweek*, 1 April 1996, p. 40.
15. United States and China: Relations at a Crossroads, policy paper, p. 10.
16. See 'Text of Anthony Lake's remarks to Johns Hopkins School of Advanced International Studies', 21 September 1993, in W. Q. Bowen

& D. H. Dunn, *American Security Policy in the 1990s* (Aldershot: Dartmouth Publishing, 1996), pp. 158–160.
17. See William Clinton, *A National Security Strategy of Engagement and Enlargement* (The White House, February 1995), p. 7.
18. Winston Lord, 'A Sweet and Sour Relationship' (Interview), *Current History*, Vol. 94, no. 593 (September 1995), pp. 248–251.
19. Winston Lord, 'For China, not Containment but True Integration', *International Herald Tribune*, 13 October 1995.
20. See William J. Murphy, 'Power Transition in Northeast Asia: US–China Security Perceptions and the Challenges of Systemic Adjustment and Stability', *Journal of Northeast Asian Studies*, Vol. 13, no. 4 (Winter 1994), p. 80. This view, of course, is based on the assumption that Chinese leaders are divided into conservative and moderate (reformist) factions.
21. 'Strategic Divergence of China and US: Interview of James Lilley', *Open Monthly* (Hong Kong) (August 1995), p. 30.
22. See Les Aspin, *Report of the Secretary of Defense to the President and the Congress 1994*, January 1994, in Bowen and Dunn, p. 161.
23. Zheng Yin, 'Asia–Pacific Region: Multiple Angles and the Five Parties', *Contemporary International Relations* (Beijing), No. 60, October 1994, p. 4.
24. Jia Qingguo, 'Reconsidering Sino–American Relations'.
25. House voted 396 to 0, Senate 97 to 1.
26. See David Shambaugh, 'The United States and China: A New Cold War?', *Current History*, vol. 94, no. 593 (September 1995), p. 244
27. See the various issues of *Cheng Ming Monthly* (Hong Kong), in 1995.
28. N. B. Tucker, *Taiwan, Hong Kong and the United States, 1945–1992: Uncertain Friendship* (New York: Twayne Publishing, 1994), pp. 5–6.
29. See the press conference of Qian Qichen in Beijing, reported by *World Journal* (Chinese daily published in New York), 11 March 1996. p. A2.
30. It is stipulated by the authoritative *Jane's Defence Weekly* that 'China lacks the amphibious lift capability to sustain a massive surprise operation'. Other weaknesses of the Chinese military are force projection, logistics, training, command and control, and the most important of all, the air force. See the analysis by Barbara Starr, in *Jane's Defence Weekly*, 20 March 1996, p. 17. In another analysis, it is said that in the first phase of an assault on Taiwan, China should send at least 60,000 soldiers across the Strait, but she lacks the capability to do so. See *Newsweek*, 1 April 1996, p. 41.
31. See E. Friedman, 'The Challenge of a Rising China: Another Germany?', in R. Liebert (ed.), *Eagle Adrift: American Foreign Policy at the End of the Century* (New York: Longman,1997), pp. 215–45.
32. See 'Testimony of Winston Lord before the Subcommittee on East Asia and the Pacific, Senate Foreign Relations Committee, 7 February 1996', *Foreign Policy Backgrounder,* USIS Hong Kong, 9 February 1996, p. 4.
33. Taipei consistently seeks diesel submarines, P-3 anti-submarine aircraft, Harpoon anti-ship missiles and individually-operated anti-aircraft missiles from the US, but is always denied access. Nevertheless,

Taipei obtains 150 F-16 fighters, 4 AWACS detection airplanes, and the patriot anti-missiles.

34. See the *White Paper on Arms Control and Disarmament of China*, in *Ta Kung Pao*, 17 November 1995, p. A7.
35. See E. W. Eikenberry, 'Explaining and Influencing Chinese Arms Transfers', *McNair Paper* 36, February 1995 (Washington, DC: Institute for National Strategic Studies, National Defense University), p. 27.
36. *Newsweek*, 1 April 1996, p. 42.
37. Information on US official figures are supplied by United States Information Service (USIS) Hong Kong for detailed explanation on calculation of 'real deficit' see also Nicholas Lardy, 'Normalizing Economic Relations with China', *NBR Analysis*, 1997, pp. 15–21.
38. *Newsweek*, 1 April 1996, p. 40.
39. See *World Journal*, 26 February 1996, p. A2; *World Journal*, 27 April 1996, p. A2.
40. *New York Times*, 16 April 1996, p. D4.
41. For Taiwan's position, see *World Journal*, 20 April 1996, p. A2; for Hong Kong's position, see the interview of Chris Patten before his visit to the US, *New York Times*, 29 April 1996, p. A8. Patten stresses that if China loses MFN, Hong Kong's growth in GDP will be cut by half and 90,000 jobs eliminated.
42. See Robert S. Ross, *Negotiating Cooperation: the United States and China, 1969–1989* (Stanford: Stanford University Press), 1995. p. 261.

6 Sovereignty Disputes across the Taiwan Straits

Chen Yu Hsi

An appropriate sub-title for this chapter is: 'A deviant case of divided nations'. In the discourse about sovereignty disputes in connection with divided nations, two controversial points which have theoretical implications need to be addressed. The first arises from a gap between political science and national governments in the perception of sovereignty. Political scientists generally perceive sovereignty as a functional concept, which can be defined as 'a formal autonomy (of a nation-state) combined with real limitations on this autonomy' imposed by the rules of the international system and the power of other states in that system. As such, 'no state in the interstate system, even the single most powerful one at any given time, is totally autonomous, but certainly some enjoy far greater autonomy than others'.[1] From this functional perspective, sovereignty is a matter of degree and relativity; it is not absolute. On the other hand, national governments tend to add an ideological hue to the term, regarding it as something supreme and absolute, sacred and inviolable. It is partly on the basis of this ideological perception that a government in a divided nation claims total sovereignty over the entire national territory at the expense of its rival counterparts.

A second point concerns the divisibility or indivisibility of sovereignty. Drawing on classic political philosophy, some political theories interpret sovereignty of a modern state as 'absolute and indivisible'.[2] This implies that a nation can be repesented by only one sovereign state or government which exercises national sovereignty in its entirety – a notion that follows from the traditional conception of nation-state, and perhaps also from the Enlightenment political view that the people are the ultimate source of sovereignty. However, contemporary political reality has rendered that notion questionable.

Indeed, the political developments in the world's divided nations since 1945 have opened up new perspectives that challenge the indivisibility of nation-state sovereignty. For instance, the conclusion of a

Basic Treaty between the Federal Republic of Germany (FRG) and its communist counterpart, the German Democratic Republic (GDR), in 1972 provided for mutual recognition of the two Germanies as separate sovereign states. This was done despite the FRG constitutional claim that East Germany (GDR) is an integral part of the FRG territory. It is important to note that the recognition of separate sovereignty was carried out within the framework of a nation. The famous remarks by Willy Brandt, then Prime Minister of FRG and architect of the German rapprochement, that East Germany was 'sovereign but not foreign', and the FRG official vision to create 'two German states in one German nation' drive home the point that one nation can have two sovereign states at least temporarily with an ultimate goal of national reunification.[3]

In the Korean peninsula, the political upheavals in the Soviet Bloc at the beginning of the 1990s ushered in a new era in which North Korea agreed to dual diplomatic recogniton of the two Koreas by its communist allies. Seoul and Pyongyang simultaneously joined the United Nations in September 1991, a move that clearly indicated that both sides accepted each other as a sovereign state, though no formal agreement or treaty has ever been signed to that effect. One year before the UN move, North Korean leader Kim Il Sung proposed 'one nation, two governments' as a basis for reunification, saying that Pyongyang would not object to Japan retaining its diplomatic recognition of South Korea if it also recognised the North.[4] The theme of a homogeneous national identity shared by the two Korean states has also been stressed by political leaders of South Korea, who are committed at least rhetorically to the goal of 'national reconciliation and reunification'. Thus the German model of 'one nation, two sovereign states' has come to form the underpinning of the new South–North Korean relations as well.

This notion of 'one nation, two sovereign states' implies that under the present-day reality of divided nations, national sovereignty is no longer considered as indivisible.[5] As a matter of fact, the *de facto* split of sovereign power comes into being simultaneously as a nation is territorially divided. The People's Republic of China, for instance, exercised its sovereignty over mainland China effectively even in the first 20 years after its founding, when a majority of the world's nations still recognised the Republic of China (ROC) on Taiwan as the sovereign government of China. East Germany prior to 1972 was also denied diplomatic recognition by the Western allies of West Germany, but internationally it was considered as an 'established state'.[6] A question arises, however, over the sovereign status of the Taiwan Government today. In light of the above-stated political science concept that sovereignty is a matter of relativity and degree, it can be observed that the 'Republic of China on Taiwan' is a valid sovereign state insofar as it effectively exercises its 'internal sovereignty' while externally it still enjoys the diplomatic recognition of some 30 countries. But its sovereign status may become problematic if Beijing succeeds some day in its bid to deprive Taiwan of its diplomatic ties with these small countries.

The German and Korean experiences are different in that the two rival governments in question accept each other's sovereign status in the international arena. By contrast, there is no such mutual acceptance in other divided nations such as China and the former Vietnam and Cambodia. On the contrary, disputes over sovereignty were – and still are in the case of China – prolonged indefinitely, with at least one rival party claiming sovereignty and even administrative jurisdiction over the national territory not under its control.[7]

The mutual acceptance of sovereignty in a divided nation may lead us to coin the term 'sovereignty sharing' if one insists on the philosophical 'indivisibility' of national sovereignty. It implies that national sovereignty belongs to the people of a nation as a whole, and insofar as the rival parties cherish the oneness and integrity of the nation and her people, that sovereignty is not to be 'divided', but can be 'shared' by consent. Rather than merely a play on words, 'sovereignty sharing' appears to be a useful concept with positive implications for regional peace and development, which may otherwise be affected by the sovereignty disputes of a divided nation. It can also form a philosophical basis on which rival governments of a divided nation agree to the functional division of administrative jurisdiction.

But the separation or sharing of sovereignty by consent does not come easily. Both the two Germanies and the two Koreas had come a long way before they agreed to meet each other halfway. The rapprochement is part of a long process of evolution in the intra-national relations of a divided nation. Some political scientists have attempted to construct a sort of general theory to account for that evolution process. Henderson and Lebow present a four-stage model which hypothesizes the evolution process as the four stages of intense hostility, declining hostility, rapprochement and unification. Partly based on the German experience, the model was accurate in predicting the course of development of the East–West German relations in which rapprochement has led to unification. But the four stages appear to represent merely the static results of a dynamic evolutionary process, which warrants a careful study in its entirety. Presumably to account for the dynamic process, Weng has reconstructed a modified model in which the evolution consists of five stages, namely, hostility, competition, cooperation, negotiation and settlement, wherein competition, cooperation and negotiation can be conceived as the dynamic processes that yield the results of rapprochement and final settlement in terms of national unification or partition.[8]

DEVIATIONS FROM DIVIDED-NATION MODEL

This chapter explains the sovereignty disputes of China as a deviant case based on the evolution model. It is true that mainland China and Taiwan have gone through the stages of hostility and competition, and have, since the beginning of the 1990s, engaged in limited semi-official cooperation with regard to certain civilian matters. But political negotiations have been indefinitely postponed because, unlike the German and Korean cases, the easing of hostility across the Taiwan Straits has failed to usher in a new phase of relations in which both sides learn to accommodate each other politically. As a result of this political stalemate, the process of evolution in the bilateral relations has been disrupted, and there has been no progress towards economic and non-economic cooperation on an official level, not to speak of a settlement of sovereignty disputes in terms of unification or peaceful coexistence. The characteristics of the cross-Straits relations as a deviant case of a divided nation will become clear as we explore the root causes of the political stalemate.

In terms of the divided-nation model based primarily on the German and the Korean experiences, the following deviations are observed in cross-Straits relations. First, unlike the German and the Korean experiences, no political dialogue or negotiation has ever taken place between the mainland and Taiwan since the national division in 1949. Negotiations on civilian matters have been held only between non-governmental organisations in recent years, but even these negotiations are unable to continue due to intense political conflicts.

Second, historically there were political talks and negotiations between the Chinese Communist Party (CCP) and the Kuomintang Party (KMT) prior to the 1949 national division – an experience lacking in the German and the Korean cases. The two parties were able to achieve agreements on such national issues as fighting against domestic warlords and Japanese aggression, but when it came to the allocation of political power, both sides regarded it as a zero-sum game in which there was no room for compromise or power sharing. In a historic context, the current sovereignty disputes across the Taiwan Straits are an extension of the inter-Party power struggle. Both sides have yet to learn to accept the political rules of the game guided by the logic of compromise and power-sharing rather than the logic of zero-sum power struggle.

Third, for a number of reasons to be discussed below, there has been a lack of awareness that China is a divided nation. While Taipei has awakened to that awareness in recent years, Beijing continues to reject the divided-nation status by rejecting Taipei as a legal government or 'political entity'. Moreover, the persistent presence of the Taiwan Independence Movement (TIM), coupled with the continuing political hostility between Taiwan and the mainland, hampered the Chinese national identity on the part of many Taiwanese people, thereby causing the Chinese case of sovereignty disputes to deviate further from the established divided-nation model.

In spite of these deviations, this chapter argues that the only way in which the Chinese sovereignty disputes can be resolved peacefully is to revert to the divided-nation model, which is characterized by a strong sense of a shared national and cultural identity and a mutual acceptance of each other as a legal government or 'political entity'. To accomplish this it is proposed that Beijing and Taipei make mutual political compromises and concessions in the long-term interests of the Chinese nation as a whole.

THE 'ONE CHINA' MODEL

As in other divided nations, the hostility stage in the Chinese case began with both Beijing and Taipei claiming sovereignty over the entire national territories of the mainland and Taiwan. Both sides insisted on the 'one China' position. But instead of emphasizing a shared national and cultural identity, this 'one China' notion essentially referred to a self-centred and mutually exclusive political identity. To Beijing, it meant the People's Republic of China. To Taipei, it meant the Republic of China. Both sides vowed to overthrow the other by force. The sovereignty disputes at this stage were over the national sovereignty as a whole package, even though a *de facto* split of sovereignty had occurred simultaneously as the nation was divided into two functional states, with each possessing the four elements of a modern state: people, territory, government and sovereignty. In the international arena, both sides fought to represent China as a 'sole legal government'.

From Beijing's standpoint, the overwhelming military victory in the Chinese civil war in 1949 justified its claim as the 'sole legal government of China', in keeping with the traditional pattern of revolution. The mutually exclusive zero-sum nature of any power struggle by means of civil war implies that political legitimacy is also mutually exclusive. Moreover, the insignificant size of the territory under the control of the KMT regime as compared with the vastness of the mainland has enhanced the CCP perception that Taiwan is merely a 'runaway province' to be recovered, rather than the other half of a 'divided nation'.

Taipei has a completely different perception. It maintains that the Republic of China has never ceased to be a sovereign state since its foundation in 1912, and has enjoyed diplomatic recognition by a majority of the world's nations at least until the early 1970s. As a sovereign state it has exercised sovereignty and jurisdiction over the Taiwan region effectively since 1945. The economic development of Taiwan has won international recognition as one of the world's most successful economic stories. Furthermore, since the beginning of the 1990s, political development in the direction of pluralistic democracy has enhanced the sense of the distinct identity of the ROC as a sovereign state, with its legitimacy being recognised even by segments of the indigenous populace who used to reject the KMT regime as an 'alien regime' in exile. The heightened internal legitimacy and awareness of the ROC as a sovereign state in the face of Beijing's continuing rejection of such a legitimacy has made the sovereignty dispute even more complicated and difficult to resolve.

Nevertheless, the KMT regime under Chiang Kai-shek and his son Ching-kuo shared one thing with its Communist counterpart: it did not see China as a divided nation. This lack of a 'divided-nation' awareness can be accounted for in two ways: first, the KMT regarded its sovereignty and jurisdiction as covering the entire China, and the loss of the mainland to the Communists was only 'temporary,' with an expectation that the CCP regime would collapse in no time. Second, the ready preparedness to retake the mainland through war and the technical continuation of China's civil war until the late 1970s, had further obscured the awareness that China was a divided nation in the sense that the two rival governments were in firm control on a more or less permanent basis.

The KMT regime under Chiang Kai-shek and his son had claimed all-China sovereignty for four decades. The unrealistic persistence of such a 'national policy' cannot be explained solely in terms of 'hostility' against the Communist regime. The KMT ideologists see Chiang and his son as staunch Chinese nationalists who refused to separate Taiwan from the mainland. From the perspective of the indigenous Taiwanese, however, pretending to repesent the whole of China with an empty 'national policy' of retaking the mainland was the only way the KMT regime in exile could have justified its prolonged one-Party dictatorship in Taiwan. Whatever the case may be, the costs of maintaining such a sovereignty claim have been enormous. The constitutional civil rights and liberties were frozen under martial law, which remained in force for some 40 years under the pretext that Taiwan was in an 'extraordinary period' of 'mobilization for the suppression of the Communist rebellion'. More importantly, democratic political reforms could not be instituted as the KMT claimed that the 'Congress' of the Republic of China (the National Assembly and the Legislative Yuan) was formed by nation-wide popular elections in the 1940s to represent all of the Chinese people, and therefore no new elections could be held until the Government overthrew the Communist regime and regained its control of the mainland.

THE 'DIVIDED NATION' MODEL

In May 1991, the Taiwan Government under its president, Lee Teng-hui, declared the termination of the Period of Mobilization for the Suppression of the Communist Rebellion and abolished the Provisional Articles that had served to freeze the democratic ROC Constitution under martial law. This historical move has had profound implications for mainland–Taiwan relations as well as the political development of Taiwan itself. First of all, it signified that the ruling KMT under Lee would abandon its long-held policy of retaking the mainland, with a tacit recognition of PRC as the legitimate government of mainland China. Moreover, it is important to note that the drastic shift in the KMT's mainland policy was not merely aimed at improving relations across the Taiwan Straits; perhaps more importantly it was necessitated by the need of Taiwan to carry out democratic constitutional reforms. With the abrogation of the Provisional Articles, the constitutionally guaranteed civil rights and liberties were now available to the Taiwan people for the first time in 40 years. The tacit acceptance of Beijing's legitimacy meant that the ruling KMT recognised the reality that the jurisdiction of ROC was limited to the Taiwan region, and therefore localised elections of the legislative bodies of the Central Government could now be initiated and justified. Constitutional revisions were undertaken to reflect the new political reality while catering to the need for political reforms. The first general elections of the National Assembly in 40 years took place in the same year (1991), followed by the general elections of the Legislative Yuan in 1992 and the first direct Presidential elections in 1996.

It logically follows from the acceptance of the political legitimacy of the PRC that Taipei has begun to see China as a 'divided nation' in which two 'political entities' govern different parts of the Chinese territories. Such a new-found 'divided-nation' awareness has in turn inspired the official doctrine of 'divided jurisdiction in a divided nation' (*fenlie fenzhi*) as a basis of Taipei's new mainland policy. In the international arena, the '*fenlie fenzhi*' concept justifies Taipei's new 'pragmatic diplomacy' to develop relations with nations that recognise the PRC.

While Taipei regards *fenlie fenzhi* as reflecting the objective political reality, Beijing denounces it as a scheme to create 'two Chinas' and 'one China, one Taiwan', which in the logic of the CCP propagandists are equivalent to Taiwan Independence (*taidu*). Thus starts a new round of sovereignty disputes: Taipei proclaims that it will pursue national unification under the divided-nation model of two Chinese 'political entities' in one Chinese nation, but Beijing rejects the notion of China as a divided nation and the ROC as a legal government, accusing Taipei of attempting to 'split the motherland'. Beijing even attacks all diplomatic efforts by the Taiwan Government to boost its international status, especially President Lee Teng-Hui's private visit to Cornell University in June 1995, as a divisive scheme to promote *taidu*.

Ever since Lee's US trip, Beijing had escalated its political conflicts with Taiwan in three aspects: First, Beijing has previously used the term 'one China' in a somewhat ambiguous way to allow for semantic flexibility. For example, mainland propagandists referred to Chiang Kai-Shek and his son as 'advocating one China', where 'China' was apparently intended to mean the Chinese nation in a historical and cultural sense, not the PRC. Since the second half of 1995, however, Beijing has decided overtly to politicise the term, stating on many occasions that 'one China refers to the People's Republic of China'.

Following Lee Teng-Hui's re-election in March 1996, Beijing has made it clear that a precondition for cross-Straits dialogues to take place is that Taiwan 'return to the principle of "one China"'. Presumably alarmed by its political implications, Taipei has recently either refrained from using that term in official statements or, when pressed for an explanation of 'one China', declared that 'one China refers to the ROC'.[9]

In his inaugural address on 20 May 1996, President Lee Teng-Hui dwelt on the theme that Taiwan and the mainland belong to one nation with a shared national identity and cultural heritage and that the ROC is committed to national unification. However, he did not mention 'one China'. A week later, on 27 May China's official Xinhua News Agency criticised in a commentary that Lee's failure to mention 'one China' was 'intended to continue perpetrating "two China" and "one China, one Taiwan" in the international community'. The same criticism was repeated in an official feedback on 22 June 1996 to President Lee's inaugural address.[10] What Beijing is demanding is not just a symbolic statement of the 'one China' principle; more importantly, it wants Taiwan to abandon all 'pragmatic diplomacy' activities such as the move to rejoin the United Nations, which Taipei considers to be vital to its survival but Beijing sees as contradicting the principle of 'one China'.

Second, a corollary of the assertion that 'one China' refers to the PRC is that Taiwan is part of the territory of the PRC. Until recently Beijing has consistently said that 'Taiwan is part of the territory of China', avoiding the mentioning of the PRC when dealing with the identity of Taiwan. Now the tune has changed. On 20 July 1995, one month after Lee Teng-Hui visited the US, China's Ambassador to the United Nations, Qin Huasun, presented an official letter to the UN Secretary General, Boutros Boutros-Ghali, which says in part:

> Since October 1949, the two sides of the Taiwan Straits have been temporarily in a state of separation, but the status of Taiwan as part of the territory of People's Republic of China has never changed. Nor has the Government of PRC ever abandoned its administrative jurisdiction over Taiwan Province.

Third, conservative think-tanks in Beijing have frowned upon Taiwan's political reforms as part of a conscious effort to separate Taiwan from China, and their lines of thinking appear to have exerted an influence over the official policy-making on cross-straits relations.

As early as 1990, the proposed popular elections of the National Assembly, the Legislative Yuan and the President in Taiwan were criticized by mainland political commentators as a bid to 'separate Taiwan's political structure from the framework of China'.[11] About half a year before the Presidential elections were held, Li Jiachuan, a key researcher and think-tank member on Taiwan affairs in Beijing, denounced the forthcoming elections as 'perpetrating *taidu* [Taiwan Independence] with action'.[12] As the elections approached, pro-Beijing propagandists spread the views that the forthcoming elections were intended to elect a '*taidu* President' and to 'split the motherland'.[13] Then came the grand military manoeuvres on the eve of the elections, during which missiles were fired into the sea to the north and south of Taiwan. Beijing has repeated a statement that the purpose of these military exercises was to 'show that the Chinese people and Government have the ability and determination to safeguard the sovereignty of China'. It was clear that Beijing saw the Presidential elections as a major step toward Taiwan independence, in contrast to the Taiwanese perception that the elections were necessary for democratic reforms and had nothing to do with Taiwan independence.

THE SEPARATIST MODEL

The Chinese sovereignty dispute is complicated by the presence of the Taiwan Independence Movement (TIM), in which Taiwanese separatists seek to disengage the sovereignty of Taiwan from China. The TIM stance on the sovereign status of Taiwan was initially intended as a legal justification to overthrow the KMT regime on Taiwan rather than to resist the call for unification from Beijing. As a matter of fact, the TIM did not pay much attention to Beijing's claim to the sovereignty of Taiwan because the island was being protected by US military forces and the prospects of the 'liberation' of Taiwan by the CCP seemed as remote as the KMT's professed 'counter-attack' on the mainland. On the other hand, the CCP did not set much store by the TIM because it comprised only a handful of Taiwanese abroad with limited support from American and Japanese sympathizers. Beijing's concern over the TIM was also alleviated by the fact that the KMT regime had enforced stern measures against the movement so that it could gain little ground in Taiwan society itself. Today, however, the tables are turned. The political liberalization and localizaton in Taiwan have made it possible for the TIM freely to pursue its cause at home, with its key proponents being co-opted into the opposition Democratic Progressive Party (DPP) leadership, to the extent that the DPP has incorporated the goal of Taiwan independence into its Party platform. As a result of democratic reforms, TIM proponents have largely accepted the new political order in Taiwan as a legitimate one in which the objectives of the TIM can be achieved through democratic participation rather than revolution against the ruling KMT. As Beijing sees it, there is a KMT–DPP coalition against China's reunification, so that the sovereignty disputes in the current stage are not simply over 'divided jurisdiction in a divided nation', but are exacerbated by the latest development of Taiwanese separatism. It is under this perception that Beijing denounces 'Republic of China on Taiwan' as a scheme to 'divide China' and to promote *taidu.*

RETURN TO DIVIDED-NATION MODEL

The above analysis has attempted to present China as a deviant case of a divided nation. It is deviant in that Beijing has all along rejected the idea of China being a divided nation and refused to accept the ROC as a legitimate government, that Taiwanese separatism has distorted the divided-nation pattern in which a strong sense of shared national identity motivates both sides of a divided nation to strive for reunification, and that negotiations to normalize relations across the Taiwan Straits have been indefinitely postponed.

Paradoxically, the only hope for a peaceful settlement of the Chinese sovereignty disputes appears to rest on the divided-nation model, in which the rival parties learn to accept each other's different political identity while cherishing a shared national and cultural identity. To achieve this end, Beijing and Taipei need to make major political compromises and concessions to each other. To Beijing, compromises and concessions mean that it recognizes the reality that there are two Chinese governments or 'political entities' in one Chinese nation and on this basis proceeds to work towards the normalisation of cross-Straits relations and the ultimate goal of national reunification. To Taiwan, compromises and concessions mean that it renounces separatism while making conscious efforts to promote national reconciliation and eventual reunification through increased cultural exchanges and economic cooperation with the mainland. This signifies a return to the divided-nation model that makes the German and Korean rapprochements possible.

There has been a pro-Beijing argument that the German and Korean experiences cannot be applied to China because these divided nations do not have the problem of separatism as Taiwan does. If Beijing accepts the Taiwan authorities as a legal government, according to that argument, it can only facilitate the declaration of Taiwan independence. However, if we reflect on the histories of those nations with a separatism problem, we will realise that an argument in reverse may be closer to the truth. It is indeed a historical irony that separatist movements in such places as Quebec, Puerto Rico and Hawaii cannot achieve their goals for decades in spite – and perhaps because – of the liberal and accommodative policies which the central governments concerned (that is, the Canadian and the US Governments) are obliged by their federalist constitutions to take towards the separatist causes. The point is that in these countries separatism has been 'internalized' as a democratic political process whose outcome needs to be decided by popular ballots instead of gun barrels. Conversely, attempts to suppress separatism by force – a recent example being the case of Russia against Chechenia – have more often than not ended up in failure and bloodshed because violent suppression gives ammunition to the separatists for the necessary mobilization to achieve their goals through armed struggles. Taiwan today fits into the former category, as the Taiwan Government has shifted its policy from violent suppression to legalization of the TIM, with the result that the *taidu* issue, if it comes to a head at all, will have to be decided by Taiwan's voters, who have overwhelmingly expressed their wish to maintain the status quo rather than pursue unification or *taidu*. It can be argued that precisely because of the presence of Taiwanese separatism, Beijing needs to opt for a liberal-minded approach to dealing with the political status of Taiwan. Implementing a liberal and accommodative policy to induce the Taiwan people and government to revert to the divided-nation model appears to be in the best national interest of China as a whole.

A peaceful settlement of the Chinese sovereignty disputes on the basis of the divided-nation model can give rise to the following scenario where the 'evolutionary process' of the cross-Straits relations can be expected to move on towards the stages of official cooperation and negotiations on national unification.

1. *'One China' principle and international relations.* Beijing's unification policy of 'one country two systems' which Taipei sees as implying that the Taiwan Government is a local government of

the PRC would be revised to reflect Beijing's respect for Taiwan's unique political status. In the international community, the 'one China' principle, under which most nations of the world are obliged at Beijing's insistence to acknowledge the PRC as the 'sole legal government of China', could also be revised to give Taiwan a certain diplomatic standing agreeable to both sides, following the example of West Germany renouncing in 1972 the Hallstein doctrine whereby the Bonn Government had threatened to break off diplomatic relations with any nation intending to recognise East Germany. While Taiwan cannot expect to enjoy an equal diplomatic standing with the mainland as in the German and Korean cases, a suitable niche in the international community for Taiwan would prove conducive to improving political relations across the Taiwan Straits and thereby to the eventual national unification.

2. *No use of force.* Beijing would announce that it would not use force against Taiwan unless it declares independence from China. Thus a peace pact could be concluded by both sides, with Taipei declaring a clear-cut official policy against Taiwan independence and pledging to work towards the unification of China in return for Beijing's assurance not to achieve unification by force.
3. *Official cooperation.* With the political stumbling blocks removed, the two governments could engage in large-scale economic and non-economic cooperation programmes on an official level. When Hong Kong and Macau are added to this cooperation scheme, an envisioned greater-China economic-cultural community would take shape, paving the way for national unification.
4. *Negotiation on unification.* On the basis of improved cross-Straits relations and official cooperation, negotiations on the terms of peaceful unification could be initiated. The immediate aims of such negotiations might not be unification itself, but rather a set of interim arragements such as the establishment of an intergovernmental institution charged with the drafting of a unified constitution and other bilateral affairs arising from the need for political integration.

Once Beijing and Taipei have accepted the divided-nation model, the disputes over sovereignty can give way to a consensus on 'sovereignty sharing' mentioned earlier in this chapter. The concept of 'sovereignty sharing' should be compatible with Beijing's position that the sovereignty of China is not divisible. On the other hand, Taipei has a constitutional basis to accept a shared sovereignty, as Article 2 of the ROC Constitution stipulates that 'the sovereignty of Republic of China belongs to all Chinese nationals'. 'Sovereignty sharing' follows from the principle of 'people's sovereignty' and forms a philosophical basis on which an agreed separation of jurisdiction can be justified. It also has a symbolic meaning, in that both Beijing and Taipei identify themselves with China as a nation.[14]

CONCLUSION

No one should expect the above scenario to become a reality in the foreseeable future. On the mainland side, the difficulties lie in a leadership mentality that rejects the notion of two governments in one nation and a political system that tolerates no power sharing by oppositional political parties. On the Taiwan side, the Government insists on pursuing a course of diplomatic activities considered by Beijing as a move to 'split China'. And the pervasive influences of the TIM, combined with the continuing political hostility between the two governments, have increasingly eroded a sense of Chinese national identity in segments of the Taiwan populace and a firm official commitment to China's national unification. A real political rapprochement between the mainland and Taiwan cannot materialize until both sides are prepared to accept the political rules of the game guided by the logic of compromise and power sharing rather than that of power struggle. To ensure that Taiwan remains motivated towards the goal of unification, both sides should play down political differences while making concerted efforts to cultivate such non-political relations as will deliver tangible benefits to both sides and simultaneously strengthen a sense of the shared Chinese national and cultural identity.

On the international scene, both sides have yet to negotiate on how to reinterpret the 'one China' principle to give Taiwan an appropriate international standing commensurate with its political and economic achievements. Continuing confrontation on this issue could prove counter-productive, as Taipei has raised a concern that if it loses all its diplomatic ground to Beijing, internal political instability would ensue to lend the TIM an opportunity to replace the 'Republic of China' with the 'Republic of Taiwan.' It is estimated that such a critical point may come when the number of countries recognising Taipei is reduced from the current 30 to below 20.[15] Even if the TIM poses no real threat to political stability, continuing diplomatic isolation, coupled with political hostility between Beijing and Taipei, has proven to be destructive to the development of a greater-China outlook and a shared Chinese national identity on the part of the Taiwan people, making it increasingly difficult for either side to achieve the goal of national unification.

While it is difficult for both sides to meet each other halfway politically under the present circumstances, developing a sense of mutual trust and goodwill seems relatively easy and will certainly be very helpful. It may be advisable for Beijing not to think of Taipei's diplomatic activities as 'splitting China' or engaging in Taiwan independence. After all, Taiwan has been striving to preserve itself as a distinct sovereign state separate from the Communist-oriented mainland polity and to maintain a decent diplomatic standing in the international arena since the days of Chiang Kai-Shek. In those days the formulas of 'two Chinas' and 'one China one Taiwan' were a real threat to Beijing because they were initiated by an American political leadership to perpetuate the separation of Taiwan from China. But today, these formulas appear obsolete as the US has withdrawn its military forces from the Taiwan region and made clear its stand against Taiwan independence and 'one China, one Taiwan'. This US policy largely reflects the political reality that a great majority of the Taiwan people wish to maintain the status quo, while shelving the issue of unification versus *taidu* for future consideration. What really needs to be addressed by Beijing, then, is not an issue of nationalism that Taiwan may be 'taken away' from China some day, but rather a reluctance of the Taiwan people and government to pursue political unification under existing circumstances. To address such a problem requires patience and goodwill. Any hostile verbal attacks or military threats based on the assumption of Taiwan heading for *taidu* appear to be counter-productive, as they can only further alienate the Taiwan people.

On the Taiwan side, TIM proponents should learn to consider the cross-Straits relations not only from their own perspectives, but also from the perspectives of China as well. For one thing, if Taiwan is allowed to declare independence, some ethnic minority regions in China are likely to follow suit and the Beijing Government will be in real trouble. Rather than attempt to play a dangerous zero-sum game with China, the TIM should be prepared to accept a compromise solution in the spirit of democratic politics. Furthermore, the ruling KMT leadership should keep the cross-Straits relations in perspective with a realisation that, given the historical, cultural and geographical affinity between the mainland and Taiwan, it will be in the interests of both sides to develop rather than shun close relations. Diplomatically Taiwan should be sophisticated enough to build its 'pragmatic diplomacy' on a sound foundation of cross-Straits relations.

Beijing and Taipei have obviously dismissed any major political compromise with each other as a compromise of principle. In this connection, both sides can learn an important lesson from the Germans. When Willy Brandt initiated the rapprochement drive at the beginning of the 1970s, he met with severe crtiticism and opposition from his political opponents, who charged that Brandt was compromising the interests of the FRG to 'prop up an illegitimate state' and to make the territorial division between East Germany and West Germany permanent. However, a far-sighted Brandt considered it in the long-term interest of the German nation to switch the policy focus to 'working for an increased permeability of the two states, with improved human contacts and communications between citizens of each Germany, to keep alive the sense of a shared national identity'.[16] History has proven him right. While the German reunification may be regarded as the result of a historic accident, its foundation would have been fragile without the people-to-people solidarity which Brandt's policy had helped to cement. If Beijing and Taipei place the long-term national interests of China above the self-interests of the respective regimes, mutual political compromises are not too dear a price to pay, and it may be well for them to take the wisdom of Willy Brandt seriously.

Notes and references

1. Quoted from Paul R.Viotti and Mark V. Kauppi, *International Relations Theory: Realism, Pluralism and Globalism* (New York: Macmillan, 1993) p. 502.
2. The political theory that interprets sovereignty as 'absolute and indivisible' is quoted and discussed in Byron S. J. Weng, 'Sovereignty Split: Towards a Theory of Divided Nation' (Professorial Inaugural Lecture Series 20, Chinese University of Hong Kong, 1994), p. 21 and p. 35.
3. See Mary Fulbrook, *The Divided Nation: History of Germany, 1918–1991* (London: Fontana Press, 1991) pp. 209–210.
4. See Chen Yu Hsi, *Nation Divided: An Anthology of the Greater-China Political Economy* (in Chinese, minzu fenlie shidai de zhengyan) (Taipei: Renjian Publishing Co., 1991) p. 456.
5. For a discussion on national sovereignty being divisible, see Byron S. J. Weng, 'Sovereignty Split', p. 21.

6. The notion of the German Democratic Republic as a sovereign state or 'established state' is mentioned in Fulbrook, *The Divided Nation*, ch. 8 and elsewhere.
7. For example, an official letter which Beijing presented to UN Secretary General Boutros-Ghali via its Ambassador to the United Nations, Qin Huasun, in July 1995 and again in July 1996 states that the PRC has 'never abandoned its administrative jurisdiction over Taiwan Province'.
8. For a discussion on Henderson and Lebow's evolution model, see G. Henderson, Richard N. Lebow and John G. Stoessinger, *Divided Nations in a Divided World*. (New York: David Mckay, 1974.) See also Weng, 'Sovereignity Split', p. 36.
9. For example, in response to questions from visiting Canadian and American legislators in March and April 1996, President Lee Teng-Hui twice stated that 'one China means ROC, not PRC'. See Taiwan newspapers published on 27 March and 10 April 1996.
10. The Xinhua commentary entitled 'Listen to What He Says and Watch What He Does' (in Chinese, ting qi yan, guan qi xing) was published in *Ta Kung Pao*, 24 June 1996, front page.
11. See Chen Yu Hsi, *Nation Divided* p. 459.
12. See a special column on the political views of Li Jiachuan, in *Wen Wei Pao*, 29 November 1995.
13. See, for example, an editorial in *Ta Kung Pao* entitled 'Splitting Taiwan from the Motherland Cannot Be Tolerated'. 6 March 1996, p. A2.
14. When this chapter was being revised for the last time in the fall of 1997, the Taiwan Government had just announced its updated mainland policy, puting forth two new concepts, that is, 'shared sovereignty' and 'one China being equal to Taiwan plus the Chinese mainland', as a policy guideline for developing relations with the mainland.
15. These concerns over the TIM attempting to replace the 'Republic of China' with 'Republic of Taiwan' were expressed by Foreign Minister Chang Hsiao-yen in an interview with *Open Magazine* (Hong Kong), November 1996, p. 61.
16. The concessionary rapprochement strategy of Willy Brandt is detailed in Fulbrook, *The Divided Nation*, ch. 8.

Part III

Economic Issues

7 China's Regional Development Issues

Li Si Ming

The question of equity versus efficiency is a thorny issue that social scientists and decision-makers all over the world, regardless of ideological predisposition, have to confront. At times these two objectives of economic and social development are complementary to each other; but, more often than not, the two are at odds, and there is a trade-off to be made. In the realm of regional analysis, the trade-off is often in the form of faster but spatially uneven development versus less rapid and yet spatially more uniform growth. A complex set of interacting political, economic, social and spatial processes together shape the outcome of this process of choice.

In China there has been a felt need for rapid industrialization and modernization ever since the late Qing period (the beginning of the twentieth century) in order to catch up with Japan and the West. The victory of the Chinese Communist Party (CCP) over Guomindang (the Nationalist Party, better known as Kuomintang or KMT), and the founding of the People's Republic of China (PRC) in 1949, only helped to reinforce this industrialization and modernization quest. Alongside this and central to the communist ideology is the stress on egalitarianism and equity. An over-riding concern of the emerging socialist state under Mao Zedong was to eradicate the three major differences – between industry and agriculture, between manual and mental labour, and between town and country – characteristic of the semi-feudal and semi-colonial past[1].

China is a country with a vast geographical extent. Its varied physical geography and five thousand years of history suggest almost at once that enormous differences exist between regions, both physically and culturally. In particular, the establishment of treaty ports along the eastern coast in the nineteenth century under the threat of Western imperialism has brought about an east–west divide, superimposed on top of the traditional north–south divide resulting from climatic, physiographical and cultural differences, and also from the fact that northern China had been repeatedly subjected to nomadic invasions from the north.[2] Consistent with, and in a sense an integral part of, the egalitarianism agenda is the elimination of spatial disparity, which implies a redeployment of scarce resources to the lagging regions and to regions currently with less potential for self-sustained growth.

Industrialization, especially the development of capital-intensive 'basic industries' such as iron and steel and petrochemicals, however, requires a concentration of resources to selected urban centres with potential for development. This, in iteslf, is consistent with central planning, another important ingredient of socialism, especially of the Leninist type. But the spatial reallocation exercise often results in a development strategy that favours not only the urban areas at the expense of the vast rural hinterlands but also regions that are already endowed with resources, especially in terms of industrial and human capital.

Adding to the quest for industrialization and the egalitarianism ideology is the concern for national security and integration. Internally, China is a country with many 'nationalities'[3] or ethnic groups. The bulk of the minority nationalities live in the frontier regions in the north, the north-west and the west. Ever since the late Qing period, with the gradual weakening of the centre, some of the largest nationalities, notably the Mongols, the Uygurs and the Tibetans, have attempted secession. Indeed the Mongols in the then Outer Mongolia succeeded and founded the Republic of Mongolia in 1912, immediately after the collapse of the Qing dynasty. Secession tendencies have persisted under the PRC. The escape of the Dalai Lama to India following the repression of the Tibetan uprising by the People's Liberation Army (PLA) in 1959 was a case in point. More recently, separatist movements in Xinjiang have been re-ignited by the collapse of the former Soviet Union, and there have been reports of sabotage and riots instigated by Uygur separatist forces both within and outside Xinjiang.[4] To the leaders of the PRC (as well as their predecessors in the KMT government and the Qing court), the question of national integration or disintegration is a real one and cannot be lightly dismissed. There is a need, therefore, to design specific policies that can enhance the inclusiveness of the minority groups, including the transfer of resources from the more developed regions populated by Han Chinese to the frontier regions with large concentrations of minority groups. Even within the geographical realm of Han Chinese, factionalism tends to surface occasionally, and historically there has been a tradition of maintaining a strong central control over the provinces.[5]

Internationally, the PRC was founded in an era of Cold War. Obviously it belonged to the socialist camp, and was encircled, in the minds of the Chinese leaders, by Western, primarily American, imperialism. Indeed the PRC fought the Korean War (1950–3) against the Americans immediately after it was founded. Moreover, the People's Liberation Army (PLA) played an active part in the Vietnam War during the 1960s and early 1970s, which ended with the withdrawal of American forces and the unification of Vietnam under the communist Hanoi regime. In both instances the PRC risked the very real likelihood that the war might be extended to China itself. Furthermore, the KMT forces under Generalissimo Chiang Kai-Shek, with the support of the United States, still occupied Taiwan. Military confrontations between the two sides of the Taiwan Straits persisted until at least the late 1960s. To this date, the issue of unification remains top on the agenda of the Chinese leaders (see Chapter 6). On the northern front, the initially cordial relations with the former Soviet Union gradually broke down, culminating in the sudden withdrawal of Soviet technical experts in 1958 and military clashes on Zhenbao Island in Heilongjiang River (Amur) in 1969. Mao thought that a Third World War was inevitable, and that there was a need for China to prepare for it. Both the industrialization agenda and the development of the interior, especially in the remote mountainous areas which are least vulnerable to air strikes, should thus go hand in hand, hence the famous *sanxian* or 'third front' construction strategy of the 1960s and early 1970s.

Deng Xiaoping's rise to power after Mao's death marked a fundamental shift in China's foreign policy. The overriding concern since then has been to maintain a dialogue, firstly between China and the Western nations and secondly between China and countries in the former socialist camp, so that China can focus on economic construction. Efforts have been made to re-integrate China into the world economic system. Efficiency considerations become important, and the utilization of international capital is seen to be a key to economic success. But still, tension between China and the Western powers, especially the United States, continues to re-surface occasionally. The Tiananmen Incident in 1989 and the collapse of the Soviet Union two years later have helped to highlight the ideological differences between China under the CCP and the West. Recently there appears to be a concerted effort, at least in the United States, to 'demonize' China (see also Chapter 5), despite the tremendous progress that China has made, both on the economic front and in terms of human rights, since the launching of the reforms.[6]

The history of regional development in the PRC is thus one which is full of self-contradictions and ironies, reflecting the competing sets of objectives. The rest of this chapter will further elaborate this theme. First, data on China's changing spatial disparites, which are full of apparent anomalies, will be presented. Efforts will then be made to explain these anomalies by reference to the salient features of China's economic institutions in both the pre-reform and post-reform periods. The chapter will then examine the likely impacts of some of the recent developments affecting China's regional scene, including the growing importance of foreign direct investments. A reference to Hong Kong's return to China and its implications for China's regional development serves to conclude the chapter.

CHINA'S CHANGING SPATIAL DISPARITIES

Earlier it was pointed out that China is a big country with a varied geography as well as a long history. One would expect, therefore, the degree of difference between regions to be large. Figure 7.1 maps the distribution of the per capita gross domestic product (GDP) over China's provincial-level administration units in 1995. It can be seen that the level of economic development, as measured by per capita GDP, indeed varies a great deal over the provinces.[7] Shanghai, being ranked one in the list, has a per capita GDP of RMB17 403, which is nearly ten times that of Guizhou (RMB1796), the province with the lowest per capita GDP. Perhaps it may not be appropriate to include the three directly administered municipalities in a comparison of provinces. However, even if we restrict ourselves to the other 27 provincial-level units, the differences among the provinces are still substantial. Provinces at top of the list, including Zhejiang, Guangdong and Jiangsu, have per capita GDP in excess of RMB7000, or two to three times those of the poorest provinces, such as Guizhou, Gansu, Tibet and Shaanxi. Figure 7.1 also shows that provinces with high per capita GDP in general are located in the south and along the eastern coast, whereas provinces with low per capita GDP are generally found in the hilly and mountainous regions in the central and western parts of the country.

Many have attributed these big regional differences in the level of economic development to Deng Xaioping's Open Policy launched in 1978, which has adopted a 'gradient development strategy' favouring the eastern coastal region.[8] However, in recent years a number of

Figure 7.1 China: per capita GDP by province, 1995

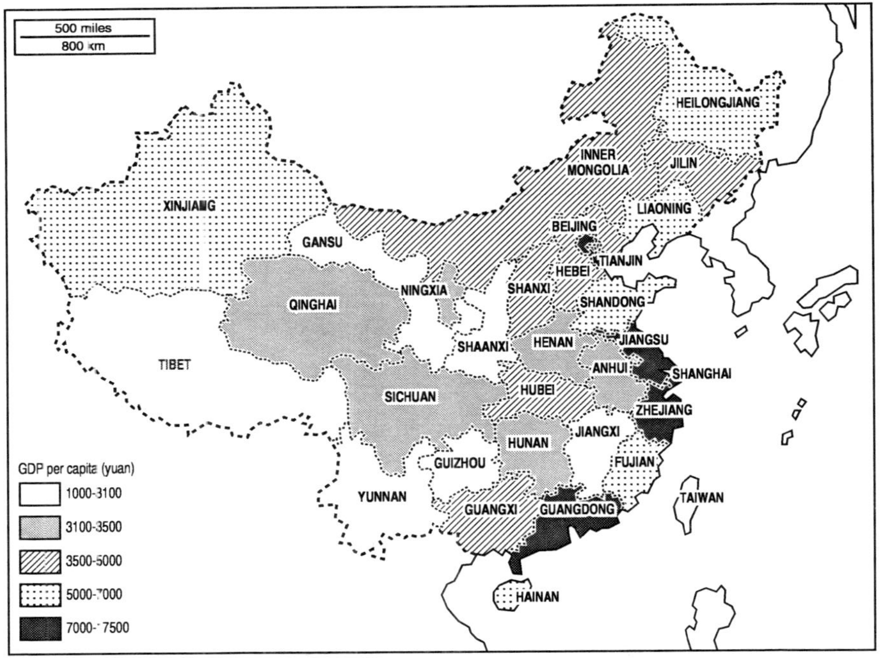

Source: *Zhongguo Tongji Nianjian* (*China Statistical Yearbook*), 1996. Zhongguo Tongji Chubanshe.

authors have employed recently released provincial-level economic data and found many surprises.[9] Regardless of the measure employed, be it per capita GDP, per capita national income or per capita gross industrial output value, indices of spatial disparity such as the Gini coefficient and the coefficient of variation (CV) all show substantial and continual declines throughout the 1980s and early 1990s. More surprising even, these indices generally exhibited a rapid increase in the late 1960s and peaked during the 1970s, roughly the same time as the *sanxian* construction period, when large amounts of resources were allocated to the remote provinces in the south-western part of the country. Consider, for example, the per capita gross industrial output value (GIOV) which is an indicator of the level of industrialization. The CV based on this measure experienced a rapid decline during the early years of the People's Republic, but rose sharply again during the *sanxian* construction period (from 1.50 in 1965 to 1.72 in 1974). Thereafter, a consistent downward trend has been manifested. In 1979 it was 1.49; in 1989; 1.03; and in 1995; 0.96. The national income (NI) is a more broadly based measure, akin to the GDP employed in the West, and does not suffer from the problem of double counting, a problem inherent in most economic indicators such as the GIOV used in socialist countries. Computation of the CV using provincial per capita NI shows an inverted U trend. The CV rose rapidly from 0.73 in 1963 to 0.92 in 1971, and peaked around 1976 at 0.96. Thereafter, the index showed a consistent and rapid decline: from 0.79 in 1981 to 0.62 in 1992.[10] Recently the Statistical Bureau of China (*Guojia Tongjiju*) has begun to compile national account data following the Western practice, and hence the gross national product (GNP) and the gross domestic product (GDP) have replaced the NI as the most comprehensive measures of national economic strength. Figure 7.2 presents results of the CV computations using the per capita GDP. It can be seen that, aside from the bulge of the 1990–2 period, which followed immediately after the 4 June Incident of 1989 and the economic retrenchment exercise of 1988–91, the degree of inter-provincial disparity, as measured by the per capita GDP, remained more or less stable in the late 1980s and in the first half of the 1990s. Contrary to popular beliefs, regional disparity in China has not deteriorated in recent years. In fact, if anything, the degree of disparity has decreased rather substantially since the launching of the reforms.

To many, including China's political leaders and economic planners, the results presented above would be surprising. Of course, these

Figure 7.2 Coefficient of variation of provincial per capita GDP, China, 1988–95

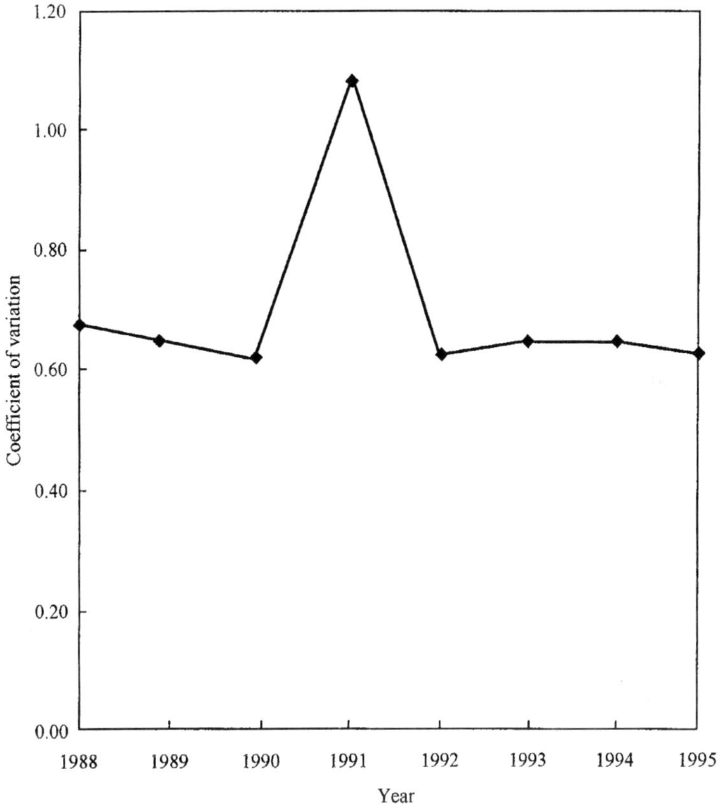

Source: *Zhongguo Tongji Nianjian* (*China Statistical Yearbook*), 1989–96. Zhongguo Tongji Chubanshe.

results mainly pertain to inter-provincial differences. If we re-organize the data and examine, say, the differences between and among the three broad regions – the eastern coastal region, the central region and the western region[11] – a scheme of regionalization adopted in the Seventh Five Year Plan (1986–90) and commonly employed by students of China's regional development ever since, we will arrive at a largely similar conclusion. The eastern coastal region's position *vis-à-vis* the others had strengthened considerably during the *sanxian* construction period. In the reform period, at least up to 1990, the growth rates recorded for the three broad regions had been quite similar. Only in recent years have the comparative advantages of the eastern coastal region become apparent again.

The findings are somewhat unexpected, but they are consistent with the highly subtle and often paradoxical regional policies alluded to above. In Maoist China, especially during the Cultural Revolution, it appeared that egalitarian considerations had become paramount. A large amount of resources, including human capital, was redeployed to the lagging regions in the interior provinces, especially during the *sanxian* period. Yet capital accumulation, which provides the necessary funds for further industrialization, was also a major concern, especially at a time when the country had to prepare itself for possible military attacks. The 'scissors difference' in pricing had been an integral feature of China's socialist central planning. On the one hand, prices of rural produce and other raw materials were set at artificially low levels so as to keep down the cost of industrial production and the cost of living in the urban-industrial centres. On the other hand, prices of manufactured consumer items were set at artificially high levels in order to generate funds for re-investment and expanded production. The *hukou* or household registration system,[12] in conjunction with the system of the People's Communes and grain rationing, to a very large extent reinforced the effectiveness of the pricing system. The *hukou* system effectively divided the country into the rural and the urban, with only minimal interchanges between the two. Despite the existence of huge differences in living standards and in welfare provisions between the urban areas and the country's vast rural hinterlands, rural to urban migration was kept under very tight control. In fact, farmers would have lost their very means of existence once they left the Commune without the proper documents. In effect the farmers were trapped in the system. Under such circumstances, resources continued to be siphoned from the rural areas to the urban centres, and from the lagging interior provinces to the more prosperous coastal provinces. Moreover, there did not appear to be any escape for the under-privileged, as even 'voting with their feet' was not possible. Massive geographical transfer of value, basically in favour of the established industrial centres and at the expense of the lagging regions, underlies much of China's socialist planning.[13]

Another distinguishing feature of socialist central planning is the central allocation of resources. Priorities were given to the various industrial ministries or *tiaotiao* (lines of authority) over the various localities or *kuaikuai* (blocks). In this sense regional development policy in China existed on paper only, as investment decisions were made in the interests of the specific ministries rather than in terms of regional needs.[14] The problem of *tiaokuai fenge* or line and block compartmentalization was, in a sense, inherent in socialist planning. There had been a lack of communication, or what was labelled *hengxiang lianxi* or 'horizontal linkages' in the Chinese language literature, between production enterprises belonging to the different ministries or government departments, let alone between different localities. The geographical manifestations of the input–output chains can appear absurd. To this date, 'transactions' involving the flow of raw materials and semi-finished products tend to take place only between enterprises belonging to the same ministry or government department, even though this could necessitate the transportation of materials over a long distance when the necessary materials could be obtained from nearby sources belonging to other lines of authority. As a case in point, Qilu Petrochemicals and Shengli Oil Fields are both located in Shangdong Province. Theoretically they should have had a wide range of input–output linkages. Yet these two organizations are under two different lines of authority. The former is a member of the China Petrochemical Group of Companies, while the latter is under the jurisdiction of the Department of Petroleum Industry. A mismatch between the supply of gas and oil produced by Shengli Oil Fields and the demand for the product by Qilu Petrochemicals has persisted for a long time. On the one hand, Qilu Petrochemicals has to purchase oil and gas from afar in order to make up for deficiency in the supply; on the other hand, Shengli Oil Fields has to find markets for its product even though there is an obvious demand from the nearby Qilu Petrochemicals.[15] Industries appear to agglomerate in a given industrial region; yet agglomeration economies have been quite limited.

The overwhelming emphasis on military considerations during the *sanxian* construction period further exacerbated this problem. Many of the industrial enterprises that were installed in the third front region were like something dropped from outer space, with minimal integration with the local economy. Even the production workers, let alone the managerial and technical personnel, were brought in from the major industrial centres on the eastern coast such as Shanghai and Tianjin. Multiplier effects at the local scale tended to be very limited. For military reasons, the premises concerned were often hidden behind high barbed walls, maintaining a high degree of seclusion. The only regional spillovers were likely to be negative externalities such as air and water pollution. So these third front enterprises played a very limited role in fostering growth in the lagging regions. The deployment of resources to build new production enterprises in the third front region meant that fewer resources were available to maintain and upgrade existing facilities in the older industrial centres. Tang and Chu argued that this would inhibit improvement in production efficiency and, given the scissors' difference in pricing, would thus further drain resources from the lagging regions which, in general, were the suppliers of raw materials to the country's industrial centres.[16] Moreover, the inefficiency arising from their isolation meant that the third front enterprises could only survive on continual injection of heavy subsidy. In the post-reform period, when the redistributive power of the central state has been very much circumscribed, this has added to the burden of the lagging regions themselves.

REGIONAL DEVELOPMENT ISSUES UNDER REFORM AND OPENNING

The contract responsibility system and central–local fiscal relations

The reforms introduced since 1978 can be seen as actions to rectify some of the irrationalities and inefficiencies which had developed under a highly centralized planning system. The quest for rapid industrialization continues under the reform, but there is now less emphasis on heavy or 'basic' industry. Investment decisions, to a large extent, have been decentralized, both to the provinces and to the individual enterprises. Greater reliance is placed on the market and the market-oriented economic levers such as the taxation and credit system. A system of fiscal responsibility was introduced in the early 1980s and lasted until 1994.[17] Each province signed a contract with the central government, stipulating the amount of funds that had to be forwarded to the centre annually. Revenues generated over and above this stipulated sum could be retained in whole or in part for provincial usage. Under this system, the provinces not only have more resources at their disposition but also have a greater influence on the enterprises located within their respective boundaries, whether or not these enterprises are under the direct jurisdiction of the respective ministries of the State Council. Indeed throughout the 1980s and into the early 1990s, the provinces had a substantial control over the flow of resources.

Local protectionism was evident, especially in terms of the protection of scarce resources. A dukedom economy, reminiscent of a system of feudal states, according to many Chinese economists, was in its embryonic stage.[18] The central government had formulated the Coastal Development Strategy, envisioning a regional division of labour in which the coastal areas concentrate on developing labour-intensive processing industries geared toward the international market, and the interior provinces play an essentially supporting role by concentrating on the development of resource-based industries.[19] Hence there were first the designation of the Shenzhen, Zhuhai, Xiamen and Shantou 'special economic zones', then the designation of 14 coastal cities as 'coastal open cities', and then the delineation of the 'open regions' of the Yangzi Delta, Pearl River Delta and Minan Triangle.[20]

Yet the fact was that most provinces, regardless of location, devoted their energies to developing essentially the same types of processing industries, that is, the types which could yield a larger profit. This is understandable, given the continual existence of 'scissors difference' in the pricing structure, along with dual or even multi-level pricing of products of the 'basic industries', that is, products that will be used as raw materials for other industries. A series of 'wars' – wars involving the grabbing of resources of various kinds such as silk cocoons, wool, iron ore, coal, and so on – broke out in the late 1980s, reflecting the determination of the resource-rich provinces to protect their own interests.[21] 'Policy on the top, and counter measures down below' (*shangyou zhengce, xiayou duice*) is indeed a vivid description of central–local relations in post-reform China. The marketization reform was intended to rectify the line and block compartmentalization and to bring about a rational spatial division of labour based upon the market signals; but ironically the end result was an even greater degree of spatial compartmentalization and a trend toward homogenization of the space economy. Nevertheless, this has somewhat mitigated the seriousness of the problem of geographical transfer of value arising from the 'scissors difference' in pricing.

By the late 1980s the shortcomings of the contract responsibility system, especially in terms of inhibiting the centre's ability to redistribute resources and in terms of the formation of the dukedom economy, had become apparent. The centre has since tried to rectify the situation by launching a series of reforms. Instead of giving certain regions or certain industrial sectors preferential treatment, these recently introduced measures are primarily aimed at promoting an environment in which all localities and all enterprises, regardless of their ownership structure, compete on an equal footing. In the Fourteenth Party Congress held in October 1992, soon after Deng's famous southern tour, it was formally proclaimed that the construction of the 'socialist market economy', despite the apparent contradiction in terminology, would be the main task for the country to accomplish for a prolonged period of time. Earlier, in July of the same year, measures were introduced to transform the state enterprises into modern corporations, and to dissociate their links with the respective state organizations, including local governments.[22] The state enterprises, at least in theory, are now free to set their own developmental goals, identifying their respective niches in an increasingly competitive environment. They are given the right to issue shares and raise capital in the stock exchange, and to form joint ventures with foreign companies. They are also given the authority to design their respective remuneration packages and recruitment policies. The market, under such circumstances, has a much larger role to play. The 'scissors difference' in pricing will be very much curtailed with the penetration of market forces. Increased mobility, both in terms of flow of capital and labour, and in terms of the movement of the goods produced over different spatial domains, consequent upon the deepening of the market-oriented reform, will help break down the barriers erected because of local protectionism.

In 1994, a 'tax sharing' system, which formally delineates local and central taxes, was introduced to replace the contract responsibility system. More specifically, customs duties, customs-levied value added tax, consumption tax and income tax from centrally owned enterprises are designated to be central tax. Personal income tax, income tax of locally owned enterprises, urban land use tax and property gains tax are considered to be local tax. Value added tax on domestic products, securities transactions tax and resources tax are to be shared between the central and the local governments.[23] Perhaps the value added tax is the single most important item, and is to be shared on a 3 : 1 basis – three parts to the central government for every one part to the local government. The aim was to strengthen the centre's financial position *vis-à-vis* that of the local governments and to sever the direct link between the revenues of the local government and those of the enterprises located within their respective geographical jurisdictions. Protracted arguments have taken place between the provinces and the central government over such issues as: (i) whether the tax sharing system should be implemented on a gradual basis or as a single package all at one time; (ii) what exactly constitutes the central taxes, the local taxes and the shared taxes; and (iii) how the respective expenditure responsibilities of the central and provincial governments are delineated. Irrespective of the outcome of the bargaining process, the new universalistic tax sharing system, as opposed to the particularistic form of revenue sharing under the contract responsibility system, will further erode the base of the dukedom economy. Of course, it does not mean that it will no longer be in the interests of the local governments to protect their own industries and foster growth in their own areas. Nevertheless, there will be far fewer incentives for the provinces to bargain on behalf of the enterprises located within their respective boundaries, especially if these enterprises are centrally-owned. Every locality will, however, strive to provide a favourable environment in order to attract business undertakings, given that revenues associated with any increase in land values will go to the local coffers. The problem of homogenization of the space economy alluded to earlier is unlikely to disappear with the introduction of the tax sharing system. Even worse, there is now a strong incentive for the localities to rely on income derived from land. This, coupled with the myopic behaviour of local government officials, has often resulted in unjustifiable urban development and rapid loss of valuable farm land.

Rural industrial development

Another unintended consequence of the devolution of decision-making power was the rapid development of rural industry or township and village enterprises (TVEs)(see also Chapter 8).[24] These enterprises are mainly collectives, that is, they do not constitute part of the state-owned sector and fall outside the annual state plan. In the pre-reform period this meant that the central state was not responsible for marketing their products or for supplying the relevant raw materials. In other words, they were more or less left on their own; hence they were in a rather weak position especially in comparison with the state-owned firms. The history of TVEs can be traced back to the setting up of the people's communes in 1958. Indeed prior to the formal dissolution of the people's communes in 1983, these enterprises were labelled commune and brigade enteprises. At first these enterprises were meant to augment the rural agricultural sector, and serve basically the local population. Farm machinery repairing, the manufacturing of bricks, cement and other construction materials, and the processing of agricultural products were then the main production items. Those located close to major urban centres also engaged in limited subcontracted work, acting as a buffer for the state-owned enterprises, especially at times when additional production targets had to be met.

The household production responsibility system, which constituted the main corpus of reform measures in the early reform period and which led to the collapse of the people's communes, only applied to the agricultural sector. The commune and brigade enterprises remained as collectives under the control of the respective local governments – now renamed township and village governments. The greater degree of flexibility associated with the household responsibility system provided these enterprises with an abundant supply of cheap labour, as some one-third to one-half of the agricultural labour force has been estimated to be in surplus. The TVEs also capitalized on the business networks that they had built up in the past, including the networks of connection with the various government departments and the state-owned enterprises. As the reform gained momentum, the relative autonomy of the TVEs and their previous experience in operating in a market setting provided them with an edge over the state-owned enterprises. TVEs in the Sunan region, which has a long history of rural industrial development and which has since the Song Dynasty been the most prosperous part of China, have shown the strongest performance. The Pearl River Delta, because of its proximity to Hong Kong and hence ready access to foreign capital and the international market, also recorded phenomenal growth. In addition, TVEs flourished in Shangdong, Henan, and more recently Sichuan and other interior provinces as well. Between 1978 and 1995, the number of workers employed by the TVEs increased from 28 million to 128 million; and the gross output value from RMB49 billion to RMB6891 billion. In fact there are now more workers working in TVEs than in state-owned enterprises (the latter employed 109 million people in 1995).[25] Almost by definition, the TVEs are scattered geographically. A consequence of the rapid development of the TVEs is the narrowing of the gap between the urban and the rural, and hence a more equitable distribution of the productive forces over space. Perhaps this is another reason why indices of spatial disparity have shown a consistent downward trend in the reform era.

While one of the objectives of the reform is to separate the state from the enterprise and to bring about a system of market coordination, in the case of the TVEs, at least at the micro-level, the reverse is closer to the truth. The majority of the TVEs are the under the direct control of the township and village government. In many respects, the concerned township or village government operates as though it is a corporation, trying to compete in the national and international market. However, it is still a state organ and performs state functions. In a sense it acts both as the referee and as the players in the field. The fusion of local kinship networks into the local state apparatus further complicates the matter. Again this seemingly paradoxical development appears to be a built-in feature under China's partial reform. Whether this local state corporatism,[26] a term coined by some authors to describe China's current political economy at the local level, will be able to sustain itself and continue to play a positive part in fostering China's economic growth, particularly in the vast rural hinterland, is subject to debate.

Foreign direct investments

The 1989 Tiananmen Incident might have a long-lasting effect on China's internal politics and international relations; however, its effects on the course of economic reform proved to be short-lived. In fact, there has been a massive increase in foreign direct investments (FDIs) in the 1990s, especially since Deng's famous southern tour in 1992. The amount of FDI utilized averaged about US$3 billion in the late 1980s. It was US$4 billion in 1991, US$11 billion in 1992, US$27 billion in 1993, US$33 billion in 1994, and US$37 billion in 1995.[27] For comparison, the total investment in fixed assets in 1994 and 1995 were, respectively, RMB1704 billion and RMB2001 billion, or US$205 billion and US$241 billion at current rates of exchange.[28] In other words, FDIs now contribute more than 10 per cent of fixed capital formation in China. Earlier it was pointed out that measures have been taken in recent years to end the particularistic treatment of enterprises and regions, which was characteristic of the 1980s, so as to minimize the malaise of the dukedom economy. Among these are measures to give the foreign-funded enterprises the same legal status as the local firms so that they can sell their products in the domestic market. However, at the same time, some of the privileges formerly accruing to the foreign-funded firms, especially in the special economic zones and coastal open cities, such as tax breaks and the right to import machinery and other capital goods duty free, will be taken away.[29] Apparently such policy changes have not inhibited the flow of FDIs to the country. Obviously the flow of foreign capital is guided by the prospects for profit, and it is the more developed regions on the eastern coast which offer the best prospects. Officially the coastal development strategy is no longer in practice. In fact, if anything, the state in the Ninth Five Year Plan has called for accelerated development in the interior provinces. Measures have been introduced to channel FDIs as well as investments from the more developed regions to the lagging areas in the central and western regions.[30] First, the state will encourage foreign investments into those areas in which the manpower and natural resources of the interior provinces can be ulitilized. Second, permission will be given to those foreign investors whose principal investments are in the 'basic industries' and capital intensive projects such as infrastructure developments, especially if these projects fall into the central and western regions, to extend their business to 'related activities'. Third, the interior provinces will be given priority in the use of external loans, especially loans from the World Bank, the Asian Development Bank and other international agencies.[31] However such efforts have as yet to produce any significant impacts. The published data point to the fact that the eastern coastal region still receives the lion's share of FDIs.

Table 7.1 gives the distribution of FDIs according to provinces for the period 1992–5. Figure 7.3 maps the same set of data, but uses the provincial-level units as the level of spatial resolution. It can be seen that the eastern coastal region consistently accounts for close to 90 per cent of all FDIs in China. Guangdong, Fujian, Shangdong, Jiangsu and the three centrally administered municipalities of Shanghai, Beijing and Tianjin, all on the eastern coast, are the provinces or provincial-level units that benefit most from the inflow of foreign capital. On the other hand, provinces in the remote western regions, which in general have a high concentration of minority populations, receive very little FDI, generally not more than a few million US dollars per year. Given the relative importance of FDIs in the national economy, especially in terms of fixed capital formation in recent years, the high concentration of FDIs in the eastern coastal region naturally leads to a widening of the development gap between the eastern coast and the rest of the country. Woo has compiled data on per capita GDP, tabulated according to the three broad regions.[32] Woo's results show that in 1990, if the per capita GDP in the eastern coastal region was 100, that in the central region would be 63.8, and in the western region 55.8. In 1994, the corresponding figures were 100, 53.0 and 44.5. It is somewhat ironic that during the heyday of the coastal development strategy in the 1980s, the eastern coastal region, on the whole, was not able to outperform the others by any substantial margin. Instead, it is in the 1990s, at a time when the central government is consciously promoting

Table 7.1 China: foreign direct investments by province, 1992–1995 (US$10 000)

Provinces	*1992*	*1993*	*1994*	*1995*	*Total*
Beijing	34 985	66 694	137 157	107 999	346 835
Tianjin	10 778	61 368	101 499	152 093	325 738
Hebei	11 309	39 654	52 340	54 668	157 971
Shanxi	5 384	8 643	3 170	6 383	23 580
Inner Mongolia	520	8 526	4 007	5 781	18 834
Liaoning	51 642	127 913	144 014	142 461	466 030
Jilin	7 534	27 527	24 192	40 802	100 055
Heilongjiang	7 217	23 232	34 759	51 686	116 894
Shanghai	49 361	316 025	247 309	289 261	901 956
Jiangsu	146 324	284 371	376 315	519 082	1 326 092
Zhejiang	23 978	103 175	115 026	125 806	367 985
Anhui	5 466	25 764	37 000	48 256	116 486
Fujian	142 364	287 444	371 318	404 390	1 205 516
Jiangxi	9 972	20 817	26 168	28 888	85 845
Shangdong	100 342	187 413	255 242	268 898	811 895
Henan	5 316	30 491	38 673	47 855	122 335
Hubei	20 313	54 053	60 186	62 512	197 064
Hunan	13 271	43 746	33 114	50 773	140 904
Guangdong	370 111	755 576	946 343	1 026 011	3 098 041
Guangxi	18 201	88 456	83 633	67 263	257 553
Hainan	45 255	70 710	91 809	106 207	313 981
Sichuan	11 214	57 141	92 174	54 159	214 688
Guizhou	1 979	4 294	6 363	5 703	18 339
Yunnan	2 875	9 702	6 500	9 769	28 846
Tibet	N.A	N.A	N.A	N.A	N.A
Shaanxi	4 553	23 430	23 880	32 407	84 270
Gansu	35	1 195	8 776	6 392	16 398
Qinghai	68	324	241	164	797
Ningxia	35	1 190	727	390	2 342
Xinjiang		5 300	4 830	5 490	15 620
Total	1 100 402	2 734 174	3 326 765	3 721 549	10 882 890

Source: *Zhongguo Tongji Nianjian* (*China Statistical Yearbook*), 1996, p. 600; 1994, p. 530. Zhongguo Tongji Chubanshe.

Figure 7.3 Distribution of foreign direct investments in China, 1992–5

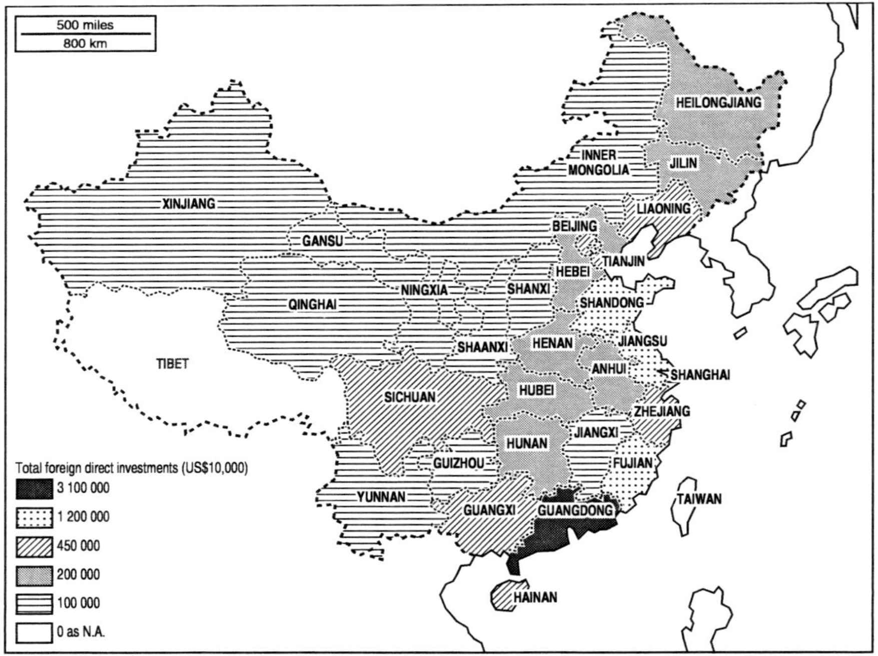

Source: *Zhongguo Tongji Nianjian* (*China Statistical Yearbook*), 1996, p. 600; 1994, p. 530. Zhongguo Tongji Chubanshe.

geographically non-discriminatory policies, especially if they favour the more developed regions, that the gap has widened.

HONG KONG'S RETURN TO CHINA AND ITS IMPLICATIONS FOR REGIONAL DEVELOPMENT

It is clear from the foregoing that regional development in China is a highly complex issue. Not only are there competing developmental goals, which have often produced a spatial distribution of investments and resource transfers that contradicts common-sense expectations; but there are also factors largely external to and perhaps beyond the control of the Chinese state. These include the attitudes of the transnational corporations towards investing in China and the changing international relations, including the sudden collapse of the Soviet Union and the consequential changes in the international balance of power, which have impinged directly and indirectly upon the way regional priorities are set and the degree to which international capital is allowed to penetrate into the country. In 1997, Hong Kong's sovereignty reverted to China, and Hong Kong became a 'special administration region' (SAR) of the People's Republic under the concept 'one country, two systems'. The implications of this for the contents and directions of flow of international capital, and hence the pattern of regional development in the Chinese mainland, could be far-reaching. For one thing, Hong Kong has been, and is likely to continue to be, the single most important source of FDIs in China. How the Hong Kong-based companies perceive investment opportunites in the mainland and deal with the various central and local authorities at a time when their 'foreign status' is in question will have an important bearing on the flow of FDIs in the country. Perhaps the business tycoons in Hong Kong will value *guanxi* or connections with the centre even more, and thus respond to the call to invest in the lagging interior provinces in a more serious manner. Moreover, there is a need for the SAR government to maintain good working relations with each and every province in the country, and yet to avoid subordination to any one of them, including its powerful neighbour, Guangdong. This is important if Hong Kong wants to play the role of international financier for the entire country. If this is the case, then geographic proximity will play a lesser part in future mainland – Hong Kong relations, and the relative importance of Guangdong as a recipient of FDIs may decline as a result.

In the period prior to the return of Hong Kong to China, FDIs from overseas were often channelled through Hong Kong. In a sense Hong Kong became the hub of doing business in China. For political reasons, investments from Taiwan and many South-east Asian countries are often carried in the guise of Hong Kong investments. The hub function of Hong Kong could be strengthened even further upon its return to China, as it might be more convenient for the various enterprises and local and central government departments in the mainland to make use of this international financial centre to raise capital and to do business with the outside world. However, as far as investments from Taiwan and from ethnic Chinese businessmen in South-east Asia are concerned, the historical function of the Territory as a buffer for conducting business with China will be curtailed. It is difficult to assess how this will affect the size and geographical distribution of Taiwanese and overseas Chinese investments in China, although it may be argued that, had it not been for Hong Kong, a substantial part of such investments would not have been channelled to Guangdong, in particular to the Pearl River Delta.

The future is full of uncertainties. The tone of this concluding section is speculative, and is deliberately meant to be so. In the past China's regional scene has experienced drastic changes, and the foci of development, as far as the official regional policy is conerned, have shifted alternately from the interior provinces to the coastal areas, and back again to the interior region. With regard to the actual regional growth patterns, however, more often than not the observed patterns have contradicted the patterns expected from the overt policy. Hidden transfers of all kinds prevail. There are limits as to what the market-oriented reforms can do to eliminate such transfers. The centre has to respond to various demands from the provinces, including the need to extend special policies to provinces with large concentrations of minorities, thus trying to maintain a delicate balance. The return of Hong Kong further complicates the matter. In addition to dealing with internal politics, especially with inter-provincial relations, the centre also has to define China's niche in the fast-changing international environment, which has direct bearing on the country's regional development strategies. Now that Hong Kong's status has been settled, the issue of Taiwan's reunification with the motherland will be sure to feature prominently on Beijing's agenda. The Hong Kong SAR may serve as a model for reunification, and Hong Kong's prosperity, if maintained, will very much strengthen China's claim that the 'one country, two systems' arrangement can apply to Taiwan as well.

But the chances are that the Taiwan authority will resist any attempt at reunification. The possibility of military confrontations is there. Equally, in order to win the hearts of the Taiwanese people, China may adopt a more accommodating attitude and offer certain special privileges and business opportunities to Taiwan firms. Again this would have geographic implications for the country's economic development.

Notes and references

The author would like to thank Miss Tang Yin-ha for her assistance in drawing the maps. This research is supported in part by Hong Kong Baptist University research grant FRG95–96/I–07.

1. See, for example, Rozman Gilbert, *The Modernization of China* (New York: The Free Press, 1981), pp. 477–8.
2. Hu Zhaoliang, 'China's Cultural Resources and China's Geography', a lecture delivered at Hong Kong Baptist Univesity on 19 February 1997.
3. According to the Population Census of China, 1990, there are a total of 56 different nationalities in China, with Han Chinese, which account for some 93 per cent of the population, constituting the largest nationality group.
4. Bus bombing which was claimed by Uygur exiles, for example, struck Beijing in March 1997. *South China Morning Post*, 10 March 1997.
5. For a discussion of the national integration issue, see, for example, David S. G. Goodman, 'The Politics of Regionalism: Economic Development, Conflict and Negotiation', in David S. G. Goodman and Gerald Segal (eds), *China Deconstructs: Politics, Trade and Regionalism* (London: Routledge, 1994), pp. 1–20.
6. See, for example, *Yazhou Zhoukan* (*Asia Weekly*), 27 January – 2 February 1997.
7. Unless otherwise stated, the term 'provinces' means provincial-level administrative units, which include also the three directly administered municipalities of Beijing, Shanghai and Tianjin, and the 'autonomous regions' of Guangxi, Inner Mongolia, Ningxia, Qinghai, Tibet and Xinjiang.
8. Li Si-ming, '*Zhongguo de kaigang zence yu quyu fazhan: Guangdong Shen de qishi*' ('The open policy of China and regional development: the hints of Guangdong Province'). *Hong Kong Journal of Social Sciences*, No. 1, 1993, pp. 135–166. See also Zhao Ziyang, *Yanzhe You Zhongguo Tese de Shehuizhuyi Daolu Qiangin* (*Marching on the Road of Socialism with Chinese Characteristics*) (Hong Kong: Joint Publishing Co. 1987).
9. Li Si-ming, '*Zhuanbianzhong de Zhongguo quyu chayi: shizheng yanyiu de huigu*' (China's changing spatial disparities: A review of empirical evidence'), In Li Si-ming, Wing-shing Tang, Nan-hung Nora Chiang and Sue-ching Jou (eds), *Zhongguo Quyu Jingji Mianmianguan* (*Perspectives on China's Regional Economy*) (Hong Kong and Taipei: David C. Lam

Institute for East–West Studies, Hong Kong Baptist University, and Population Research Centre, National Taiwan University, 1996), pp. 19–24; Simon Xiaobin Zhao, 'Spatial Disparities and Economic Development in China, 1953–92: A Comparative Study', *Development and Change*, Vol. 27 (1996), pp. 131–63.

10. The *China Statistical Yearbook* (*Zhongguo Tongji Nianjian*) has, since the 1995 edition, stopped publishing data on the national income. More recent data using this measure are thus not available.

11. These three broad regions are composed of: (i) the Eastern Coastal Region: Liaoning, Hebei, Beijing, Tianjin, Shangdong, Jiangsu, Shanghia, Zhejiang, Fujian, Guangdong, Guangxi and Hainan; (ii) the Central Region: Jilin, Heilongjiang, Inner Mongolia, Shanxi, Henan, Hubei, Anhui, Hunan and Jiangxi; and (iii) the Western Region: Ningxia, Gansu, Sichuan, Guizhou, Qinghai, Yunnan, Xinjiang and Tibet.

12. Western scholars in the 1970s and early 1980s generally thought that China under Mao practiced a pro-rural or anti-urban development policy. However, later works, such as that of Chan and Kirkby, have shown how the *hukou* system helps to channel resources from the rural to urban regions. See for example, R. Yin-Wang Kwok, 'Recent Urban Policy and Development in China: A Reversal of Anti-Urbanism,' *Third World Planning Review*, Vol. 58, No. 4, 1987, pp. 283–399; Richard J. R. Kirkby, *Urbanization in China* (London: Croom Helm, 1985), pp. 1–18; Kam-Wing Chan, 'Economic Growth Strategy and Urbanization Policies in China 1949–1982', *International Journal of Urban and Regional Research*, Vol. 16, No. 2, 1992, pp. 252–305.

13. Wing-Shing Tang has estimated the extent of this geographical transfer of value under Maoist China. See Wing-Shing Tang, 'Regional Uneven Development in China, with Special Reference to the Period between 1978 and 1988'. Department of Geography, The Chinese University of Hong Kong, Occasional Paper No. 110 (November 1991).

14. Zhao and Kwan, for example, hold such a view. See Zhao Xiaobin and Kwan Wing-Kai, '*Zhongguo quyu fazhan moshi yu konjian celefenxi*' (Analysis of China's model of regional development and spatial policy'), in Li Si-ming, Yat-ming Siu and Henry T. K. Mok (eds), *Zhongguo Shehui Fazhan* (*China's Social Development*) (Hong Kong: Commercial Press, 1995), pp. 17–59.

15. Fei, Hongping, '*Qiye yu jingjiqu de guanxi ji qi xietiao*' ('The relationship between economic regions and enterprises'), *Jingji Dili* (*Economic Geography*), Vol. 13, No. 3, pp. 23–9.

16. Chu, David K. Y. and Wing-Shing Tang, '*Zhongguo quyu fazhan and zhengjing guanxi; huigu yu qianzhan*' ('The political and economic relations of China's regional development: retrospects and prospects'), in Yue-man Yeung (ed.), *Zhongguo Chengshi yu Quyu Fazhan: Zhanwang Ershiyi Shiji* (*Urban and Regional Development in China: Prospects of the Twenty-first Century*) (Hong Kong: Chinese University of Hong Kong, Hong Kong Institute of Asia–Pacific Studies, 1993) pp. 53–70.

17. Zhao and Kwan, 'Analysis of China's model' Ho, Lok-sang, 'Central-fiscal relations', in Joseph Yu-Shek Cheng and Maurice Brosseau (eds), *China Review 1993* (Hong Kong: Chinese University Press,

1993), pp. 12.1–12.23; Woo Tun Oy, 'Regional economic development and disparities', in Maurice Brosseau, Suzanne Pepper and Tsang Shu-ki (eds), *China Review 1996* (Hong Kong: Chinese University Press, 1996), pp. 281–314.

18. The reference to *zhuhou jingji* or a dukedom economy was quite popular among China's economists during the late 1980s and early 1990s. See, for example, Shen, Liren and Yuanchen Dai, '*Wuoguo zhuhou jingji de xingcheng ji bituan he genyuan*'('The origin and adverse consequences of the dukedom economy in China'), *Jingji Yanjiu*, No.3, 1990, pp. 12–17.
19. This point had been reiterated by Zhao Ziyang, first Premier of the State Council (1982–7) and subsequently General Secretary of the CCP until his departure from the central echelons in June 1989. See Li, Si Ming, 'The Open Policy of China and regional development'.
20. Li Si Ming, 'The Open Policy of China and regional development'.
21. Shen, Liren and Dai,'The origin and adverse consequences'; Zhang Keyun, '*Zhongguo qyyu jingji yunxing wenti yanjiu* '('Problems of the running of China's regional economy'), *Jingji Yanjiu* (*Economic Research*), No. 6, 1996, pp. 52–8.
22. Joseph Y. S. Cheng and Wang Ting, 'Administrative reforms in China in 1992: streamlining, decentralization and changing government functions', in Joseh Y. S. Cheng and Maurice Brosseau, (eds) *China Review 1993* (Hong Kong: Chinese University Press, 1993), pp. 4.1–4.20.
23. Chung Jae Ho, 'Central-provincial relations', in Chi-Kin Lo, Suzzane Pepper and Kai-Yuen Tsui (eds), *China Review 1995* (Hong Kong: Chinese University Press, 1995), pp. 3.1–3.45.
24. The volume edited by Byrd and Lin provides a detailed account of the various aspects of the township and village enterprises, including the general pattern of growth, the major characteristics of the various types of TVE, the form of industrial organization, including their relations with the various levels of government, and the role of the local kinship network, and so on. See William A. Byrd and Qingsong Lin, *China's Rural Industry: An Introduction* (Washington, DC: The World Bank, 1990).
25. *Zhongguo Tongji Nianjian 1996* (*China Statistical Yearbook 1996*) (Beijing: Zhongguo Tonji Chubanshe, 1996), p. 96; pp. 388–9.
26. For a discussion, see Jean C. Oi, 'Fiscal Reform and the Economic Foundation of Local State Corporatism', *World Politics*, Vol. 45, No. 1, 1992, pp. 99–126; and Nan Lin, 'Local Market Socialism: Local Corporatism in Action in Rural China', *Theory and Society*, Vol. 24, 1995, pp. 301–54.
27. *Zhongguo Tongji Nianjian 1996* (*China Statistical Yearbook 1996*). (Beijing: Zhongguo Tongji Chubanshe, 1996), p. 597.
28. Ibid. p. 139.
29. See Woo Tun Oy, 'Regional Economic Development in Disparities', in Maurice Brosseau, Suzanne Pepper and Tsang Shu-ki (eds), *China Review 1996* (Hong Kong: Chinese University Press, 1996), pp. 281–314.
30. Ibid.
31. Ibid.
32. Ibid.

8 Rural Industrialization and International Trade

Zhang Xiaohe

Chapter 7 has described the phenomenal growth of rural industry and its impact on China's regional development. This chapter takes a closer look at its impact on the growth of China's international trade, a major policy issue of concern to Beijing's leadership. The growth of China's rural enterprises was very impressive in the 1980s and early 1990s. From 1980 to 1995, the total output of the township and village enterprises (TVEs) grew at an average annual rate of 30 per cent. In 1995, TVEs produced about 56 per cent of China's total industrial products, 43 per cent of total exports and provided employment for 128 million people.[1] The TVEs' growth of output and capability in providing employment far exceed those of the state owned enterprises (SOEs). Along with the foreign-funded enterprises (FFEs), TVEs have become the main components of the so-called non-state sector in China.

One distinguishing feature of the TVEs is the significant role they play in foreign trade. In 1994, there were more than 130 000 outward-looking TVEs, of which more than 320 firms gained the right of direct international transactions. The export value of the TVEs reached US$39 billion in 1994 and US$53 billion in 1995, accounting for 33 per cent and 43 per cent respectively of the national total.[2] The participation of the TVEs in international trade greatly contributed to China's export growth. In 1978, China's total exports were only US$9 billion. This increased to US$27 billion in 1985, and further to US$62 billion in 1990 and US$148 billion in 1995.[3]

Along with a rapid growth in China's total exports, its export pattern has also changed dramatically. As shown in Figure 8.1, China's primary exports declined sharply over the reform decade and its manufacturing exports increased dramatically, along with the diminishing of the importance of its mineral exports after the 1986 oil price drop. Indeed, by 1995 manufactures had grown to 86 per cent of total

Figure 8.1 The change in China's exports pattern, 1980–1995

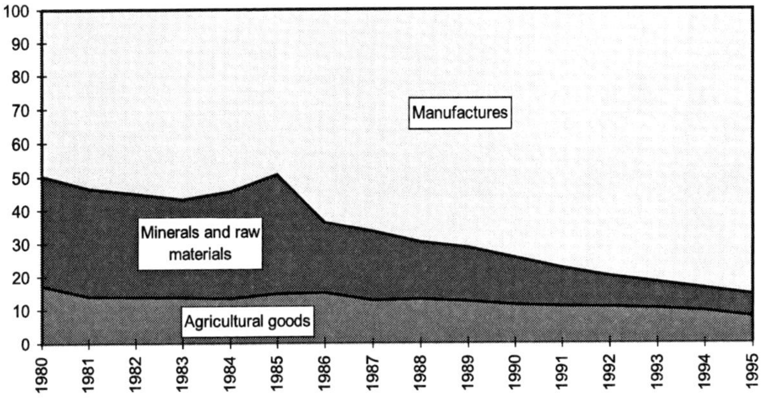

Sources: *Zhongguo Tongji Nianjian* (*Chinese Statistical Yearbook*), various years.

exports.[4] Although this structural change has been widely observed by some distinguished scholars,[5] none of them has attributed it to the growth of outward-looking TVEs in China.

Two questions are raised in this chapter. First, is the emergence of rural industrial exports a main source of the rapid growth of China's international trade? Second, how and to what extent did the development of TVEs' exports change China's export pattern? In order to provide a background to China's economic reforms, the next section reviews the reform process with particular reference to the growth of the TVEs. Then the nature of the rural industry exports and their impact on the pattern of China's exports as a whole are discussed.

RAPID GROWTH OF THE TVEs

China's labour allocation is characterized by restrictions on labour mobility between different sectors, especially between rural and urban areas. This policy was established in the late 1950s and it has been maintained for more than 40 years. In the pre-reform era, the rural economy was restricted to merely producing farm products while the urban sector monopolized manufacturing production. After the reforms, the restrictions on rural manufacturing activities were relaxed by permitting the development of rural industries. But the real wage differential between rural and urban areas, and different treatments in other welfare aspects such as housing and transportation subsidies, still exists.

In the allocation of capital, restrictions on urban–rural capital flow were stricter before the 1980s. Between 1952 and the late 1970s, fixed assets per industrial worker rose from 3000 yuan for each of 5 million workers to nearly 9000 yuan for each of 50 million workers in the urban sector.[6] By contrast, in the late 1970s, there were just 814 yuan of fixed assets for each rural worker, less than one tenth of those for each urban industrial worker.[7] Because non-agricultural activities were discouraged in rural areas, the capital available for those activities was very limited. The rural manufacturing activities were confined to industries such as primary product processing and agricultural machinery repairs, as a complementary part of agricultural production. Since 1980, the restrictions on developing non-agricultural activities have been partially relaxed. Capital mobility was also permitted across different sectors.

The existence of cheap rural labour and access to urban capital are the most important reasons for the rapid growth of the TVEs.[8] This is because the isolation and segmentation of the factor (labour and capital) market will create gaps in marginal productivity of each factor in different sectors. In China's case, the marginal productivity of capital will be higher, and the marginal productivity of labour will be lower in the rural sector than that in the urban sector. As a result, capital moves into the rural sector to earn high profits, which in turn fuels the development of rural manufacturing activities.

The process of rural industrialization was also accelerated by China's price distortion and price reforms. Prior to 1978, China's commodity prices were artificially decided by the government rather than determined by market forces. The price structure was set based on its traditional level of the 1950s. But later, as the amount of production rose and costs fell due to economies of scale and technical improvements, the manufacturing sector did not have to reduce its prices, or did so only with a considerable lag.[9] Before the 1978 reforms, China's prices were stable but distorted by a sector exploitation pattern, the so-called 'scissors difference' gap between industrial and agricultural products. This price regime was designed to support an urban development strategy biased towards heavy industry at the expense of rural agriculture and raw materials' production. Along with the factor market restrictions, the biased prices for most of the agricultural products and most of the raw material inputs dominated China's price structure for decades until 1978, when a market-oriented reform started.

The bias in China's price structure was partially corrected by the reform. However, the government kept the purchases and sales of the so-called 'key agricultural products', grain and cotton, tightly under its control until the beginning of the 1990s. This reduced the relative price of agricultural produce and enhanced the people's desire to participate in high income-earning manufacturing activities.

The total number of rural enterprises increased to over 22 million in 1995, more than triple the figure of 1984. Their total labour force was over 128 million, compared to a total rural labour force of 450 million and a total urban labour force of 173 million in the same year.[10] The employment in TVEs has surpassed the total employment in the SOEs since 1993. Table 8.1 shows the significant growth of rural enterprises in the national economy after 1984. In 1984 the share of rural enterprises was 13 per cent of national output value and about one third of rural output value. These shares rose to 32 per cent and 66 per cent respectively by 1992. The gross output value of rural enterprises jumped from 49 billion yuan in 1978 to over 6892 billion yuan in 1995, a 140-fold increase over 17 years.

In contrast, the performance of the SOEs, though often under government protection, has been disappointing. They have been the losers in competition with the rural enterprises. Table 8.2 provides a comparison of the output shares between state-owned industry and rural industry in the national economy over the period 1985–95.[11] The share of state-owned industry declined from 65 per cent in 1985 to 34 per cent in 1995. The share of rural industry, on the other hand, increased dramatically from 18 per cent to 56 per cent over the same period.

Another important non-state sector, which often overlaps the TVEs in statistics, is the foreign funded enterprises (FFEs). In 1995, these FFEs accounted for about 16 per cent of total industrial output above township level in China.[12] Rural TVEs attracted some of the foreign investment. It is reported that the total accumulated utilization of foreign capital in the TVEs was US$31 billion in 1996, accounting for about 16 per cent of total accumulated and actually utilized foreign investment in China in that year.[13] The FFEs also account for quite a large proportion of China's total exports, and this proportion has grown considerably: from less than 1 per cent in 1982, to 3 per cent in 1987, 12 per cent in 1990, 20 per cent in 1992 and 31 per cent in 1995. Nevertheless, it is very hard to distinguish the exports generated by the FFEs from those generated by the TVEs.

Table 8.1 Rural enterprises in the national economy, 1984–1995

Year	*A* *Gross output value of rural enterprises RMB Billion*	*B* *Gross output value of rural society RMB billion*	*C* *Gross output value of national society RMB billion*	*A/B* *%*	*A/C* *%*
1984	170	503	1 316	34	13
1985	272	634	1 658	43	16
1986	354	755	1 906	47	19
1987	474	943	2 303	50	21
1988	649	1 253	2 980	52	22
1989	742	1 448	3 451	51	22
1990	985	1 661	3 803	51	22
1991	1 162	1 900	4 414	61	27
1992	1 797	2 538	5 482	66	32
1993	3 154	4 253		74	
1994	4 258	5 834		73	
1995	6 891	8 925		77	

Notes: RMB: *Renminbi*, Chinese currency. The data of 'gross output value of rural society' in the period 1993–5 are estimated by summing the gross output values of industry, agriculture, forestry, husbandry, fishery and sideline production sectors.
'Rural enterprises' include all enterprises in the rural sector.
Sources: *Chinese Statistical Yearbook* (1988), pp. 37, 214, 294; (1990), pp. 49, 333, 401; (1991), pp. 7, 52, 65; (1992), pp. 47, 327, 390, (1995), p. 365; (1996), p. 388.
Yearbook of China's Rural Enterprises (1990), pp. 72–7.
A Statistical Survey of China (1993), pp. 8, 54, 67; (1996), p. 62.

Table 8.2 Gross output value of the SOEs and the TVEs in the industrial sector, 1985–1995

Year	*State-owned enterprises RMB billion*	*%*	*Rural enterprises RMB billion*	*%*	*Others RMB billion*	*%*	*Total RMB billion*
1985	630	65	183	19	159	16	972
1986	697	62	241	22	181	16	1 119
1987	825	60	324	23	232	17	1 381
1988	1 035	57	453	25	334	18	1 822
1989	1 234	56	524	24	443	20	2 202
1990	1 306	55	605	25	481	20	2 392
1991	1 496	56	871	33	296	11	2 663
1992	1 782	52	1 364	39	314	9	3 460
1993	2 273	47	2 345	48	223	5	4 840
1994	2 620	37	3 234	46	1 164	17	7 018
1995	3 122	34	5 126	56	942	10	9 189

Notes: 'Rural enterprises' include private and cooperative rural industries.
'Others' are derived by subtracting the value of SOEs and rural enterprises from the total. This item thus includes urban collective, cooperative and private industries.
Source: *A Statistical Survey of China* (1992), p. 403: (1996), pp. 389, 403.

GROWTH IN RURAL INDUSTRIAL EXPORTS

The reforms in China's foreign trade sector are characterized by a process of liberalization and marketization. These reforms will naturally induce a shift in China's export pattern toward its comparative advantage. Since unskilled labour is the most abundant factor in China, one may expect that China's labour-intensive exports will increase, and its capital-intensive and natural resource-intensive exports will decline over time. This direction of change has been confirmed by several studies on recent developments in China's foreign trade pattern.[14]

As China's foreign trade sector moves toward a more liberalized stage, the TVEs will overtake the urban sector to play an even more significant role in exporting labour-intensive manufacturing goods. And since the real wage rate in the rural sector is lower than that in the urban sector, the TVEs will be more profitable if they specialize in producing labour-intensive products. Even if the two sectors produce the same products, the TVEs will, as a result of the differences in factor prices, use a more labour-intensive technology. They are therefore more likely to represent China's comparative advantage. As a result, the TVEs' share in total exports will increase over time. In contrast to the urban sector, the TVEs have an advantage in producing and exporting labour-intensive manufactured goods. These goods, as described in Figure 8.1, are the main source of China's export growth in the post-reform era.

Thanks to low labour costs, the TVEs can compete internationally with the SOEs. It is reported that the foreign exchange earning for each unit of RMB expenditure in the TVEs was US$0.81, which was much higher than the amount earned by the SOEs (US$0.5–0.6). The cost of earning one unit of foreign exchange in TVEs was 5 to 30 per cent lower than that in the SOEs. The recycling period of capital investment for rural exporting enterprises was 6 to 12 months shorter than that in the SOEs in 1988.[15]

In Table 8.3 the value of exports from TVEs is compared with the value of total exports, for the period 1985 to 1995. It is clear that the exports of the TVEs grew much more rapidly than national exports as a whole. As a result, the share of TVEs' exports in total exports increased dramatically, from less than 5 per cent in 1985 to 41 per cent in 1993, and 43 per cent in 1995, calculated at current prices.

The TVEs' exports are mainly labour-intensive products. For instance, the top three commodities exported by the TVEs in 1992

Table 8.3 Growth of TVEs' exports, 1985–1995

Year	*National exports [1] RMB million*	*Annual growth (%)*	*Exports of the TVEs [2] RMB million*	*Annual growth (%)*	*Share of TVEs' exports [2]/[1] %*
1985	80 890	4.9	3 900		4.8
1986	108 210	29	9 949	94	9.2
1987	147 000	31	16 196	49	11.0
1988	176 670	18	29 871	61	16.9
1989	195 600	10	37 144	22	19.0
1990	298 580	42	46 230	22	15.5
1991	382 710	25	95 884	73	25.0
1992	467 630	20	119 279	22	25.5
1993	528 480	12	219 300	61	41.5
1994	1 042 180	68	339 831	44	32.6
1995	1 245 100	17	539 500	46	43.3
Average annual growth (1985–94)		**27**		**49**	

Notes: Average annual growth rate is defined as $Ln(Y_t/Y_o)/t$, where Y_o is base year value, Y_t is report year (1991) value and t is the total years under calculation.

Sources: *A Statistical Survery of China* (1991), pp. 65, 93; *Chinese Statistical Yearbook* (1992), p. 627; (1995), p. 537; *Yearbook of China's Rural Enterprises* (1990), p. 174; (1993), p. 148; (1994), p. 202; (1995), p. 100.
People's Daily, 12 November 1992, p. 1.
Qi Jingfo, 'Great achievement: A report on TVEs in the Eighth Five Year Plan', *Zhongguo Xiangzhen Qiye* (*Chinese Rural Enterprises*), No. 11 (1995), pp. 4–5.

were clothing, arts and crafts, and light manufactures, which accounted for 90 per cent, 63 per cent and 54 per cent of China's total, respectively, in the same year.[16] As a result of the rapid growth of rural enterprise exports, the national export composition will tend to be more labour intensive. In order to verify the factor intensity of rural industrial exports, a comparison of export compositions between the urban and rural sectors is called for. Distinguishing the exports from different sectors is difficult in China in the absence of separate statistics of the relevant export data in the two sectors. However, approximate estimations are still available. Table 8.4 shows that labour-intensive exports accounted for a dominant share of about 80 per cent in 1989, 1993, and 1995 by average.[17] Furthermore, if we take into account labour-intensive activities that are included in rural capital-intensive industries, the proportion will be even higher than 80 per cent.[18]

A combination of China's export pattern, in terms of agricultural, minerals and raw materials, urban and rural manufactured products is shown in Figure 8.2. The classification is based on an estimation. A total manufacturing export is derived from netting out the agricultural exports and natural resource exports from the total national exports. The total rural manufacturing exports is derived by netting out the share of total rural minerals and raw materials exports (weighted at 8 per cent on average) from total exports of the TVEs. The urban manufactured exports are thus a residual between total manufactured exports and the rural manufactured exports.

Figure 8.2 Composition of manufacturing exports by sectors

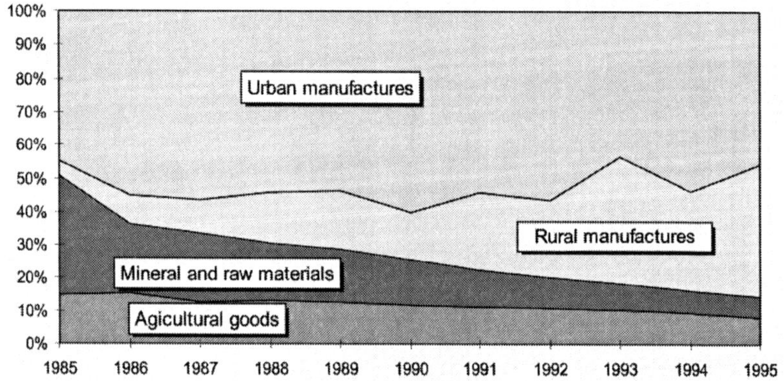

Sources: from various issues of *A Statistical Survey of China* and *Yearbook of China's Rural Enterprises*.

Table 8.4 Export composition of rural enterprises, 1989, 1993 and 1995

		1989 *RMB million*	*%*	*1993* *RMB million*	*%*	*1995* *RMB million*	*%*
1. Industrial branches							
chemical	P	2 553	5.5	13 327	5.2	34 543	5.5
machinery	H	2 141	4.6	18 204	7.1	44 577	7.1
mineral	N	2 179	4.7	8 116	3.2	24 737	4.0
light industrial	L	6 350	13.7	49 002	19.1	114 572	18.4
foods	L	3 996	8.6	15 296	6.0	45 506	7.3
native products	N	719	1.5	2 970	1.2	5 698	0.9
animal products	L	1 688	3.6	5 844	2.3	22 336	3.6
textiles	L	7 389	15.9	33 002	12.9	81 024	13.0
silk products	L	1 844	4.0	9 223	3.6	21 030	3.4
clothing	L	6 322	13.6	39 371	15.4	88 766	14.2
arts & crafts	L	5 766	12.4	24 935	9.7	65 740	10.5
others	L	5 448	11.7	37 183	14.5	75 000	12.0
total exports		46 395	100	256 071	100	623 529	100
2. Factor intensity groups							
natural resource intensive (N)		4 586	10	16 930	7	52 771	8
labour intensive exports (L)		37 115	80	208 012	81	491 639	79
human capital intensive (H)		21 41	5	13 327	5	34 543	6
physical capital intensive (P)		2 553	6	18 204	7	44 577	7
total exports		46 395	101	256 071	100	623 529	100

Source: *Yearbook of China's Rural Enterprises* (1990), p. 13; (1994), pp. 202–27; (1995), pp. 100–1, B17; (1996), pp. 124–47.

The result is very interesting when one compares it with Figure 8.1, which shows that the share of China's manufactured exports increased by more than 36 per cent over the decade 1985–95. Figure 8.2 shows that while the share of urban manufacturing exports fluctuated after 1985, rural manufacturing exports increased dramatically. Compared with Figure 8.1, one can conclude tentatively that the increase of China's manufactured exports is attributable to the increases of rural manufactured exports. Therefore the rapid growth of China's exports and the radical changes in its export pattern are mainly due to the rapid growth of China's rural labour-intensive manufactured exports. If foreign trade growth is the engine of China's economic growth, the TVEs provide the fuel for that engine.

CONCLUSION

This chapter explores the origins of the rapid growth in China's international trade and the radical changes in its export pattern. Applying standard international trade and development theory, it provides some new insights on these issues, in contrast to previous studies. It attributes the rapid growth of China's labour-intensive exports and radical changes in its export pattern to the nature of China's partial economic liberalization in general, and to the rapid growth of labour-intensive TVEs in particular.

In terms of empirical investigation, it is verified that when the distorted Chinese economy was liberalized in a particular way, by keeping the isolation of the rural and urban sectors unchanged but promoting the development of rural industries by partially releasing the capital mobility restrictions, labour-intensive manufacturing production and exports were encouraged but agricultural exports declined. Price distortions accelerated this trend over time.

Combining both the theoretical analysis and empirical examination may lead to the following conclusion. The rapid growth of China's international trade is not only due to a strategic change in China's foreign trade policy, but also due to a partial liberalization of its domestic factor markets. Changes in foreign trade policy provided a necessary condition for export promotion in the 1980s, but these changes alone might not have been sufficient to bring about a radical structural change in production structure and export composition. The partial factor market liberalization led to a boom of rural enterprises and generated labour-intensive production and exports, thus increasing allocative efficiency and economic welfare in the country. The boom in rural enterprises is not, however, without a cost. The loosely regulated or unregulated rural enterprises are reluctant to comply with the government's environmental protection regulations and become a major source of industrial pollution, an issue to be dealt with in the next chapter.

Notes and references

1. *Zhongguo Tongji Nianjian* (*Chinese Statistical Yearbook*), 1996, p. 388: and *Zhongguo Tongji Zhaiyao* (*A Statistical Survey of China*), 1996, p. 103.
2. It is reported that the total export value of the TVEs in 1994 was 339.8 billion yuan. If converting it into US dollars (US$1=RMB8.6187), it is US$39.43 billion, accounting for 32.6 per cent of the national total. See *Zhongguo Xiangzhen Qiye Nianjian* (*Yearbook of China's Rural Entesprises*), 1995, p. 297; and 1996, p. 103.
3. *Zhongguo Tongji Nianjian* (*Chinese Statistical Yearbook*), 1996, p. 580.
4. Ibid. p. 581.
5. See, for example, Kym Anderson and Rod Tyers, 'Economic growth and market liberalization in China: implication for agricultural trade', *The Developing Economies*, Vol. 25 No. 2 (1987), pp. 124–51; and Nicholas R. Lardy, *Foreign Trade and Economic Reform in China*, 1978–1990 (Cambridge : Cambridge University Press, 1992).
6. Mark Selden, *The Political Economy of Chinese Development* (New York : M.E. Sharpe, 1993), p. 167.
7. See Zhang Xiaohe, 'Urban–rural isolation and its impact on China's production and trade pattern', *China Economic Review*, Vol. 3, No. 1 (1992), p. 92.
8. See a theoretical analysis of Zhang Xiaohe, Christopher Findlay, and Andrew Watson, 'Growth of rural enterprises: impact on rural–urban relations,' *Journal of Development Studies*, Vol. 31, No. 4 (1995), pp. 567–84.
9. Nicholas R. Lardy, *Foreign Trade and Economic Reform in China, 1978–1990*, p. 90.
10. All data are collected from *Zhongguo Tongji Nianjian* (*Chinese Statistical Yearbook*), 1996, pp. 90–1, 387–9.
11. Since consistent and comparable statistics between rural enterprises and SOEs are limited due to different accounting regimes used in the two sectors, the direct comparison of all enterprises between the two sectors is impossible. Therefore only the data in the *industry* sector, not including construction, transport, commerce and service sectors are displayed in the table.
12. This figure may under-estimate the contribution of the FFEs to China's industrial output, due to the exclusion of the village enterprises into the aggregation. See *Chinese Statistical Yearbook*, 1996, p. 31. The overseas Chinese (Hong Kong, Macao and Taiwan) funded enterprises are treated as FFEs.

13. *Yearbook of China's Rural Enterprises*, 1996, p. 323.
14. See Zhang Xiaohe, 'Urban–rural isolation and its impact on China's production and trade pattern'; and Nicholas Lardy, 'Chinese foreign trade', *The China Quarterly*, No. 131 (September 1992), pp. 691–720.
15. *Renmin Ribao* (*People's Daily*), 1 December 1998.
16. Zhou Handa, 'A great success of the outward looking rural enterprises', *Zhongguo Xiangzhen Qiye Nianjian* (*Yearbook of China's rural Enterprises*), 1993, p. 272.
17. This estimation is on the basis of a rough classification of China's industries by factor intensity; see Zhang Xiaohe, 'Classification and the dualism of China's industries in the 1980s', *Industry and Development*, No. 34 (1993), pp. 61–91.
18. There are many stages of a production process in each industry and the different stages could involve quite different factor-intensive activities. In this case the broad division of the industries may be misleading. For example, the machine-building industry in China is classified so broadly that it includes some extremely capital-intensive sub-industries such as mineral equipment and some other extremely labour-intensive sub-industries such as bicycle making. It should be classified as a labour-intensive industry in the rural sector.

9 The Challenge of Sustainable Development

K. K. Wong

China, like most developing countries, faces great challenges from its large population, relative shortage of natural resources and serious environmental degradation. It is, therefore, necessary for China to explore a new path to balance economic growth and environmental protection. For instance, in the report delivered by Chairman Jiang Zemin at the Fifteenth National Congress of the Chinese Communist Party (CCP) on 12 September 1997, he urged: 'As a populous country relatively short of natural resources, China must implement a sustainable development strategy in the modernization drive.'[1] He further argued that China should stick to the basic state policies of family planning and environmental protection, correctly handling the relationship of economic development versus population, natural resources and the environment. Apparently, the idea of sustainable development has been considered by some of China's central leaders as the only viable option to reconcile the tension of the inter-related problems of environmental destruction and economic growth. The notion that the types and levels of production and consumption of goods must be brought in line with the nation's finite resource base is now getting more support from the state.

The term 'sustainable development' was popularized by the United Nations World Commission on Environment and Development (WCED) in its seminal work, *Our Common Future,* published in 1987.[2] The report defined sustainable development as 'development that meets the needs of the present without compromising the ability of future generations to meet their own needs'. It urged nations to adopt 'sustainable development' strategies to alleviate poverty, feed the people and safeguard the environment. At the Earth Summit held in Rio de Janeiro in June 1992 over 120 nations endorsed 'sustainable development' as the most important economic and environmental policy for the twenty-first century. The *Agenda 21* adopted at the

Earth Summit is a blueprint on how to make development socially, economically and environmentally sustainable.[3]

China's impetus to pursue rapid economic growth is inevitably strong. In contrast to the Maoist era, the current regime adopts Deng Xiaoping's pragmatic notion that 'to get rich is glorious'. The nation as a whole regards economic growth as the only means of achieving higher living standards for the growing population. However, there are also increasing concerns that China's current mode of development might not be able to be sustained in the future because of its huge population and meagre per capita share of many essential resources such as food, water, fossil fuels and minerals.[4] This chapter first examines the characteristics and trends of China's development. It then discusses the problems confronting China's various attempts to synchronize economic development and environmental protection.

CHARACTERISTICS AND TRENDS OF CHINA'S DEVELOPMENT

In order to understand China's current development trends from a broader perspective, this chapter first compares selected developmental indicators for China with three other countries, namely India, the United States and Japan.[5] Each of these countries has unique characteristics in its population size, resource endowment and development stage (see Table 9.1). China is a rapidly growing less developed country (LDC) with huge population and moderate natural resource endowment. India is a moderately growing LDC with large population and moderate natural resource endowment. On the other hand, the United States is a slow-growing more developed country (MDC) with large population and rich natural resource endowment. Japan, though much smaller in area, is a moderately growing MDC with large population size and poor in natural resource endowment.

Overall trend

As the twentieth century draws to a close, China has managed reasonably well to meet the basic health and nutritional needs of its huge population. The per capita average number of calories available is greater than the need; the per capita total protein consumption is improving, and the life expectancy at birth of the Chinese people compares favourably with many MDCs (see Table 9.2). Moreover, with its

Table 9.1 Country profiles

Country	*Area*	*Population*	*Natural resource endowment*	*Development stage*
China	Large	Very large	Moderate in total/poor in per capita	Rapidly growing LDC
India	Medium	Very large	Moderate	Moderate-growing LDC
USA	Large	Large	Rich	Slow-growing MDC
Japan	Small	Large	Poor	Moderate-growing MDC

Note: The classification is based on the subjective judgement of the author.

Table 9.2 Basic indicators

Countries	*Population (millions) mid-1993*	*Area (thousands of sq. km)*	*Average annual population growth rate (%) 1980–93*	*Life expect. at birth (years) 1993*	*Per capita average calorie available (as per cent of need) 1987–9*	*Per capita total protein consumption (grams/day) 1987–9*	*Urban population*			
							As % of total population		*Average annual growth rate (%)*	
							1970	*1993*	*1970*	*1993*
China	1178.4	9 561.0	1.4	69.0	112	63	17.0	29.0	3.0	4.3
India	898.2	3 288.0	2.0	61.0	99	53	20.0	26.0	3.7	3.0
USA	257.8	9 809.0	1.0	76.0	138	111	74.0	76.0	1.1	1.2
Japan	124.5	378.0	0.5	80.0	125	95	71.0	77.0	1.8	0.6
World	5501.5	133 690.0	1.7	66.0		71	37.0	44.0	2.6	2.6

Source: *World Development Report 1995* and *World Resources 1992–1993*.

very stringent one-child population policy, its population growth rate is among the lowest in the LDCs (see Chapter 11). Although China's living standards are still relatively low, its achievements in meeting the basic needs of its people are ahead of many LDCs.

Virtually all economies in the world today seek to increase their economic growth; this is usually reflected in an increase in a country's gross national product (GNP). China's performance over the last decade is well ahead of many countries in this regard. For instance, it has the highest average annual per capita GNP growth rate (8.2 per cent) among the countries shown in Table 9.3. Moreover, China's gross domestic product (GDP) maintained an annual 9.6 per cent growth rate between 1980 and 1993, which is more than three times the world's average. The data also reveal that there is a remarkable shift in the sectoral distribution of the GDP. The most rapidly growing sectors were industry and services; these maintained a double-digit growth rate during the 1980 to 1993 period. By contrast, agriculture's share of GDP dropped from 34 per cent in 1970 to 19 per cent in 1993. In 1993, 85 per cent of the merchandize imported comprised machinery, transport equipment and other manufactured products. Food, fuels and other primary commodities accounted for the rest of the merchandize imported. On the other hand, over 80 per cent of the exports were manufactured products such as textile fibres, textiles, and clothing (see Table 9.4). Between 1970 and 1993, the urban population increased from 17 per cent to 29 per cent. The annual urban growth rate in 1993 was as high as 4.3 per cent, which is the most rapid urban growth in the history of China. Evidently, China's economic growth is now driven mainly by the secondary and tertiary sectors. Two decades of economic reforms have driven China to enter a new era of rapid industrialization and urbanization.

Natural resource endowment

China possesses rich and varied natural resources. Its dilemma is that it has a large population but a meagre per capita share of most essential resources. For instance, with 22 per cent of the world's population, China has only 7 per cent of its water and cropland, 3 per cent of its forests, and 2 per cent of its oil. Despite these limits, China has managed reasonably well as a rural, agricultural, and relatively poor country.[6] As the economy develops, China's shortage of resources threatens to become a serious impediment to its ambitious modernization plans.

Table 9.3 Growth and structure of production

	Average annual growth rate (%)		*Average annual GDP growth rate (%) by sector*							
	GNP	*GDP*	*Agriculture*		*Industry*		*Manufacturing*		*Service*	
Countries	*1980–93*	*1980–93*	*1970–80*	*1980–93*	*1970–80*	*1980–93*	*1970–80*	*1980–93*	*1970–80*	*1980–93*
China	8.2	9.6	2.6	5.3	8.9	11.5	10.8	11.1	5.3	11.1
India	3.0	5.2	1.8	3.0	4.5	6.2	4.6	6.3	4.6	6.4
USA	1.7	2.7	..	..	..	..	..	..	..	..
Japan	3.4	4.0	-0.2	0.6	4.0	5.0	4.7	5.6	4.8	3.7
World	1.2	2.9	..	..	..	..	..	..	..	..

	Distribution of gross domestic product (%) by sector							
	Agriculture		*Industry*		*Manufacturing*		*Service*	
Countries	*1970*	*1993*	*1970*	*1993*	*1970*	*1993*	*1970*	*1993*
China	34.0	19.0	38.0	48.0	30.0	38.0	28.0	33.0
India	45.0	31.0	22.0	27.0	15.0	17.0	33.0	41.0
USA	3.0	..	34.0	..	25.0	..	63.0	..
Japan	6.0	2.0	47.0	41.0	36.0	24.0	47.0	57.0
World	..	..	..	..	..	..	..	..

Source: *World Development Report 1995* and *World Resources 1992–93*.

Table 9.4 Structure of merchandise imports and exports

	Percentage share of merchandise imports									
	Food		*Fuels*		*Other primary commodities*		*Machinery & transport equip.*		*Other manufactures*	
Countries	*1970*	*1993*	*1970*	*1993*	*1970*	*1993*	*1970*	*1993*	*1970*	*1993*
China	..	3.0	..	6.0	..	7.0	..	42.0	..	43.0
India	21.0	4.0	8.0	30.0	19.0	10.0	23.0	14.0	29.0	42.0
USA	16.0	5.0	8.0	10.0	12.0	4.0	28.0	43.0	36.0	38.0
Japan	17.0	18.0	21.0	21.0	37.0	13.0	11.0	17.0	14.0	32.0
HK	20.0	6.0	3.0	2.0	9.0	3.0	17.0	33.0	52.0	56.0
World										

	Percentage share of merchandise exports									
	Fuels, minerals, metals		*Other primary commodities*		*Machinery & transport equip.*		*Textile fibres, textiles and clothing*		*Other manufactures*	
Countries	*1970*	*1993*	*1970*	*1993*	*1970*	*1993*	*1970*	*1993*	*1970*	*1993*
China	..	6.0	..	13.0	..	16.0	..	31.0	..	65.0
India	13.0	7.0	35.0	18.0	5.0	7.0	27.0	30.0	47.0	68.0
USA	9.0	4.0	21.0	14.0	42.0	49.0	3.0	3.0	28.0	33.0
Japan	2.0	2.0	5.0	1.0	41.0	68.0	13.0	2.0	53.0	29.0
HK	2.0	2.0	3.0	5.0	12.0	26.0	44.0	..	84.0	67.0
World										

Source: *World Development Report 1995* and *World Resources 1992–93*.

Energy is the thread that sustains and integrates all life and supports all economies. Post-1978 increases in China's primary energy consumption have been considerable. The per capita energy consumption in China has increased 2.3 times since 1978 and is still rising. However, the current consumption level represents only 44 per cent, 8 per cent and 17 per cent of those of the world, the United States and Japan respectively (see Table 9.5). Coal provides three-quarters of the primary energy in China today, compared with 22 per cent in the United States and 17 per cent in Japan. Moreover, China's energy efficiency is extremely low. For instance, from the data given in Table 9.5, the GDP output per kilogram of oil equivalent in 1993 was only US$0.6 for China, while the GDP outputs for the United States and Japan were US$3.1 and US$9.3 respectively. The low energy efficiency and the over-reliance on coal, the dirtiest fuel, as a primary energy source are the major causes of China's air pollution problem.[7] China's cities have some of the world's highest sulphur and particulate contamination, especially cities in northern China where coal is used for winter heating.[8] In southern China, where the local coal has lots of sulphur, acid rain has become a serious pollution problem[9] which causes serious damage to crops, forests and buildings in South and South-west China.[10]

There is growing concern over water scarcity in many parts of China. Although its total fresh water resource is similar to that of the United States, its per capita water availability is only one-fourth of the United States' level. The water supply problem is most acute around big cities in northern China. In 1993, the Minister of Water Resources reported that more than 300 Chinese cities were short of water, with 100 in acute distress that resulted in enormous economic loss. Moreover, the groundwater table in northern China has been dropping at a rate of 50 centimeters per annum since the beginning of the 1990s.[11] Despite the acute water shortage, inefficiency of water use in agriculture, industry and households is widespread. In recent years, water shortages are exacerbated by a growing proportion of 'fresh' water being polluted by industrial effluent and domestic sewage; this has created serious 'human-induced' water-shortage problems in many municipal areas.[12] Naturally, as the economy continues to escalate, the competition for water between domestic, industrial and agricultural sectors will become more acute. Apparently, China has reached a stage where the availability of fresh water has become a significant factor constraining the future development of the nation.

Table 9.5 Natural resources

Countries	Forest: Total area (thousand sq km) 1990	Forest: Annual deforest, 1981–90 (thousand sq km)	Freshwater: annual withdrawal, 1970–92: Total (cu km)	Per capita (cu m): Total	Per capita (cu m): Domestic	Per capita (cu m): Industrial and agricultural
China	1247.0	8.8	460.0	462.0	28.0	434.0
India	517.0	3.4	380.0	612.0	18.0	594.0
USA	2960.0	3.2	467.0	1868.0	244.0	1624.0
Japan	238.0	0.0	89.3	732.0	125.0	607.0
World						

Countries	Average annual growth rate (%): Energy production 1980–93	Average annual growth rate (%): Energy consumption 1980–93	Energy use (oil equivalent): Per capita (kg) 1993	Energy use (oil equivalent): GDP output per kg ($) 1993	Electric power production (kwh per person) 1992
China	4.9	5.1	623.0	0.6	647.0
India	6.6	6.7	242.0	1.2	373.0
USA	0.7	1.4	7 918.0	3.1	12 900.0
Japan	4.6	2.7	3 642.0	9.3	7 211.0
World	..	..	1 421.0	3.1	

Source: *World Development Report 1995* and *World Resources 1992–93*

Vegetation cover is another seriously degraded resource in China, particularly its forests. Official statistics indicate that China has forest cover equal to 13 per cent of the country's total area, which is far below the world average of 31 per cent. Although China and the United States have comparable land area, the area of forest in the US is 2.4 times that in China. The long history of massive deforestation has not been reversed in the past decade. Both legal and illegal logging activities have been widespread in richly forested provinces such as Sichuan, Yunnan, Heilongjiang and Hainan, especially as the market economy makes it easy to sell timber. In addition, China loses 8800 square kilometers of its forested land annually for other uses, such as for agriculture, urban or industrial development. The shrinking forested area not only reduces the ability of China to produce adequate timber to meet its growing demand, it also adversely affects the ecological balance of the country. Among other undesirable side effects, deforestation has meant that droughts and flooding are now annual occurrences in major river basins in China.

Agriculture and food

Undoubtedly, food production in China increased quite substantially after the economic reform of 1978, particularly with the introduction of the 'production responsibity system' in the early 1980s. However, the increase in food production has been sustained by an immense increase in fertilizer input. For example, between 1980 and 1993, the fertilizer consumption in China doubled. As the standard of living rises, the Chinese people begin to switch from a heavily grain-based diet to one richer in meat and dairy products. In other words, the demand for livestock feeds, which are mostly grains, will increase substantially. At present about 20 per cent of the grain consumed in China is used to feed livestock (see Table 9.6). As the diet continues to change, China will encounter more difficulty in meeting its grain needs.[13]

In order to play down the concerns about China's food prospects and their impact on global food markets voiced by Western scholars,[14] the State Council issued a White Paper on *The Food Problem of China* in October 1996.[15] The White Paper reaffirmed China's commitment to a policy of food self-reliance and stated that China will not, at any time, impose a threat to the world food market. The White Paper argued that China can achieve its food self-reliance

Table 9.6 Agriculture and food

	Cropland		*Irrigated land as a percentage of cropland*		*Fertilizer consumption (hundred grams per hectare of arable land)*		*Average production of cereals*		*Average yields of cereals*		*Grain fed to livestock as percentage of total grain consumption*	
	Total (000 ha)	*Per capita hectares*					*(000 metric tons)*	*Per cent change since*	*Kilograms per hectare*	*Per cent change since*		
Countries	*1989*	*1990*	*1977–79*	*1987–89*	*1979/80*	*1992/93*	*1988–90*	*1978–80*	*1988–90*	*1978–89*	*1970*	*1990*
China	96 115.0	0.08	47.0	47.0	1 497.0	3 005.0	369 576.0	31.0	4 057.0	38.0	8.0	20.0
India	168 990.0	0.22	22.0	25.0	329.0	720.0	193 601.0	42.0	1 861.0	42.0	1.0	2.0
USA	189 915.0	0.76	10.0	10.0	1 127.0	1 011.0	267 965.0	5.0	4 341.0	6.0	80.0	70.0
Japan	4 637.0	0.04	67.0	62.0	3 721.0	3 951.0	14 214.0	7.0	5 662.0	3.0	34.0	48.0
World	1 479 190.0	0.28	14.0	16.0	817.0	874.0	1 859 005.0	18.0	2 638.0	20.0	38.0	38.0

Source: *World Development Report 1995* and *World Resources 1992–1993*.

objective through increasing agricultural investment and developing modern, intensified, sustainable agriculture based on advances in science and technology. Apparently, the White Paper tries to depict an over-optimistic assessment of China's food production capability, and to some extent reflects the wishful thinking of Chinese officials.

The reality is that China's agriculture is still confronted by many problems. For instance, land, the irreplaceable foundation of food production, is degrading in many ways, such as soil erosion, desertification, salinization and toxification by pollutants.[16] In addition to these processes of degradation, arable land is lost at an alarming rate[17] to real estate development, industries and urban expansion.[18] China's current food output comes mainly from unsustainable farming practices, such as too much mono-cropping, too few crop rotations, inadequate cultivation of legumes, unbalanced fertilization, and very high levels of nitrogen application.[19] Moreover, water shortages and diminishing returns from additional fertilizer use have begun to impact. In the late 1990s, agricultural investment has become insufficient and the cost of farming continues to soar, which has significantly weakened farmers' incentives to produce food. Can China maintain its agricultural sustainability in an increasingly hostile environment? The answer, of course, depends on the ability of the Chinese government to resolve the aforementioned problems.

Summary

China's economy is developing very rapidly against the background of a huge population, limited per capita resources and relatively backward economic, scientific and technical levels. The reliance on coal as the primary energy source causes much air pollution. In most cities and regions, especially those in the north, there is a serious shortage of fresh water and water pollution has exacerbated the problem. There is the conspicuous conflict between more people and less cultivated land, and the keen competition for land between agriculture and urban industries or other undertakings. Only a small proportion of land is forested. Moreover, the problems of ecological degradation, desertification and destruction of habitat are not yet under effective control. Overall, the state of China's environment is still very vulnerable.

ECONOMIC GROWTH NEEDS A GREEN THEME: CHINA'S AGENDA 21

China's sustainable development is being challenged by a quantitative decrease in the amount of resources available and by a qualitative worsening of the ecological environment. Many analysts predict that the current development trends in China will carry over into the twenty-first century; these will then overload the country's resource base and exceed its carrying capacity.[20] Therefore, in order to achieve sustainable development, China requires a bold new approach to development, one that builds around population stabilization, efficient use of resources, greater reliance on renewable energy sources, pollution prevention, waste reduction and the preservation of biological diversity.[21]

Seemingly, the current regime has given more attention than hitherto to incorporating environmental concerns into its economic and social development plans and programmes. New laws have established comprehensive regulations for the environment. For instance, a clause on environmental protection was included in the 1978 *Constitution of the People's Republic of China* for the first time.[22] The Environmental Protection Law of the People's Republic of China was first promulgated in draft form in 1979 and subsequently in its current form implemented ten years later in 1989. The law contains generalized guidelines, in the nature of policy statements, that provide the broad directives for environmental protection and resource conservation. In fact, in 1983 China declared environmental protection a 'basic national policy' during the Second National Environmental Protection Work Conference. The Chinese government has also encouraged local administrations to map out their own policies, targets, norms, rules and regulations on environmental protection. Building upon the foundation of China's environmental legislation, a framework of an environmental management system has begun to take shape and has started to tackle the worsening environmental problems.[23] In the late 1980s, China introduced an 'environmental protection responsibility system' in which provincial governors, city mayors, and county administrators have to sign 'responsibility contracts' containing details of the measures used to prevent environmental degradation.[24]

China participated enthusiastically in the United Nations Conference on Environment and Development held in Rio de Janeiro in June 1992. The *Agenda 21* produced during the conference committed signatory nations to produce national plans for reconciliation of the conflicts between the needs of development and environmental concerns. China responded promptly and positively. Soon after the conference, in July 1992, the Environmental Protection Committee of the State Council decided to designate the State Planning Commission and the State Science and Technology Commission to take charge of organizing more than 50 departments and over 300 experts to formulate *China's Agenda 21* and to identify priority programmes.[25] It took the team merely 15 months to draw up the *China's Agenda 21* document, which was formally adopted by the State Council in March 1994.[26] In fact, China was the first LDC to come up with a national *Agenda 21*. This helps to reinforce its aim to be a political leader among LDCs on environmental issues, and to allay some international fears about China as a possible global polluter.[27]

In recent years, the Chinese government has taken more specific actions to promote the implementation of a sustainable development strategy. For instance, the State Council decided to use *China's Agenda 21* as the guide in the formulation of medium and long-term national and social development plans and programmes. Its main ideas and content had been included first in the Ninth Five Year Plan (1996–2000) and the long-term objectives to the year 2010, and then in a report delivered by Jiang Zemin at the Fifteenth National Congress of the CCP,[28] *China's Agenda 21* is the overall strategy for China's sustainable development, which will be implemented through specific programmes. The first group of priority programmes consisted of 62 priority programmes in nine fields.[29] If these plans could be successfully implemented, the changes would lead to greater production efficiency, a reduction in the amount of waste generated, more rational pricing of raw materials, better pollution-control technologies, and closer links with the international arena in environmental protection cooperation. In broad terms, China's effort should, over a considerable period, contribute to a greener environment for the Chinese people.

THE CONSTRAINING FACTORS

China's Agenda 21 is a significant policy document that takes an holistic view of development and specifically rejects the development policy of polluting now and cleaning up later. The Agenda attempts to put forward China's objectives and guidelines for action, so as to make its economic and social development compatible with its population, resources and environmental requirements. It is, therefore, a good beginning towards the attainment of China's sustainable development goals. However, to redirect China's economic development on to a sustainable development track is a formidable and difficult task. There are still numerous obstacles impeding the implementation of the plans and programmes, which include institutional defects, problems of policy failure and implementation gap, as well as the weak environmental and legal awareness of the Chinese people.

Institutional defects

Institutions affect the management of natural resources by allocating decision-making authority among different individuals, agencies and levels of government. Institutional structures also affect whether rules and regulations can be effectively enforced.[30] What is unique about China is that the national environmental laws are implemented by local agencies that are part of the national agency system (via the *xitong*, with the National Environmental Protection Agency, NEPA, at the top level) and part of local government (with attendant *tiao kuai* relationships).[31] Therefore, to a very large extent, an environmental protection bureau (EPB) director's ability to carry out environmental protection functions is not only tied to the NEPA, but also to the nature of the director's *guanxi* (or relationships) with other leaders of local government.[32] In addition, EPB officials typically view the development of *guanxi* with the people they regulate as a key to carrying out their jobs effectively.[33] The over-reliance on *guanxi* to resolve problems weakens the legal enforcement of environmental regulations and this, to a great extent, accounts for the looming non-compliance cases in environmental management nationwide.

In China, the EPBs are an integral part of local governments and are funded locally and with only meagre support from the central government. Therefore, their strengths and weaknesses in enforcing environmental regulations are related to the workings of local government. For instance, actions taken by EPBs to implement regulatory programmes are motivated and constrained by their positions within local government, and the operations of local government shape the development of EPBs and the implementation of environmental regulatory programmes.

Since local EPBs receive little budget allocation from the central government, they have sought financial support largely from those regulatory programmes that they are chartered with implementing. For instance, the pollutant discharge fee programme and the related services fee generate the basic funding for the bureaux. Paradoxically, the revenue of the EPBs is directly proportional to the scale and extent of the pollutants generated within their own jurisdictional areas. Under such circumstances, whether local EPBs can be sufficiently impartial regulators, without a government allocation of revenue that frees them from compromising regulatory goals in order to survive financially, is questionable. An institutional design that relies on fees and fines to support the EPBs simply produces a license for industries and enterprises to contaminate the environment with full legal and administrative support.[34]

Policy failure and implementation gap

Often the EPBs are a 'tiger without the teeth'. Even where higher-level administrative units exist, the old systemic bias in favour of the production organization remains. The National Environmental Protection Administration, for example, has a lower bureaucratic rank than that of the various production ministries[35]. While it can raise issues and draft regulations, it cannot issue binding orders either to the ministries or to the provinces, which have ministry rank, and thus lacks the authority to force their compliance.[36] This is, therefore, one major source of the 'implementation gap' and 'policy failure' in environmental policy implementation in China.[37]

While there is a strong claim of a national commitment to promote environmental protection, yet this commitment is often weakened by the desire to achieve economic gains. The major source of disharmony is in the unique Chinese conception of 'development'. For instance, *China's Agenda 21* clearly stated that for a developing country like China the precondition for sustainable development is [economic] development. Today, China's per capita incomes are still so extraordinarily low that the drive for economic growth remains overwhelming. Therefore, it is not surprising that many officials still regard economic growth *per se* as having higher priority than sustainable development. It is still common for decision-makers, especially those in the economic field, to claim that pollution and ecological disruption are the necessary evils of economic development. They still maintain that 'control after pollution' is the historical sequence of economic development that cannot be bypassed, and from which China cannot be exempt.[38]

Local government, in particular, has an overriding interest in faster economic growth even at the expense of environmental damage.

Clearly, this is contrary to the stated national policy that demands that environmental protection is incorporated into every economic development plan and programme. Qu Geping condemned this situation as a major 'economic policy failure' of local government officials.[39] They generally wish to maximize the growth of local industry and commerce, both to reap the immediate profits and to expand the employment base for the growing population. Besides, there are too many exaggerated expectations on the part of many local officials who have great difficulty shedding their Stalinist fondness for new megaprojects, a strategy that places its emphasis on industrialization. Such growth has made the already insufficient resources and fragile environment face even greater pressure.

Weak environmental and legal awareness

Another constraint on implementing sustainable development programmes in China is the weak environmental and legal awareness among the Chinese people. According to the findings of the first nation-wide survey on people's environmental awareness, it was found that 76 per cent of the 4000 respondents said they knew what environmental protection was, but did not know much about the State regulations on environmental protection.[40] They also lack an in-depth understanding of many environmental issues. Therefore, it would be difficult for them to participate actively in the environmental protection programme. Enhanced public awareness on environmental issues would be necessary for successful monitoring of large numbers of polluting industrial operations, and to make existing complaint mechanisms more effective.

Moreover, in an empirical survey of the environmental awareness of environment protection officials in three Chinese cities during the early 1990s, the findings revealed that officials were sympathetic toward environmental values but they also aspired to develop material wealth.[41] The street-level regulators of the EPBs did not rate environmental values highly. In the present era of economic reform, it is typical for many officials to contend that economic growth has a higher societal value than environmental protection. These officials work in an unsupportive work constituency and a pro-growth social environment. The findings show that measures to protect the environment in China, in fact, make inroads into the economic viability of investments.[42] Undoubtedly, to the EPB officials 'economic sustainability' has a higher priority than 'environmental sustainability'.

The weak environmental awareness of people is also demonstrated by the low participation of ordinary citizens in environmental protection. To date, there are still no non-government environmental organizations in the China mainland. China's policy of prohibiting the formation of such organizations inevitably consigns environmental concerns to a subsidiary position in the structure of power. Unfortunately, the fear on the part of the authorities associated with the prospect of establishing any type of autonomous organization has made it very unlikely that real autonomous green movements will be tolerated by the current regime.[43] Nevertheless, China is gradually recognizing that an environmentally informed and articulate population is the key to the successful implementation of sustainable development programmes. The government is now assuming a more active role in disseminating the environmental protection message to its people. For instance, to raise the environmental and legal consciousness and to encourage public participation, the government in 1993 initiated a campaign entitled 'A Journey into the next Century for Environmental Protection'. The reporting teams, composed of reporters from different presses, covered thousands of miles in 19 provinces and autonomous regions. They commended examples of environmentally friendly actions and behaviour, and brought to light cases of serious environmental problems and lack of law enforcement. This is by far the largest single environmental publicity campaign launched by the Chinese government.[44] But the Chinese government should encourage rather than prohibit 'green' movements among the populace. Experience elsewhere has shown that the works of many non-governmental green groups complement the government's endeavour, especially in arousing public awareness on environmental issues and in mobilizing public participation in environmental protection campaigns.

Due to the lack of both financial and technological resources, China turns to reliance on 'intensified management' to tackle the rising environmental problems of the country. This, in turn, demands the establishment of the regulatory system and a set of enforceable environmental laws and regulations.[45] China has developed an impressive collection of environmental laws and regulations. Beginning in 1993, China launched a three-year large-scale national inspection on environmental law enforcement.[46] The purposes of the inspection included: (1) to crack down on illegal activities causing serious pollution and destruction of the ecological environment; (2) to change the situation characterized by weak enforcement of environment laws; and (3) to send out a strong signal to society that the government is resolved to use all legal means to strengthen the protection and improvement of the environment. The 1993 inspection concluded that environmental pollution had worsened in some parts of the country because of the relaxed enforcement of state laws and regulations on environmental protection. The investigation found numerous cases of non-compliance, and many local officials sacrificed their environment for the sake of economic profit.[47] Similarly, the 1994 inspection found more than 3000 non-compliance cases, and the pollution caused by poorly regulated rural enterprises warranted special attention.[48] The law enforcement inspection represents China's determination to improve the effectiveness of the legal system for environmental and resources protection.

However, the Communist state-centred conception of administrative law determines that environmental law is predominately an instrument for effective and efficient environmental management. Environmental law, therefore, is a way to legitimize the state's environmental policy and to facilitate its management rather than to limit its power.[49] Although Article 6 of the Environmental Protection Law granted citizens (*danwei*, or unit and individual) the legal right to bring legal suits to reduce damage-causing pollution, Chinese people do not often use courts to resolve environmental problems. In reality, environmental law is not an effective means for the public to regulate the government's performance in environmental management. Even in the case of government failure, no non-governmental entity can file a lawsuit against the government in the name of public interest. Therefore, the Chinese perceive 'law' as an instrument protecting the interests of the state rather than the rights of individuals. The weak legal awareness of the Chinese people is actually an outgrowth of their distrust of the existing legal system. If China is concerned to raise the legal consciousness of its people and to enhance law enforcement in environmental management, it should reform its legal system (for a detailed analysis of China's current legal reform, see Chapter 4) by approaching environmental law from the perspective of the individuals' right to be protected from the abuse of power, rather than as a policy-enforcement instrument. Hence, the system of environmental management by law should be augmented with a democratic and 'rights' content.[50]

CONCLUSION

Undoubtedly, the post-1978 economic reform in China has progressively unleashed market forces and dramatically improved the material well-being of most Chinese people. During the same period, however, China's environment has deteriorated significantly. The environmental protection endeavour is one characterized by a mixture of good intentions, admirable achievements, and astonishing negligence. For instance, giving the opportunity to earn a profit during the reform era has increased the incentive and ability of people to use resources more efficiently. On the other hand, the quest for short-term profit has abruptly escalated irrational resource exploitation and environmental damage. The Chinese government hopes to be able to control the environment, particularly the population pressure on natural resources, through planning and law enforcement. However, this approach is often still taking a back seat to short-term economic gains. Therefore, the net result is that the environmental conditions have been worsened appreciably during the reform era.

In sum, if China does not want to be trapped into an unreconcilable conflict between economic growth and environmental protection, it will require the political will and commitment of the Chinese leaders to reorient fundamentally the country's development from one that pursues 'quantity growth', that is, economic growth measured by GNP *per se*, to one that emphasises 'quality growth', that is, sustainable development in the economic, social and environmental domains. To attain this goal, China needs, apart from strict population control and rational resource development, a more open society where individuals' rights are respected and information can be obtained and opinions freely expressed. Sustainable development entails reform not only in the economic sectors, but also in the social and political arenas. The prognosis might be somewhat mitigated if the Chinese government were to carry out reforms to tackle problems such as institutional defects, policy failure and the implementation gap. At the same time, China needs to reform its legal systems by addressing people's environmental rights. And more resources should be committed to educating the public on environmental issues in order to raise their environmental awareness. Obviously, the mounting battle for a greener and more habitable China will require courageous and visionary leadership to set a course for the sustainable development of the country.

Notes and references

1. *China Daily's 15th Party Congress Supplement*, 23 September 1997.
2. The World Commission on Environment and Development, *Our Common Future* (Oxford: Oxford University Press, 1987).

3. Daniel Sitarz (ed.), *Agenda 21: The Earth Summit Strategy to Save Our Planet* (Boulder, Colorado: Earthpress, 1994).
4. Megan Ryan and Christopher Flavin, 'Facing China's Limits,' in Lester R. Brown (ed.), *State of the World 1995* (Washington, DC: World Watch Institute, 1995); Vaclav Smil, *China's Environmental Crisis: An Inquiry into the Limits of National Development* (Armonk, NY: M.E. Sharpe, 1993).
5. The data were compiled from two international sources: (1) the *World Development Report 1995* published by the World Bank; and (2) the *World Resources 1992/93* published by the World Resources Institute.
6. Megan Ryan and Christopher Flavin, 'Facing China's Limits', p. 113.
7. Wang Qingyi, *Energy in China* (Beijing: Metallurgical Industry Publisher, 1988).
8. Koon Kwai Wong, 'The Three-wastes Pollution in China: The Current State and Future Prospects', in Si-Ming Li *et al.* (eds) *Social Development in China: Reflections of Hong Kong Scholars* (Hong Kong Educational Publishing, 1995), pp. 225–251.
9. According to a report published in *China Daily* on 27 January 1995, acid rain affects 29 per cent of China's land area. South and South-west China constitute one of the world's three biggest acid-rain-affected regions.
10. Acid rain is blamed for causing an estimated economic loss of 14 billion yuan (US$1.6 billion) a year in South and South-west China (*China Daily*, 11 January 1995).
11. Liu Changming, 'Underground Water Table under Heavy Pressure', *China Environment News*, No. 44 (March 1993), p. 6.
12. An official survey showed that about 37 billion tons of liquid waste, mostly untreated, are poured into China's rivers, lakes and reservoirs annually (*China Daily*, 14 January 1995).
13. Lester R. Brown, *Who Will Feed China: Wake-up Call for a Small Planet* (London: Earthscan, 1995).
14. The debate was initiated by a report by Lester R. Brown, the Director of the World Watch Institute, entitled: 'Who Will Feed China?', *World Watch,* September/October 1994.
15. *White Paper on the Food Problem of China,* issued by the State Council in October 1996. See *China Daily*, 25 October 1996, p. 2.
16. Cai Yunlong and Barry Smit, 'Sustainable Agriculture and the Chinese Perspective', *ACTA Geographica Sinica* 50(2), (1995), pp. 97–106.
17. According to a China Daily News report (*China Daily*, 10 February 1995), China has consistently diverted 400 000 to 466 000 hectares of farmland annually for non-agricultural uses in recent years. And this trend seems difficult to control, despite some specific farmland protection rules that have been issued by the central and local governments.
18. Koon Kwai Wong and Xiaobin Zhao, *An Institutional Process of the Drastic Shrinkage of Farmland in Mainland China: The Pearl River Delta Case* (Hong Kong: Working Paper Series, No. 9602, Faculty of Social Sciences, HKBU, 1996); Graham Johnson, 'From Farms to Factories: Some Consequences of Economic Transformation', *China Perspectives,* No. 4 (1996).

19. Vaclav Smil, *China's Environmental Crisis: An Inquiry into the Limits of National Development* (Armonk, NY: M.E. Sharpe, 1993).
20. Megan Ryan and Christopher Flavin, 'Facing China's Limits'; Lester R. Brown, *Who Will Feed China?*; and Vaclav Smil, *China's Environmental Crisis.*
21. Gu Geping, *Environmental Management in China* (Beijing: UNEP & CESP, 1991).
22. The *Constitution* of 1978 stipulated that 'the state protects the environment and natural resources, prevents and eliminates pollution and other hazards to the public.'
23. Koon Kwai Wong and Hon S. Chan, 'The Development of Environmental Management System in the People's Republic of China', in Maurice Brosseau and Lo Chi Kin (eds), *China Review 1994* (Hong Kong: The Chinese University Press, 1994), pp. 21.1–21.21.
24. This is one of the environmental management systems in China developed in the late 1980s, which was first introduced in Gansu province in 1986 and later in other provinces and large cities. For discussion see *Zhongguo Huanjin Guanli Zhidu* (*China's Environmental Management System*) (Beijing: China Environmental Science Press, 1991).
25. *Introduction to China's Agenda 21* (Beijing: China Environmental Science Press, 1994), pp. 2–3.
26. *China's Agenda 21 – White Paper on China's Population, Environment. and Development in the 21st Century* was adopted at the Sixteenth Executive Meeting of the State Council of the People's Republic of China on 25 March 1994.
27. Clem Tisdell and Zhu Xiang, 'Reconciling economic development, nature conservation and local communities: Strategies for biodiversity conservation in Xishuangbanna, China', *The Environmentalist* No. 16 (1996), pp. 203–211.
28. See *China Daily's Business Weekly*, 14–20 April 1996; *China Daily's Fifteenth Party Congress Supplement*, 23 September 1997.
29. *Introduction to China's Agenda 21* (Beijing: China Environmental Science Press, 1994) pp. 27–29.
30. Carlos Wing-hung Lo and Shui-Yan Tang, 'Institutional contexts of environmental management: water pollution control in Guangzhou, China', *Public Administration and Development*, No. 14 (1994), pp. 53–64.
31. The vertical bureaucracies are called lines (*tiao* or *sitong*), while the horizontal coordinating bodies at various levels are called pieces (*kuai*). The relationships between the vertical and horizontal bodies are called *tiao/kuai guanxi.*
32. Barbara J. Sinkule and Leonard Ortolano, *Implementing Environmental Policy in China* (Westport, CT: Praeger Publishers, 1995).
33. Hon S. Chan and Kenneth K. K. Wong, 'Environmental Attitudes and Concerns of the Environmental Protection Bureaucrats in Guangzhou, People's Republic of China: Implications for Environmental Policy Implementation', *International Journal of Public Administration*, Vol. 17, No. 8 (1994), 1523–54.
34. Sinkule and Ortolano, *Implementing*, p. 201; Chan and Wong, 'Environmental Attitudes'.

35. The National Environmental Protection Administration is an 'administration' rather than a 'ministry'.
36. Kenneth Lieberthal, *Governing China: From Revolution Through Reform* (New York: W. W. Norton, 1995).
37. Hon S. Chan, Koon Kwai Wong, K. C. Cheung and Jack Man-keung Lo, 'The Implementation Gap in Environmental Management in China: The Case of Guangzhou, Zhengzhou, and Nanjing', *Public Administration Review,* Vol. 55, No. 4 (1995), pp. 333–40.
38. Qu Geping, *Environmental Management in China* (Beijing: United Nations Environmental Program & China Environmental Science Press, 1991) .
39. Qu Geping, the then NEPA Director and now the Chairman of the Environmental and Resource Protection Committee under the National People's Congress, in a speech entitled 'A Comprehensive Assessment of Environmental Pollution Trends in China', delivered in the 1995 National Environmental Protection Work Conference. In *China Environment Yearbook 1995*, p. 47.
40. The survey was organized by the China Environmental Protection Foundation. Reported by *Ming Pao* on 21 March 1996.
41. Koon Kwai Wong and Hon S. Chan, 'Environmental Awareness of Environmental Protection Bureaucrats in the People's Republic of China', *The Environmentalist,* Vol. 16, No. 3 (1996), pp. 213–19. The empirical survey conducted in 1991 and 1992 interviewed 180 environmental protection officials working at the Environmental Protection Bureaux in Guangzhou, Nanjing and Zhenzhou.
42. Chan, Wong, Cheung and Lo, 'The Implementation Gap'; Chan and Wong, 'Environmental Attitudes'.
43. Kenneth Lieberthal, *Governing China*, p. 291.
44. The campaign was organized by the Environmental and Resources Protection Committee of the National People's Congress and several mass media and government departments related to environmental protection. The theme for the 1994 campaign was 'Maintaining Ecological Balance: Building a Green China for the Future Generations'. See China, *Environment Yearbook 1995,* p. 23.
45. Richard L. Edmonds, *Patterns of China's Lost Harmony: A Survey of the Country's Environmental Degradation and Protection* (London: Routledge, 1994).
46. The inspections have been jointly organized by the Environmental and Resources Protection Committee of the National People's Congress and the Environmental Protection Committee under the State Council.
47. *China Daily*, 8 December 1993.
48. *China Environmental Yearbook* 1995, p. 95.
49. Carlos Wing-hung Lo, 'Environmental Management by Law in China: The Guangzhou Experience', *Journal of Contemporary China,* No. 6 (Summer 1994).
50. Ibid.

Part IV
Social Issues

10 The Political Economy of Anti-Poverty in Socialist China

Luk Tak Chuen

The Chinese government declared war against poverty in 1994 and aimed to eradicate it completely by the year 2000. Poverty eradication is not just a social relief, but an economic development strategy and a political task. The political discourse of poverty eradication not only creates hope for the poor, but also enables the current leadership to silence their opponents and any public dissent against the growing economic polarization. Therefore, the performance of anti-poverty efforts not only indicates how much the poor might have their living standards improved, but also reveals the effectiveness of the reform and tests the political credibility of the leadership.

Since the Chinese government admitted the existence of poverty in 1978, it began to formulate various poverty alleviation policies. In 1994, the State Council pronounced a grand plan to end poverty by 2000 – the National Seven Year Poverty Eradication Programme 1994–2000. In order to demonstrate its political commitment to fighting poverty, it held a series of conferences in the International Anti-Poverty Year of 1996. Major leadership figures attended the conferences. President Jiang Zemin and Premier Li Peng delivered keynote speeches, Vice Premier Zhu Rongji – the so-called Gorbachev of China – convened the meetings. Chinese Central Television (CCTV) and *The People's Daily* (*Renmin Ribao*) were full of images and reports that President Jiang paid home visits to workers and peasants in poor regions during the New Years of 1996 and 1997.

These high personal profiles in the propaganda operation seem to demonstrate the political commitment of the top leadership to fighting poverty; however, this chapter questions the effectiveness of these anti-poverty efforts and thus the leaders' political commitment. The policies and programmes are severely handicapped by the market myth, bureaucratic politics and the emerging market economy of

China. This chapter explores how politics and economics enter the process of poverty definition, policy formulation and programme implementation. The market myth, bureaucratic politics and marketization not only hinder poverty alleviation, but also intensify the relationship between the state and society in the localities.

THE POLITICS OF POVERTY DEFINITION AND INCIDENCE

The discourse on poverty is a politically sensitive issue in China. Orthodox Maoists denied the existence of poverty in Chinese socialism. They maintained that poverty was created by feudalism, capitalism and imperialism in Old China. Thus when the Chinese Communist Party built the New Socialist China in 1949, poverty should have disappeared. Anyone who invoked the discourse on poverty was framed as part of the bourgeois conspiracy to defame the Chinese Communist Party and Chairman Mao. Many sociologists who advocated the study of poverty were purged and re-educated during the Anti-Rightist Campaign.[1]

The official position on poverty changed dramatically when Deng Xiaoping assumed power in 1976. In 1978, the central government admitted the prevalence of rural poverty in the third plenary meeting of the Eleventh Party Congress. A report in the meeting indicated that more than 100 million peasants suffered from food insecurity and 25 per cent of production brigades earned less than 40 yuan per capita income per annum. The 40 yuan per capita income became the first official 'poverty line' in 1978.

The origin of the living standard of 40 yuan per capita in 1978 remains obscure. Other estimates adopted by the Ministry of Agriculture might provide a hint. The Commune Management Bureau of the Ministry defined 150 kg of wheat per capita per annum in North China and 200 kg of rice in South China as the poverty line in 1979. Wang estimated that 50 yuan per capita was roughly equivalent to 150 kg of wheat in North China and 200 kg of rice in South China.[2] Therefore, both 40 yuan and 50 yuan per capita were used as poverty measures, and sometimes interchangeably.

Using statistics from the Commune Management Bureau, Table 10.1 shows that the average per capita incomes of 12 per cent of counties (283 counties) were lower than 50 yuan, and the poor population was 87 million. The geographical distribution in Table 10.2 reveals that poor counties were concentrated in Guizhou, Gansu and Henan. The poor

Table 10.1 Distribution of poor counties, 1977–1979[3]

Year	*Number of counties below 50 yuan per capita average income*	*Proportion of all counties (%)*	*Number of counties under 40 yuan*	*Proportion of all counties (%)*	*Brigades under poverty line*	*Proportion of all brigades (%)*
1977	515	22.5	182	7.9	180	39
1978	381	16.3	97	4.3	139	29.5
1979	283	12.4	81	3.5	137	27.2

Table 10.2 Provincial distribution of poor counties with per capita income lower than 50 yuan for 3 consecutive years, 1977–1979[4]

Province	*Number of poor counties*	*Ratio to all poor counties (%)*	*Ratio to counties in the same province (%)*	*Population of poor counties (millions)*	*Ratio to agricultural population in the same province (%)*	*Number of poor counties below 40 yuan*
Guizhou	43	19.6	49.4	13.7	61.1	10
Gansu	26	11.8	32.5	6.6	41.2	10
Hennan	26	11.8	20.2	17.3	27	1
Shandong	24	10.9	19.7	12.8	19.7	3
Yunnan	23	10.4	18	5.5	20	4
Shaanxi	11	5	14.7	1.8	7.7	1
Fujian	11	5	15.9	4.6	22.6	4
Hebei	11	5	7.1	3.2	7.1	
Anhui	10	4.5	12.3	9.4	22.4	3
Shanxi	8	3.6	7.2	1.2	5.8	
Xinjiang	8	3.6	9.4	1.1	16.3	2
Guangxi	5	2.3	5.8	1.6	5.4	
Guangdong	3	1.4	2.8	1.7	3.9	
Ningxia	3	1.4	16.7	0.9	32.4	
Zhejiang	3	1.4	4.3	1.3	4.2	1
Jiangsu	2	0.9	2.7	2.0	4.1	
Sichuan	2	0.9	0.6	1.6	1.9	1
Neimeng	1	0.4	1.2	0.06	0.4	1
Jiangxi	1	0.4	1.1	1.4	5.4	
National total	221			87.9		41

population in Henan alone reached 17 million and accounted for 20 per cent of the national total.

The poverty line provided by the Ministry of Agriculture was replaced by one formulated by the LGEDPA (the Leading Group for the Economic Development of Poor Areas under the State Council) in 1986. Instead of one poverty line, LGEDPA adopted a poverty line which varied with the political importance of the counties. The poverty lines helped the LGEDPA to identify counties as 'nationally designated poor counties' which could apply for poverty alleviation programmes.

While ordinary counties with per capita income below 150 yuan attained the status of nationally designated poor counties, counties of political importance with higher per capita incomes also attained the same status. The poverty line was 200 yuan per capita for counties in old revolutionary base areas, minorities and border areas and 300 yuan for counties in old revolutionary base areas with special contributions. Under the variable poverty line, Table 10.3 indicates that more than two-thirds of all poor counties belonged to the categories of county with political importance.

Once it had selected the designated counties, the LGEDPA seldom adjusted the poverty line officially nor reviewed the status of nationally designated poor counties. Informal adjustment of the poverty line appeared only in fragmentary reports, and the adjustment has been discretionary and unsystematic. For instance, the LGEDPA mentioned that the poverty line for ordinary counties was 200 yuan per capita in 1990, and another report in 1991 suggested 300 yuan.[6] Moreover, the LGEDPA maintained the same list of nationally designated poor counties for more than ten years from 1986. It does not

Table 10.3 Distribution of poor counties under the LGEDPA poverty line, 1986[5]

Ordinary counties with annual per capita income lower than 150 yuan	83
Counties in old revolutionary base area, minorities and border region: annual per capita income between 150 and 200 yuan	95
Counties in old revolutionary base area with special contribution, i.e., Jinggang Shan, Dabi Shan, Taiheng Shan: annual per capita income 200–300 yuan	93
Total number of poor counties	271
Agricultural population	94.5 million
Population under poverty line	45 million

regularly review the list of poor counties. It does not remove counties from the list when their incomes rise over the poverty line nor add to the list new counties that fall below the poverty lines.

PROBLEMS OF POVERTY DEFINITION

These official poverty estimates exhibit many problems of definition, measurement, fairness and vulnerability to bureaucratic manipulation. First, the official estimates are vague and unsystematic. The official definition represents the poverty problem through a vocabulary of solving the *wenbao wenti*, or to help those with inadequate food and clothing. The government only provides a vague monetary value, but never defines the basic standard of food and clothing.

Second, the official poverty line is well below the international standard of absolute poverty. Wang estimated the calorie level of the official Chinese poverty line in 1979 and found that it was only a half to two-thirds of the international standard of absolute poverty.[7] He calculated from the procurement price that 50 yuan in 1979 was equivalent to 150 kg of wheat or 200 kg of rice. 200 kg of rice produce 140–150 kg after processing, which in turn provide 1260–1500 kilocalories per day. This daily consumption is much lower than the international standard of absolute poverty – 2150 kilocalories.

Inflation continues to drive down the official poverty line below the international standard. Wang argues that the poverty line of 150 yuan in 1986 seemed to meet the international standard of absolute poverty when calculated with the procurement price only. Since peasants with insufficient grain have to buy grain from the market rather than from the state, they have to pay higher market prices for grain of lower quality. Furthermore, the food problem intensifies when poor peasants have to sell their grain to the government even though their food is inadequate for domestic consumption. When they buy the grain deficit from the market, they cannot afford to buy the same amount of grain they sold to the government if the procurement price is lower than the market price. Thus, adjustment of the 1986 poverty line shows that it was still below the international standard. If the official poverty line is inadequate to cover basic daily calorie consumption, other basic needs – in clothing, shelter, education and medical services – really become luxuries.

Third, any estimation based on county average per capita income is inaccurate. Although this estimation method can locate high concentrations of poor people, it cannot capture the poor who are dispersed in well-off counties. Poor peasants may cluster at the regional level, and may disperse in townships, villages and households as well. The estimation method over-estimates the incidence of absolute poverty in the 'poor counties', and under-estimates the size of the poor population in well-off counties.

Fourth, the political definition of poverty is inaccurate and unfair. The Chinese government obviously manipulates the definition of poverty and the development programme to pacify the minorities and the populations living in the border areas, and to reward their long-time supporters in the revolutionary bases. This definition thus under-estimates the poor population in ordinary regions and over-estimates the poor population in regions of political importance. As far as fairness is concerned, this method discriminates against the poor in ordinary regions and favours those in special regions.

Fifth, the official estimation is vulnerable to bureaucratic manipulation. Since the method is unstandardized and unsystematic, the bureaucracy can easily manipulate the estimates for its own purposes. The State Council and various departments can manipulate the poverty line, control the proportion of the population defined as 'poor', and proclaim success in poverty eradication. Thus, poverty will definitely be eradicated by the year 2000 under this estimation method.

ALTERNATIVE POVERTY ESTIMATES

An expert group from the World Bank provides an alternative set of poverty estimates, which are more standardized and systematic. First, the group adopts the international definition of absolute poverty – minimum daily consumption of 2150 kilocalories. This redefinition adjusts the poverty line from 50 yuan to 98 yuan at 1978 prices. Second, the study takes account of the inflation effect and adjusts the poverty line systematically from 1978 to 1990 by the inflation index. Third, the study takes account of the dual price system, a feature of the economic reform, and estimates the poverty line both by planned and market prices. Fourth, the estimates take note of statistical error and allow a 10 per cent price adjustment in the poverty line. Finally, the most important improvement this study adopts is the unit of analysis. This expert group uses household per capita income rather than county per capita income. The household income and expenditure data provide more reliable poverty estimates than the county income.

Table 10.4 National poverty lines and incidence of rural population[8]

	1978	*1980*	*1981*	*1982*	*1983*	*1984*	*1985*	*1986*	*1987*	*1988*	*1989*	*1990*
Poverty line (yuan)												
Planned	98	134	158	167	175	179	190	199	210	231	262	275
Procurement	99	135	160	170	175	178	193	206	222	249	292	301
Poverty line index (1985=100)												
Planned	52	71	83	88	92	94	100	105	111	122	138	145
Procurement	51	70	83	88	92	94	100	107	115	129	151	156
Absolute poverty (percentage of households)												
Planned	32.8	26.8	23.4	16.3	14	10	10.7	11.2	10	9.0	11.4	10.7
Procurement	33	27.2	24.3	17.4	14.1	9.9	11.1	12.5	12.1	11.9	14.7	13.3
Absolute poverty (million)												
Planned	260	218	194	140	123	89	96	97	91	86	103	97
Procurement	262	221	202	148	123	88	100	108	109	106	132	121
Absolute poverty (+10%) (million)												
Planned	306	272	255	186	163	119	131	133	124	113	128	121
Procurement	310	276	264	195	164	118	138	146	144	136	168	160

Table 10.4 summarizes the estimates. Taking account of the dual system, the poverty line in 1990 was 275 yuan (planned price) and 301 yuan (market or procurement price); poverty incidence was 10.7 per cent and 13.3 per cent of rural households; the population size was 97 million and 121 million. If we count the 10 per cent estimation error, the number of people in poverty was 121 million and 160 million respectively.

The geographical distribution shown in Table 10.5 illustrates that Gansu (30.4 per cent), Qinghai (21.8 per cent) and Inner Mongolia (20.8 per cent) in 1989 have the highest proportion of poor households in their total populations. Provinces in the north-west and south-west have the highest proportion of poor households and 15–20 per cent of their rural households were below the poverty line.

Although the estimation method proposed by the World Bank study group is more systematic, there is no obvious evidence that the Chinese government has adopted a similar method. The estimates that the Chinese government offers are still vague, unstandardized and unsystematic. For instance, the national seven year poverty-eradication programme never explicitly states the poverty line. The plan suggests helping the poor to attain an income of 500 yuan at the constant price of 1990, but it does not state clearly whether the 500 yuan was the poverty line.[10]

On the other hand, several reports hint that the poverty line in 1995 was 530 yuan, but this amount is inconsistent with 500 yuan at the 1990 constant price. One report in 1996 stated that the size of the poor population with per capita income below 530 yuan had dropped to 65 million, but the source of the figure is unknown.[11] The poverty alleviation meeting convened in 1996 suggested the size of the poor was 65 million but it did not explicitly indicate the poverty line.[12] These reports and meetings converged to indicate the official poverty line at 530 yuan in 1995. This poverty line in 1995, however, is highly inconsistent with the standard in the national seven year plan of poverty eradication – 500 yuan at the constant price of 1990. The average inflation index between 1990 and 1995 increased by double digits each year, so the accumulated inflation index between 1990 and 1995 should result in a figure much in excess of 530 yuan, or about 1000 yuan, in 1995. When the official estimates remain unstandardized and unsystematic, it is difficult to evaluate objectively the effectiveness of poverty alleviation in China. Without objective criteria, the Chinese government can easily manipulate the poverty line for political purposes to claim success in poverty eradication to the public and to the international community.

Table 10.5 Provincial poverty lines and incidence of poverty 1989[9]

		Incidence of poverty: % of households		
	Poverty line (yuan)	*National poverty line*	*Provincial poverty line*	*Difference*
National average	262	11.3	11.3	
North				
Beijing	250	0.2	0.1	0.1
Tianjin	253	0.4	0.4	0.1
Hebei	249	13	11.7	1.3
Henan	254	16.5	15.2	1.4
Shandong	250	6.8	5.9	0.8
North-east				
Liaoning	249	8	7.1	0.9
Jilin	244	12.2	10.7	1.5
Heilongjiang	259	18.3	17.9	0.4
North-west				
Inner Mongolia	247	23.5	20.8	2.7
Shanxi	246	17.4	14.8	2.6
Shaanxi	253	20.3	18.4	1.9
Ningxia	259	18.9	18.4	0.5
Gansu	250	34.2	30.4	3.7
Qinghai	252	23.7	21.8	1.9
Xinjiang	254	18.7	17.6	1.1
Yangtze River				
Shanghai	274	0	0	0
Jiangsu	268	3.4	3.6	–0.2
Zhejiang	278	2	2.3	–0.4
Anhui	268	7.7	8.3	–0.5
Jiangxi	284	5	6.4	–1.3
Hubei	274	6	7	–0.9
Hunan	282	6.2	7.7	–1.5
South				
Fujian	277	1.8	2.1	–0.3
Guangdong	279	0.9	1.1	–0.2
Hainan	277	3.3	3.8	–0.5
South-west				
Guangxi	278	15.4	18.1	–2.6
Sichuan	262	11.2	11.2	0
Guizhou	259	17.8	17.4	0.5
Yunnan	258	19	18.3	0.7

THE POLITICAL ECONOMY OF POVERTY ALLEVIATION

Anti-poverty measures in the eighties

The efforts to alleviate poverty in the 1980s were disjointed and lacked coordination. When the Chinese Communist Party admitted the prevalence of rural poverty, it did not formulate a comprehensive poverty alleviation policy but instead requested various ministries to formulate their own poverty alleviation programmes. The Ministry of Finance offered the first poverty alleviation programme in 1980. It established a Backward Region Development Fund and offered grants to old revolutionary bases, minority areas, border areas and poor areas in 1980, and subsequently set up the Sanxi Agricultural Construction Fund in 1983. The Sanxi Fund helped local government to improve the agricultural and irrigation facilities in notoriously poor regions, in particular the arid regions of Hexi, Dingxi and Xihaigu at the intersection of Shaanxi, Gansu and Ningxia provinces.

The State Planning Commission adopted a Work For Relief project in 1985, which is similar to the public works programmes in other developing countries. In principle, this programme intends to stimulate local governments to invest in infrastructure projects and to stimulate the poor to earn income from participating in these projects. The local governments and peasant workers in China, however, do not get cash as subsidy, but receive food or industrial products in kind or in coupons, that is, grain, clothes or fertilizer. In 1986, the establishment of LGEDPA signified important changes in the poverty alleviation policy. First, the group and its office, PADO (Poor Area Development Office), would coordinate the disjointed poverty alleviation programmes carried out by different ministries. And, most importantly, LGEDPA transformed the spirit of poverty alleviation into economic development, and the forms of assistance from grants to loans. In other words, the central government no longer offered free assistance and the poor counties have to repay the capital as well as the interest in the future. Poverty alleviation was institutionalized in the political domain with the establishment of LGEDPA. The State Council, ministries and various levels of local government formulate their poverty alleviation policies in their Five Year Plans, and establish their *Fupinban* (Poverty Alleviation Office) to formulate and coordinate poverty alleviation programmes. Poverty alleviation programmes can be classified into two types: grant and loan programmes and special projects.

1. Grant and loan programmes offered to designated poor counties

The State Council required all levels of government to establish grants and loans for designated poor counties. As a division of labour, the State Council and ministries offered grants and loans to nationally designated poor counties while provincial governments provided funds for provincially designated poor counties. Table 10.6 indicated that funds came from three sources. First, the Ministry of Finance provided 1 billion yuan each year to improve the agricultural infrastructure of the poor regions, that is, drinking water facilities, arable land, irrigation facilities, and so on. The ministry provided constant support to the Sanxi regions (Hexi of Shaanxi, Dingxi of Gansu and Xihaigu of Ningxia) annually, but considered other applications case by case. Second, the Planning Commission offered the Work for Relief project which granted overstocked commodities worth 200 million yuan to local government, that is, grains,

Table 10.6 Types of poverty alleviation funds 1989[13]

	Million yuan per year	*Rate (%)*
Grant		
Ministry of Finance		
Sanxi Development Fund	200	NA
Development Grant	800	NA
Work for relief		
Planning Commission		
Industrial and agricultural products for work and relief	200 (for 3 years)	
Loans		
People's Bank of China		
Revolutionary bases, minority and remote areas	1 000	3.9
County-run enterprises	400	3.9
Poverty Reduction Fund	1 000	2.4
Pastoral Areas Fund	50	2.4
Agricultural Bank of China		
Economic Development Grant	300	standard rate
Industry and Commercial Bank of China		
County-run enterprises	200	20% discount
People's Construction Bank of China		
County-run enterprises	100	20% discount
Total grants and loans	4 250	

clothes, fertilizer, and so on. The third source was poverty alleviation loans. The national banks provided, in total, around 3 billion yuan of loans to the nationally designated poor counties. Half of the loans were subsidized loans, in which the central government subsidized the interest so that the rate was lower than the market rate. The other loans were reserved for poor counties at market rate or discount rate. With these loans, the central government intended to help poor counties to invest in projects, to improve the agriculture infrastructure, raise food security, and develop rural industries.

2. Special projects of ministries and mass organizations
Besides the provision of grants and loans, the State Council required all ministries and mass organizations to organize their poverty alleviation programmes. Every ministry and mass organization had established their Poverty Alleviation Office (*Fupinban*) to formulate poverty alleviation programmes. For example, the Finance Ministry offered grants to the arid region of Sanxi to improve drinking water facilities, to build irrigation canals and to reclaim land. The Science and Technology Commission set up a series of Science and Technology Poverty Alleviation programmes in the Dabi Mountains. The programme attempts to promote the diffusion of agricultural technology to tackle poverty. *The People's Daily* emphasizes the importance of information diffusion in poverty alleviation. The press thus promotes the exchange of market and technology information through setting up local newspapers with commercial news in the poor regions.[14] Two projects stand out against other programmes. Food and Clothing Engineering (*Wenbao Gongcheng*) aims at raising food security. This programme promotes food subsistence by introducing high yield seeds and agricultural technology. On the other hand, the Spark Project (*Xinhuo Jihua*) attempts to raise peasants' incomes by promoting cash crops or husbandry.

Anti-poverty measures in the nineties

The basic approach of poverty alleviation remained unchanged throughout the 1990s, but there are some changes of detail worth mentioning. First, the Work for Relief Project came to dominate the funding programmes. In 1994, the National Seven Year Poverty Eradication Program increased the annual funding of the Work for Relief Project to 1 billion yuan as grants and 1 billion as low-interest loans. The subsequent national poverty alleviation conference in 1996 further raised the annual funding to 1.5 billion as grants, and loans to 3 billion.[15] Second, the central government adjusted the allocation of poverty alleviation funds as a reaction to the economic polarization between inland and coastal provinces. It no longer funds poor counties in developed provinces and requests developed provinces such as Guangdong, Jiangsu, Fujian, Shandong, Zhejiang and Liaoning to aid their own poor counties. The central government mainly reserves its funds for inland provinces. Third, the central government set up the new China Agricultural Bank to coordinate and monitor poverty alleviation loans. The new bank tries to centralize the coordination of poverty alleviation loans previously operated by various banks. These reforms seem to reflect the determination of the Chinese government in poverty alleviation. This chapter, however, argues that the poverty alleviation policy is severely undermined by the economic myths guiding poverty alleviation policy, bureaucratic politics and market reform.

MARKET MYTH OF THE POVERTY ALLEVIATION POLICY: THE IMPOSSIBILITY OF EFFICIENCY AND TRICKLING DOWN

The poverty alleviation policy does not redistribute resources against the market bias, but rather allocates resources in line with the market bias, which in turn intensifies economic polarization. The policy shift in 1986 signified a critical transformation of the underlying principles of poverty alleviation. These new working principles emphasized marketization, efficiency of grants and loans, and the trickling down of economic development in practice. When these working principles are put into practice, however, poverty alleviation programmes deviate from the original goal. The bureaucracy does not redistribute poverty alleviation funds to develop food security programmes and to help those in need, but instead to income-generating projects and to the well-off.

The economic myths of efficiency and trickling down deflect poverty alleviation programmes from their objectives. While the objective of poverty alleviation policy emphasizes food security, the working principles of economic efficiency and marketization funds emphasizes cash crops and industrial production instead. While the policy emphasizes grants and loans to peasants and the local governments of poor regions, the concern for efficiency and repayability actually diverts the grants and loans to well-off peasants and local governments.

Food security programmes give way to cash crop and township industrialization programmes. When the banks and local governments emphasize economic efficiency rather than poverty alleviation, repayability and profiteering dictate the consideration of grant and loan applications. Food security programmes raise the subsistence level of poor households, but they are not marketized and thus not profitable. Thus local governments do not propose such programmes and the banks do not fund them. Food security programmes cannot compete with cash crops and industrial projects in gaining support. Better-off peasants get the loans and poor peasants are discriminated against. When the banks and local government are concerned with efficiency and credit worthiness, they direct grants and loans to better-off regions and peasants. When better-off local governments and better-off peasants in designated poor counties can afford the mortgage and promise to repay, they succeed in getting the grants. Local governments and peasants in need are continuously marginalized in the poverty alleviation programmes because these programmes are biased by repayability and profitability. Moreover, the poverty alleviation policy ignores basic social services in the poor regions. The concern for economic efficiency neglects basic education and health programmes since they are 'economically inefficient'. When the poverty alleviation policies do not improve basic social provisions, the population in poor regions continues to suffer from the vicious cycle of illiteracy, poor health, indebtedness and underdevelopment.

The central government is not unaware of the institutional bias against the poorest. The government, however, believes that the trickling down of development will eventually solve the inequalities. In theory, the central and local authorities anticipate that marketization and investment in county seat or township enterprises would gradually create jobs for the rural poor. Profits from township and county enterprises would help local governments to generate taxation. The taxation would finance local poverty alleviation programmes. Finally, poor peasants would gradually improve their economic conditions and self-finance their own educational and medical needs. The reality never follows this theory. The following paragraphs examine how the efficiency principles and trickling-down model work in reality.

Banks discriminate against poor communities and peasants in awarding loans. Although the central government allocates 3 billion yuan as poverty alleviation loans, the loans hardly go to the communities and peasants in need. Banks are concerned with risk aversion and profiteering even in managing poverty alleviation loans. These considerations discriminate against the poor communities and peasants in the following ways:

1. Banks suspend and misappropriate poverty alleviation loans. When financial reform emphasizes profiteering and repayability, banks are cautious in giving out poverty alleviation loans, since the loans are risky. Banks used to suspend loans and let the poverty alleviation funds lie idle in the banks. The Guizhou provincial government set aside 94 million yuan for poverty alleviation loans in 1988; the banks still had 65 million yuan lying idle at the end of that year.[16] In many cases, the banks even appropriated poverty alleviation funds as regular loans to earn higher interest. In 1989, the State Council discovered that 18 million yuan were misappropriated for other uses, about 1.5 per cent of the total poverty alleviation fund for that year.[17]

2. Requirement for compulsory local matching fund discriminates against poor communities and peasants. Most poverty alleviation loan programmes require the applicants to provide 20 per cent of equipment purchase credit and 30 per cent of current investment as the local matching fund. The matching fund is an obstacle for communities and peasants who are very poor. They are simply not eligible to apply since they cannot afford the matching funds. As a result, poverty alleviation loans usually go to better-off regions and peasants who can provide the matching funds.[18]

3. Short-term and high-interest loans discourage food security programmes. When the banks are concerned with profit and repayability, they are inclined to offer short-term loans, and higher interest rates for long-term loans. These loan practices are at odds with the objectives of poverty alleviation, discourage long-term agricultural investment, and hinder food security programmes in particular. For example, many banks offer 1 year loans at a rate of 10.08 per cent, 3 year loans at 10.8 per cent and 5 year loans at 11.88 per cent. Moreover, the banks only allow loans of from one- to four-year duration for Food and Clothing Engineering, one to three years for agricultural and husbandry programmes, and the longest five years for forestry programmes. These short-term loan programmes cannot meet the financial needs for long-term agricultural improvements, and defeat the original objectives of poverty alleviation programmes.[19]

4. The commercial and industrial bias hinders food security and agricultural development. The economic development strategy of China favours industrialization and commercial farming. When the banks and local governments are more concerned about profitability than poverty alleviation, they tend to invest in commercial farming and industrial projects. Commercial bias not only deflects from the goal of food security, but also increases the economic risks of local communities and individual peasants. Bureaucratic practices and market uncertainties are associated with the commercial bias. Bureaucratism penetrates poverty alleviation practices, since local bosses try to demonstrate their ability to the higher authorities by getting loans and running large-scale poverty alleviation programmes. Local officials tend to make cursory and irresponsible investment decisions against the will of the community and against the market. Sometimes they even obtain loans illegally to build up their job record. When they are promoted, they leave the communities behind to bear the fruits of their irresponsible decisions.

As a result, poverty alleviation loans not only fail to attain their objectives, but also increase the debts of the localities. In the case of Yilong county in Sichuan province, Fan found that the county government accumulated a total of 48 million yuan in poverty alleviation loans from 1986 to 1991. Since the county government spent most of its income to repay interest and capital, it owed county employees many months of salary. The economic difficulties of Yilong county are common among other poor counties.[20]

BUREAUCRATIC POLITICS

The organization of anti-poverty efforts in China not only exemplifies the bureaucratic politics identified by Lieberthal and Oksenberg, but also hinders the effectiveness of poverty alleviation.[21] The multiple involvement of all the bureaucratic organizations weakens the coordination and monitoring of poverty alleviation efforts. The Chinese government advocates the total mobilization of political and social forces to participate in poverty alleviation and requires all political, economic and societal organizations to formulate their poverty alleviation programmes. The National Seven Year Poverty Eradication Program has virtually required all ministries and societal organizations to bring their expertise to bear on poverty alleviation. Therefore, the various ministries and societal organizations take a variety of different initiatives.[22]

The operations of PADOs at each level of local government are significantly handicapped by the intervention of the many high-ranking bureaucracies running poverty alleviation programmes. A county PADO can hardly monitor the programmes operated by a ministry. Many PADOs fail to coordinate and monitor poverty alleviation programmes to meet the policy objectives. Moreover, when the initiatives and organizations are diverse and scattered, the local governments have to spend extra time and effort to identify and to coordinate the most appropriate policies, loans, matching funds, personnel and resources from the departments involved.[23] Red tape, competition, negligence and even corruption dominate the formulation and implementation of poverty alleviation programmes.

The objectives and practices of multiple bureaucratic organizations are diverse, divided and may even contradict each other. The departments involved can hardly build consensus among themselves, not to mention building consensus with recipients in the local communities. In some cases, the authorities just ignore the needs of local communities and impose poverty alleviation programmes against the wishes of the local community. Zhu and Jiang give an account of a typical conflict between the county and township governments in the Work for Relief project (*yigong daizhen*).[24] Since the county agricultural bureau offered the grant, it restricted local communities to using the grant to improve arable land, no matter what the real needs of the local communities were. A township government believed that the community needed a road more than improvements to arable land and thus secretly diverted the grant to build a road. Finally, the agricultural bureau discovered the 'abuses', punished the township official and forced the township government to return the grant. The interests of high-level bureaucracies are at odds with the needs of local communities. Therefore, local communities find it hard to build consensus with higher authorities on poverty alleviation.

The top-down mobilization in poverty alleviation puts pressure on local state–society relations. Top-down mobilization not only dominates the relations between higher authority and local government, but also intensifies the tensions between local government and local residents. The local residents cannot voice their needs nor oppose the poverty alleviation programmes imposed on them. In some cases, the poverty alleviation programmes cannot improve the livelihood of poor peasants and they can even make the life of poor peasants harder.

Peasants do not benefit much from the Work for Relief project, but sometimes they even suffer from the programme. The Work for Relief project intends to improve the livelihood of peasants by paying peasant workers in kind. The reality never works the way the policy intends. First, local government may withhold the grants and not pay the peasant workers. Since the Work for Relief project requires local governments to provide matching funds, local governments may withhold the compensation as the matching fund when they cannot afford to pay. In other words, local officials convert the paid work into compulsory labour without pay. Zhu and Jiang found that half of the working time that peasants contributed in the Work for Relief project was compulsory labour. In other words, the peasants only got pay for half of the working time. Even when the local government paid the compensation, it paid at a lower rate than the market. Secondly, local residents cannot learn new skills from the projects. Skilled jobs are usually dominated by subcontractors recruited elsewhere rather than from the local community. Local residents are marginalized into manual labour that requires little or no skill. Thirdly, peasants cannot improve their nutrition by receiving payment in kind. The Work for Relief project pays peasant workers not with money, but with coupons for industrial goods or food at a lower price. In many cases, the peasant workers just do not have the money to buy the goods or food that the coupon offers at lower prices. If they sell the coupons, they can only sell the coupons at a highly reduced rate rather than for the face value of the coupons. In short, the peasants regard the Work for Relief project as a levy, not an additional source of income.

This levy on peasants increased when the central government increased the annual budget from 1 billion to 1.5 billion yuan in 1996. The central and local governments only consider the efficiency of this programme, and understate the levy problem. Zhu and Jiang warned that increasing reliance on the Work for Relief project would increase the deficiency in matching funds available to the local governments. Local governments would nevertheless transfer the economic burden to peasants and increase the compulsory working days. The levy on peasants not only persists, but becomes heavier.

The imposition of official poverty alleviation loan programmes induces tension between local officials and peasants. In many cases, local officials introduce poverty alleviation programmes for their own political advantage, rather than out of a concern for the well-being of the community. They make irresponsible investment decisions and coerce peasants into borrowing money. When the local officials are promoted, they leave the peasants behind to bear the consequence of those irresponsible decisions. The Food and Clothing Engineering

Project of Migu County illustrates the tension between the peasants and the officials in an imposed poverty alleviation programme.[25] In the late 1980s, the county government promoted sheep husbandry and grass feed as the poverty alleviation programme. The local officials ignored the conflict of grass feed cultivation with the cycle of grain production. Peasants could not manage both cultivation and sheep husbandry at the same time and, therefore, refused to join the programme. Despite their rejection, the county government forced them to participate. Peasants resisted by selling grass seeds dispatched from the local government to middlemen at a low price. Ironically, the middlemen resold the seeds to the local government at a higher price. Furthermore, the county government did not provide adequate veterinary support and peasants suffered heavily from widespread sheep disease.

The case of Qianyang county reflects similar conflict between local residents and officials induced by the poverty alleviation programme.[26] In 1984, the county government promoted raising milk sheep and silk worms, regardless of the natural environment and peasants' initiative. When many peasants could not fulfil the procurement contract, the county government sent officials to supervise local production. The officials even deployed political means to discipline those who failed to fulfil the terms of the contract. Most peasants cheated the officials by borrowing and lending sheep amongst relatives and neighbours during the inspection. Moreover, the county government forced the peasants to join a brewers wheat cultivation programme but the officials did not experiment with the cultivation beforehand. The wheat grew badly and participants suffered heavily. While the officials would be promoted to other localities, it was the local residents who had to bear the collective and individual debts.

MARKET VOLATILITY AND ITS IMPACT ON POVERTY ALLEVIATION PROGRAMMES

Market volatility is another critical factor that hinders the effectiveness of poverty alleviation programmes. Even when the poverty alleviation programmes prove to be technically feasible and win popular support, their effectiveness is affected by the volatile market. While the Spark Project, and the Food and Clothing Engineering Project strive hard to promote food security and to improve agricultural technology, inflation and speculation make it difficult for poor peasants to obtain the high-yielding seeds and other necessary supplies. Even though the Food and Clothing Engineering Project had won popularity, peasants frequently complained that it was difficult for them to adopt the new cultivation methods. The poverty alleviation departments could not guarantee the supply of plastic sheet, fertilizer, pesticide and high-yield seeds at a low price. Speculation and inflation lifted the price of agricultural inputs to levels that the peasants could no longer afford. Therefore, the peasants had reluctantly to abandon the agricultural technology that they had learnt.[27]

Peasants do not benefit much from the high-yield agricultural technology. They cannot sell the surplus in the market or to the state during good harvests. Since many local governments in the poor regions are in debt, they cannot afford to buy the surplus. Many peasants even received 'I owe you' forms as payment for the contracted procurement. The popularity of high-yield grain cultivation also depressed the market price of the harvest. In many cases, the peasants could not cover the purchase price of agricultural inputs with the money they gained from the sale of their products to the market or the state.[28]

Market volatility intensifies the vulnerability of poor peasants when local officials prefer cash crop projects to food security programmes. Their preference nevertheless leads to numerous agricultural 'fevers'. While the prices of agricultural inputs are raised by intensive competition among individuals, enterprises and governments, the product prices are depressed by the cut-throat competition to sell the surplus. In many cases, the local communities and peasants lose not only the investment and fall into debt, but also the land that provides food subsistence. For example, the 'afforestation and tea fever' in Bohong county plantation transformed acres of arable land to forestry and tea plantations. When the tea and timber markets crashed, the plantations became wasteland.[29] Peasants in poor regions are the most vulnerable to the market when cash crop projects are institutionalized in poverty alleviation programmes.

CONCLUSION

The prospect for poverty eradication by the year 2000 is gloomy. The Chinese government not only fails to regulate the economic inequalities, but also institutionalizes market bias in poverty alleviation policies. These policies do not redistribute resources towards the poorest.

On the contrary, the practices of market efficiency and trickling down embodied in the policies reinforce market inequalities and divert resources to better-off regions and households. The objectives of poverty alleviation are further plagued by bureaucratic politics inherent in state socialism. The multiplicity of organizations involved in poverty alleviation fragments the line of authority and renders coordination difficult. Furthermore, the greater the number of departments and bureaucracies involved, the more difficult it is to build a consensus on the goals and practices of poverty alleviation. Bureaucratism not only hinders the effectiveness of the poverty alleviation policy, the imposition of poverty alleviation projects also leads to heightened tension between local government and local communities. Reliance on marketization increases the market vulnerability of peasants who are already at the brink of poverty.

Notes and references

1. Siu Lun Wong, *Sociology and Socialism in Contemporary China* (London: RKP, 1979).
2. Wang Sangui, 'Zhongguo nongcun de pinkun wenti' ('Rural poverty of China'), *Jingji yu shehui (Economy and Society)*, No. 6 (1991), pp. 1–26.
3. The Commune Management Bureau, Agriculture Ministry, '1977–1979 quanguo qiongxian qingkuang' ('The Profile of Poor Counties across the Country'), *Nongye jingji congkan (The Agricultural Economic Review)*, No. 1 (1981), pp. 48–52.
4. Ibid.
5. LGEDPA, 'Guowuyuan bangongting zhuanfa Guowuyuan pinkun diqu jingji kaifa lingdao xiaozu diyici quanti huiyi jiyao de tongzhi' ('The summary of the first meeting of the Leading Group of economic development and poverty alleviation'), *Zhongguo nongye nianjian 1987(The China Agriculture Handbook 1987)* (Beijing: Nongye chubanshe, 1997).
6. LGEDPA, 'Guowuyuan banggongting zhuanfa Guowuyuan pinkun diqu jingji kaifa lingdao xiaozu guanyu 1988 guojia jiguan fupin gongzuo qingkuang baogao de tongzhi' ('The report of the participation of central ministries in poverty alleviation programs'), *Zhongguo nongye nianjian 1990 (The China Agriculture Handbook 1990)* (Beijing:Nongye chubanshe, 1990), pp. 500–2; LGEDPA, 'Guowuyuan pizhuan Guowuyuan pinkun diqu jingji kaifa lingdao xiaozu guanyu jiushi niandai jin yi bu jiaqian fupin kaifa gongzuo qingshi de tongzhi' ('The report of LGEDP to further the development of poverty alleviation progams in the Nineties'), *Zhongguo nongye nianjian 1991 (The China Agriculture Handbook 1991)* (Beijing:Nongye chubanshe, 1991), pp. 512–14.
7. Wang Sangui, 'Rural poverty of China'.

8. Adapted from World Bank, *China, Strategies for reducing poverty in the 1990s* (Washington, DC: World Bank, 1992), p. 140.
9. Ibid.
10. Editorial, 'Dahao fupin gongkin jian' ('Fight a good war on poverty'), *Renmin ribao*, 27 September 1996.
11. 'Woguo nongcun pinkun renkou jianshao wu bai wan' ('The size of rural poverty has declined by 5 million'), *Shanqu kaifa (Development of Mountainous Regions)*, No. 2 (1996), p. 74.
12. 'Fight Poverty in New Ways', *China Daily,* 24 September 1996, p. 1.
13. Modified from Tong Yamin, 'Pinkun diju de jingji kaifa' ('The economic development of poor regions'), *Zhongguo nongye nianjian 1990 (The China Agriculture Handbook 1990)* (Beijing:Nongye chubanshe, 1990), pp. 125–128.
14. Editorial, 'Dahao fupin gongkin jian' ('Fight a good war on poverty'), *Renmin Ribao*, 27 September 1996.
15. 'Fight Poverty in New Ways', *China Daily,*24 September 1996.
16. Chen Junsheng, '*Guanyu dangqian punkin diqu jingjika zhong di liange wenti''*(Two issues in the economic development of poor regions'), *Kuanyu Zhongguo Fupin Wenti (Issues of Poverty Alleviation in China)* (Beijing: Sanxia Press, 1994), p. 63.
17. Chen Junsheng, '*Chedi ganqu fupin gongzuo zhong de yiche fubi xianxiang* '('Uproot all the corruption practices in poverty alleviation programs'), *Kuanyu Zhongguo Fupin Wenti' (Issues of Poverty Alleviation in China)* (Beijing: Sanxia Press, 1994), p. 56.
18. Han Fujun and Wen Youxiang, 'Guanyu fupin zijin de chouji guanli he shiyong wenti tantao' ('An evaluation of the funding, management and utilization of poverty alleviation loans'), *Kaifa yanjiu (Development Research)*, No. 2 (1991), pp. 52–56.
19. Ibid.
20. Fan Wang, 'Pinkun xian de caizheng kunjing yu chulu – Sichuan Yilong xian caizheng xianzhuang jiqi duice' ('The financial crisis and alternatives of designated poor counties'), *Shanqu kaifa (Development of Mountainous Regions)*, No. 4 (1991), pp. 278–9.
21. Kenneth Lieberthal and Michel Oksenberg, *Policy Making in China: Leaders, Structures and Processes* (Princeton, NJ: Princeton University Press, 1988).
22. 'Guojia ba qi fupin gongjian jihua 1994–2000' ('The Eighth National Seven Year poverty eradication program 1994–2000'), *Zhongguo nongye nianjian 1995 (Agricultural Yearbook, 1995)* (Beijing: Nongye chubanshe, 1995), pp. 521–2.
23. Han Fujun and Wen Youxiang, 'An evaluation of the funding, management and utilization of poverty alleviation loans.'
24. Zhu Ling and Jiang Zhongyi, *Yi gong dai zhen yu huanjie pinkun (Public Works and Poverty Alleviation)* (Shanghai: Sanlian chubanshe, 1995), p. 155.
25. Luo Zhongnan, 'Pinkun shanqu nongye zijin touru wenti zhang'ai ji duice' ('The obstacles and solutions to agricultural investment of poor mountainous regions'), *Shanqu kaifa (Development of Mountainous Regions)*, Vol. 3, No. 1 (1991), pp. 52–4.

26. Xiang Dongfang, Lei Tao, Ge Hong, Cao Huicong, 'Tuopin bixu xian songbang – dui pinkun shanqu Qianyang xian de diaocha' ('Untie before poverty alleviation: an investigation of Qianyang County'), *Jingji gaige (Economic Reform)*, No. 2 (1986), pp. 35–7; Piao Zhishui, Ren Changqing, 'Zhongguo pinkun diqu de ziyuan liudong, shichang yu jingji fazhan' ('Resource flows, market and economic development of poor regions'), *Nongye jingji wenti (Issues of Agricultural Economics)*, No. 3 (1996), pp. 20–8.
27. Yang Zhiyuan and Hong Shaohua, 'Wenbao gongcheng chuyi' ('Reflection on the Food and Clothes Engineering Program'), *Zixun yu juece (Consultation and Decision)*, No. 9 (1989), p. 35–6.
28. Ibid.
29. Luo Minhua, 'Li bi mangmu fazhantigao jidi jianshe xiaoyi – Baokang xian gaoxiao jingji lin fazhan toushi' ('Avoid the blind development, raise the efficiency of production bases'), *Kaifa yanjiu (Development Research)*, No. 1 (1996), pp. 18–20.

11 The Evolution of Family Planning Policies

Siu Yat Ming

The population of China was estimated to be 542 million at the founding of the People's Republic in 1949; the figure had more than doubled when the fourth census was taken in 1990, with the count recorded at 1134 million. The number passed the 1.2 billion mark in 1995. This figure, though large in size, was smaller than that expected by many demographers and China observers. The major reason for this low figure was that natural increase slackened as a result of the declining birth rate. Though there was under-reporting of births, the adjusted figures still showed that there was a decline in fertility in the early 1990s.[1] The major cause of China's fertility decline can be attributed to the continuing success of the state-operated family planning programme.[2] Its achievement in the late 1980s and early 1990s was remarkable, given the increase in the number of women at their prime childbearing age and the fact that the government machinery was losing influence on the people due to the reforms started in 1979. Since the implementation of the national family planning programme in 1973, about 300 million births had been averted by 1995.[3] This achievement is even more notable when China is still classified as a developing country.

Though China is now one of the strongest proponents of family planning, she was once a leading opponent. Economic development, instead of family planning, was considered to be the solution to rapid population growth. The idea that 'development is the best contraceptive' was first introduced in the Second World Population Conference held in Bucharest in 1974.[4] Representatives from Third World countries, led by China, argued that the solution to rapid population growth was fertility decline, which could be brought about by economic development. The promotion of organized family planning programmes was seen as a means used by the Western countries, led by USA, to distract the attention of the Third World countries from tackling the origin of their poverty, which was not population growth but exploitation by the Western countries. The irony is that, though China was the strongest proponent of this idea, she secretly started her national family planning programme in 1973, one year before the Conference was held. As a country which stresses central planning and as a government which has effective control over its people, the success of the family planning programme is beyond doubt. This chapter describes the evolution of China's family planning programme and discusses how it achieved success even though the country was still at a rather low level of economic development.

DEVELOPMENT OR FAMILY PLANNING?

First we need to know why China changed her position on family planning in the 1970s. Why did she use family planning, instead of development, to solve her population problems? The idea that development is the cause of fertility decline in the Western countries can be best described in the demographic transition theory. According to one of its formulators:

> These arrangements [for high fertility], which stood the test of experience throughout the centuries of high mortality, are strongly supported by popular beliefs, formalized in religious doctrine, and enforced by community sanctions. They are deeply woven into the social fabric and are slow to change. Mortality dropped rather promptly in response to external changes because mankind has always coveted health. The decline of fertility, however, awaited the gradual obsolescence of age-old social and economic institutions and the emergence of a new ideal in matters of family size. The new ideal of the small family arose typically in the urban industrial society.[5]

From this statement we can see that the origin of fertility decline is the transition of a society from an agricultural agrarian type to an urban industrial type, which is what development can achieve. However, is there an alternative pathway to achieve fertility decline? The Princeton's European Fertility Project, under the leadership of Ansley Coale, offers an answer.

After careful examination of fertility levels and socio-economic situations in each of the 700 provinces of Europe, Coale comes up with a conclusion that there are many doubts concerning particular points in the demographic transition theory.[6] The diversity of social and economic circumstances in which fertility has declined in Europe, and the consequent difficulties in defining a particular threshold of development which triggers fertility decline, suggest the existence of more than one broad pre-condition for fertility to decline. Freedman further argues that the whole complex of socio-economic factors – which can be collectively termed development – that accompany the demographic transition in the Western countries are certainly sufficient, but not necessary, conditions for fertility decline.[7]

Ansley Coale then proposes his famous 'three pre-conditions' for fertility decline:

> (1) Fertility must be within the calculus of conscious choice. Potential parents must consider it an acceptable mode of thought and form of behaviour to balance advantages and disadvantages before deciding to have another child. (2) Reduced fertility must be advantageous. Perceived social and economic circumstances must make reduced fertility seem an advantage to individual couples. (3) Effective techniques of fertility reduction must be available.[8]

In short, when there is a change in the cost/benefit ratio of children couples will then make a rational choice to practise effective contraception in order to have fewer children. Of course, the question right now is: 'How to change the cost/benefit ratio of children?' Advocates of the 'development' explanation will consider economic and social development as the solution, but advocates of the 'family planning' explanation see that this ratio can be influenced by government programmes. The situation is particularly acute in the less developed countries, since the speed of mortality decline in these countries, which is mainly caused by the importation of advanced medical technology, is faster than that of the more developed countries, resulting in a larger and more rapid population increase. Development is a long-term solution, but the less developed countries need a quicker solution to their immediate problem.

One of the effective means to reduce population growth is organized family planning. Of course, if the cost/benefit ratio of children has been changed, the family planning programme can play a more passive role by simply providing effective contraceptive means and knowledge to the public. However, if the cost/benefit ratio has not been changed or the change is small, then a *laissez-faire* approach to family planning may not achieve the desired aims. A more aggressive family planning programme, together with a change in the social structure, are needed.[9] This is the method that China chooses to adopt.

CHINESE FAMILY PLANNING: FROM THE FIFTIES TO THE NINETIES

There is a mistaken view that China started her family planning programme in the 1970s. Some even take the 'one-child policy' as China's first family planning programme. In fact, China launched her first family planning campaign in the mid-1950s, though the progress of family planning in China was not a smooth one.

In the fifties

In the early period following the founding of the People's Republic, the economy recovered after a long period of war. With an improvement in the social and economic conditions, the death rate dropped remarkably, whereas the birth rate remained at a fairly high level due to a post-war baby boom. As a result, China's population grew rapidly. At that time views on family planning were mainly negative. Western ideas, particularly the Malthusian, on population explosion were rejected by the communists. Mao Zedong said in 1949:

> It is a very good thing that China has a big population. Even if China's population multiplies many times, she is fully capable of finding a solution; the solution is production. The absurd argument of Western bourgeois economists like Malthus that increases in food cannot keep pace with increases in population was not only thoroughly refuted in theory by Marxists long ago, but has also been completely exploded by the realities in the Soviet Union and the Liberated Areas of China after their revolutions ...
>
> Of all things in the world, people are the most precious. We believe that revolution can change everything and that before long there will arise a new China with a big population and a great wealth of products, where life will be abundant and culture will flourish. All pessimistic views are utterly groundless.[10]

This kind of pronatalist idea was prevalent in the early years when the People's Republic was established. *The People's Daily* even wrote an editorial in January 1952 saying that limiting births would destroy China.

The attitude began to change in the middle of 1953 when China took her first population census. Apparently the government leaders received preliminary figures from the census which counted a population about 100 million larger than the official figure used previously.[11] In August 1953 the State Council then instructed the Ministry of Health to assist the people to practise birth control, but this instruction was not implemented because a consensus had not been reached within the government.[12]

The first public proposal for birth control was made not by a government official but by a scholar, Shao Lizi, in the People's Congress on 18 September 1955. Shao, a proponent of birth control even before 1949, further published an article in *Guangming Daily* on 19 December 1954 calling for the dissemination of contraceptive knowledge to the public.

In December 1954, the Central Government held a forum on family planning in Beijing, at which Liu Shaoqi, the premier, explicitly pointed out, 'What we must affirm here is that the Party is in favour of family planning'.[13] However, in the same speech, he also pointed out that there were people opposed to this point of view and he also instructed government officials not to promote family planning openly, especially in the rural areas.

After the forum, the government designated the departments concerned to organize research groups on family planning and to work out methods of publicizing this work. In March 1955, the CCP Central Committee issued a directive on controlling population, instructing the Ministry of Public Health to help the people to practise family planning and to improve the provisions on contraception and induced abortion.[14] Family planning was eventually discussed in public and even *The People's Daily* released an editorial on 5 March 1957 to promote family planning.

The first family planning campaign, however, did not last long. Beginning in the second half of 1957, the continuous growth of population came to be seen as the law governing population growth in socialist societies, while the idea of birth control was criticized as the Malthusian theory on population. The family planning programme was finally abandoned after Mao Zedong launched his Great Leap Forward, when statistical fabrications suggested that food supply had increased enough to feed the large and ever-growing population.

Table 11.1 Fertility in China, 1950–1996

Year	*Crude birth rate* *National*	*Total fertility rate* *National*	*Rural*	*Urban*
1950	37.00	5.81	5.96	5.00
1951	37.80	5.70	5.90	4.72
1952	37.00	6.47	6.67	5.52
1953	37.00	6.05	6.18	5.40
1954	37.97	6.28	6.39	5.72
1955	32.60	6.26	6.39	5.67
1956	31.90	5.85	5.97	5.33
1957	34.03	6.41	6.50	5.94
1958	29.22	5.68	5.78	5.25
1959	24.78	4.30	4.32	4.17
1960	20.86	4.02	4.00	4.06
1961	18.02	3.29	3.35	2.98
1962	37.01	6.02	6.30	4.79
1963	43.37	7.50	7.78	6.21
1964	39.14	6.18	6.57	4.40
1965	37.88	6.08	6.60	3.75
1966	35.05	6.26	6.96	3.10
1967	33.96	5.31	5.85	2.91
1968	35.59	6.45	7.03	3.87
1969	34.11	5.72	6.26	3.30
1970	33.43	5.81	6.38	3.27
1971	30.65	5.44	6.01	2.88
1972	29.77	4.98	5.50	2.64
1973	27.93	4.54	5.01	2.39
1974	24.82	4.17	4.64	1.98
1975	23.01	3.57	3.95	1.78
1976	19.91	3.24	3.58	1.61
1977	18.93	2.84	3.11	1.57
1978	18.25	2.72	2.97	1.55
1979	17.82	2.75	3.05	1.37
1980	18.21	2.24	2.48	1.15
1981	20.91	2.63	2.91	1.39
1982	22.28	2.86	3.32	1.58
1983	20.19	2.42	2.78	1.34
1984	19.90	2.35	2.70	1.22
1985	21.04	2.20	2.48	1.21
1986	22.43	2.42	2.77	1.24
1987	23.33	2.59	2.94	1.36
1988	22.37	2.52	–	–
1989	21.58	2.35	2.54	1.55
1990	21.06	2.31	–	–

Table 11.1 Continued

Year	*Crude birth rate* *National*	*National*	*Total fertility rate* *Rural*	*Urban*
1991	19.68	2.20	–	–
1992	18.24	2.00	–	–
1993	18.09	–	–	–
1994	17.70	–	–	–
1995	17.12	–	–	–
1996	16.98	–	–	–

Sources: 1. Crude birth rates are taken from *Statistical Yearbook of China*, 1991 and 1997 issues.
2. Total fertility rates are taken from Yao Xinwu and Yin Hua, *Basic Data of China's Population* (Beijing: China Population Publishing House, 1994), p. 144.

Hence, population growth remained out of control and more than 20 million babies were born annually, with the total fertility rate reaching six births per woman and a crude birth rate above 30 per thousand. Table 11.1 presents China's fertility data from the 1950s to the mid-1990s. China's fertility in the 1950s remained at a high level for both the rural and urban populations, except for a sudden depression during the three years of famine from 1959 to 1961, showing that the result of the first family planning programme was not promising.

In the sixties

This was a period in which the Chinese government again focused attention on controlling population growth and formally implemented family planning programmes in the urban areas with great success.

After a period of plunging fertility rates and negative population growth due to economic hardship, there began in 1962, when the economy recovered, a baby boom which pushed the fertility rate to its highest level since the establishment of the PRC. Due to the grain procurement system, the Chinese government had to provide grain for the urban residents and a large urban population meant a heavy burden on the government, particularly in times of economic hardship. In 1962, Vice-Premier Chen Yun called for reducing the size of the urban population in order to solve the economic problems at that time.[15] To achieve this aim, the government, on the one hand, reclassified cities and towns to abolish some of them or to make the size smaller and, on the other hand, launched a well-organized family planning programme in the urban areas.

Under these circumstances, the CCP Central Committee and the State Council jointly issued the directive on 'Earnestly Carrying out Family Planning'[16] on 18 December 1962, which called for family planning in cities and densely populated countryside. Population growth should be controlled and fertility would be transformed from an unplanned to a planned state. The directive explicitly pointed out this would be an established component in China's socialist construction. Since then, family planning has formally become an established policy. Consequently, in 1964, the State Council set up a family planning committee together with an office to take charge of family planning work. Similar organizations were also established in local governments.

In 1965, the Chinese government put forward a series of specific policies and measures for controlling population growth. It also set the target of population growth and concrete demands regarding the number of births: 'one is enough, two is just good, three is too many'.[17] Free and more effective contraceptives, such as pills and intra-uterine devices, were distributed to the masses. During this period, family planning was first tried out in the cities and then gradually spread to the rural areas. As a result, fertility rate in many big and medium-sized cities dropped to some extent in the 1964–7 period, but since family planning was not earnestly carried out in the vast rural areas, the fertility rate of the country as a whole remained very high. The data in Table 11.1 also clearly show that urban fertility fell drastically in 1964 and the trend continued throughout the 1970s. But women in the rural areas still maintained a high level of fertility, making the fertility rate of the country as a whole about six children per woman during this period, since over 80 per cent of the population resided in the countryside.

Then came the Cultural Revolution in 1966. Like other programmes, family planning had to come to a halt. Diffusion of the programme to the rural areas was therefore delayed.

In the seventies

This was a period in which the Chinese government had a consensus on the population problem and started to implement a nation-wide family planning programme which led to an unprecedentedly rapid decline in fertility.

After 1971, when the chaotic conditions caused by the Cultural Revolution were brought under control and the central government began to pay more attention to practical matters, family planning work resumed. Premier Zhou Enlai played a leading role, though not publicly announced, in reviving the family planning programme. On many occasions he gave personal guidance to the programme. For example, in 1969 he said in a symposium on national planning: 'too many marriages and babies were born during the Cultural Revolution. We need family planning, we need contraception.'[18] On 8 July 1971, the State Council approved a report on 'Doing Better Family Planning Work' which called for strengthening leadership over family planning work and better propaganda to promote late marriage and birth planning.[19]

Family planning work began to spread to the countryside. The Family Planning Leading Group, headed by Hua Guofeng, was formed in the State Council on 16 July 1973. The national family planning programme, well-known by its slogan *wan, xi, shao* ('later, longer and fewer') which was first put forward in a national meeting on family planning in December 1973,[20] was expanded to cover the whole country, except for the minorities. Couples were encouraged to marry at older ages, to have longer intervals between births, and to have fewer babies. *Yige bushao, liangge zhenghao, sange duole* ('One is not too few, two is enough, three is too many') was again taken as the slogan, indicating that having two children was the norm, but one was also preferred.

Unlike the previous two campaigns, the Chinese government was more serious this time. The importance of family planning could be deduced from its inclusion in the constitution. The constitution amended at the First Session of the Fifth National People's Congress in 1978 explicitly stipulated: 'the state advocates and encourages family planning', and made family planning a basic right and duty of the citizens.[21] Policies and administrative measures incompatible with family planning were revised, and policies and stipulations conducive to controlling the growth of population were formulated. Beginning in 1973, the target of population growth was incorporated into the national economic development plan.

Due to the government's strenuous efforts, fertility declined at a rapid pace. From Table 11.1 we can see that fertility in the rural areas, as well as the national figures, fell in the 1970s. There was a gradual drop in the crude birth rate from 33.4 per thousand to 17.8 per thousand during the 1970–9 period, and the total fertility rate also decreased from 5.44 to 2.75 during the same period.

A more stringent policy, commonly referred to as the 'one-child policy' by Western scholars, was introduced in 1979. The first announcement of this policy was an editorial made in the *Renmin ribao* on 27 January 1979, entitled 'Great Importance Should be Attached to Family Planning Work', and advocating a policy favouring one child per couple. Under this policy, each couple was encouraged to have only one child. As a result, the number of children will not be enough to 'replace' their parents. Such a policy, if successful and carried out for an extended period of time, will lead to a decrease in population. The major reason why this 'below-replacement' policy was introduced was an economic one. Leaders at the top believed that a large population base was detrimental to China's economic growth. The target of the policy was to limit the size of the population to no more than 1.2 billion by the end of the twentieth century. To achieve this, couples were urged to have no more than one child. On 11 August 1979, Vice-Premier Chen Muhua wrote a long essay of more than 7000 words in the *People's Daily* entitled 'To realize the four modernizations, it is necessary to control population growth in a planned way'. It was the first time that a high-ranking official in the Chinese government had publicly revealed the urgency of the population problem and argued in great detail for a more stringent family planning policy.[22]

The details of this policy, however, were not clearly stated when the policy was introduced. More concrete instructions were given in the following decade.

In the eighties

This was a period in which China's policies on population and family planning were laid down and improved, though after trial and error which led to a fluctuation in fertility.

On 25 September 1980, the CCP Central Committee and the State Council jointly issued an 'Open Letter to All the Communist Party Members and the Communist Youth League Members Regarding the Control of China's Population Growth', which explained the urgency and importance, both ideologically and practically, of family planning. The Open Letter called for every member to have only one child per couple so as to set an example to the masses. Apart from arguing against the negative consequences of a one-child-per-couple policy, the letter also pointed out that the policy might last for only about 30 years, after which a more lenient policy would be sufficient to deal with a less pressing population problem. Furthermore, in September of the same year, the Third Session of the Fifth National People's Congress adopted the new Marriage Law, which stipulated, 'both husband and wife have a duty to practise family planning', and 'late marriage and late childbearing should be encouraged'. The new Marriage Law, however, put the minimum age for marriage at 22 for men and 20 for women, which was lower than those prescribed by executive orders, though higher than those required by the previous version of the Marriage Law. One of the reasons for this change was to relieve the tension between the government and the people caused by the executive order on late marriage, which was one of the major determinants of fertility decline in the 1970s. However, an unexpected outcome of this change was an increase in the number of new marriages in the following years, which led to an increase in fertility.[23]

The family planning programme was rigorously pursued in the next few years, partly due to the upsurge of fertility in 1981 and 1982. The number of birth control operations, which included IUD insertions, sterilizations and abortions, jumped to a historical high in 1983 (see Table 11.2). Furthermore, a resurgence of infanticide, particularly of female babies, was widely discovered in many places. Numerous stories of female infanticide and mistreatment of mothers who bore female babies were reported in both local and national newspapers.[24] The situation was so disastrous that the national leaders made several statements condemning this practice,[25] showing that the government also believed that the number of infanticides had reached alarming proportions. Western scholars attributed this sad event to the stringent 'one-child policy'.[26] Female babies were more likely to be the victims since the family planning policy restricted the number of children to one or at most two; some couples who did not have a son resorted to this brutal act in order to dispose of the daughter to make room for them to have another birth, hopefully a son.

As a result, the relationship between the government and the people was damaged. Misgivings and resistance were widespread, particularly in the rural areas. A backlash from the people caused the replacement of the Minister of the State Family Planning Commission, Qian Xinzhong, by his deputy, Wang Wei.

Wang Wei followed a more moderate path and sought ways to restore the relationship between the government and the people. Coercion and command were prohibited. Instead, a more moderate work style was called for to carry out the family planning work. The essence of the newly proposed work style could be summarized as the

Table 11.2 Percentage distribution of birth control operations in China, 1972–1995

Year	*IUD insertion*	*Vasectomies*	*Tubal ligations*	*Induced abortions*	*Total operations* %	*Number*
1972	51.69	9.62	11.70	26.99	100.00	(17 836 821)
1973	58.25	8.07	12.34	21.34	100.00	(23 948 801)
1974	59.10	6.79	10.69	23.42	100.00	(21 285 442)
1975	60.31	9.56	11.82	18.31	100.00	(27 760 648)
1976	56.51	7.27	13.16	23.05	100.00	(20 572 845)
1977	54.98	11.09	11.77	22.16	100.00	(23 597 206)
1978	55.84	3.91	12.79	27.46	100.00	(19 632 676)
1979	47.62	5.92	18.70	27.77	100.00	(28 292 444)
1980	43.82	5.20	14.65	36.33	100.00	(26 225 029)
1981	48.69	3.06	7.32	40.93	100.00	(21 246 929)
1982	44.46	3.89	12.41	39.25	100.00	(31 645 718)
1983	33.57	8.24	31.01	27.18	100.00	(52 885 218)
1984	42.96	4.73	19.81	32.50	100.00	(27 351 735)
1985	40.98	2.46	9.77	46.78	100.00	(23 368 080)
1986	40.66	3.94	11.14	44.26	100.00	(26 162 349)
1987	44.68	5.82	14.64	34.85	100.00	(30 098 097)
1988	41.37	3.59	12.15	42.89	100.00	(29 555 688)
1989	40.25	5.60	15.66	38.49	100.00	(26 965 189)
1990	37.86	4.49	16.29	41.36	100.00	(32 627 200)
1991	34.61	6.71	19.02	39.67	100.00	(35 512 274)
1992	39.01	3.32	17.40	40.27	100.00	(25 866 382)
1993	n.d.	n.d.	n.d.	n.d.	n.d.	
1994	52.79	3.78	18.31	25.12	100.00	(25 028 547)
1995	56.00	3.37	17.61	23.02	100.00	(23 270 230)

Note: No data for Liaoning, Xizang, Ningxia and Xinjiang in 1989, for Guangdong and Xinjiang in 1990, for Heilongjiang, Guangdong and Sichuan in 1992, for Xizang in 1994 and 1995.
n.d.: no data
Sources: For 1972–92, *Zhongguo weisheng nianjian* (Almanac of China's Health) (Beijing: Renmin weisheng chubanshe 1994). For 1994–5, *Zhongguo renkou nianjian* (China Population Statistics Yearbook) (Beijing: Zhongguo tongji chubanshe, 1996).

'three priorities' (*san weizhu*): regular work in lieu of shock methods, contraception in lieu of abortion, and propaganda and education in lieu of economic penalties.[27] The policy of 'open a small hole to close up a large one' (*kai xiaokouzi, du dakouzi*) was introduced in 1984, which allowed more couples to have second births. This policy increased the percentage of couples who could have second births from five to ten. In 1986, a further relaxation of the policy was introduced which increased the percentage of couples who could have second births to 20. As a result of the loosening in family planning policy, fertility increased (see Table 11.1). In both the urban and rural areas, the total fertility rates rose during the period between 1985 and 1987. This raised criticisms from within and outside the government which led to the dismissal of Wang Wei.[28]

Peng Peiyun succeeded Wang Wei as Minister of the Commission in 1988. She believed that the problem was not in the content of the policy itself but in the implementation. She insisted that family planning policies should be stabilized and, with this reason, she rejected the suggestions put forward by hard-liners to overturn the relaxed policy. Instead, she further expanded the quota of couples who could have second births to about 50 per cent by introducing the notion of *dunu hu* ('single daughter household'), allowing couples whose first birth was a girl to have a second birth. By 1989, four policy categories emerged for couples living in the rural areas.[29] The first category, comprising 18 provinces and autonomous regions, allowed *dunu hu*: couples whose first child was a girl could have a second child after a spacing of several years. The second category followed a more stringent policy under which parents could have only one child. This was operated in 'progressive' areas such as Beijing, Tianjin, Shanghai, Jiangsu and Sichuan. The third category allowed all couples to have second births, irrespective of the sex of their first child. Six provinces and autonomous regions were in this category, namely Guangdong, Hainan, Yunnan, Ningxia, Qinghai and Xinjiang. The fourth category referred to the minority nationalities who were allowed to have more than two births. Urban residents and government employees, however, were still restricted to having no more than one child.

Though the restrictions had been relaxed, fertility levels did not show an upward trend but declined instead after 1988 (see Table 11.1). In short, the 1980s saw an oscillatory cycle in terms of 'loosening or tightening up' the family planning policy,[30] which resulted in fluctuations in the fertility rate.

In the nineties

The economic reform continued into the 1990s, resulting in the rapid growth of the national economy. The family planning policy in the 1990s kept being revised and adapted to the improving economic situation. Fertility continued to decline.

Table 11.1 shows that the crude birth rate started to decline in the mid-eighties and kept on declining throughout the first half of the 1990s, despite an increase in the number of women at the prime child-bearing age during this period. Though there was a relaxation in the content of the policy as compared with the mid-eighties, Peng Peiyun attributed the decline to increased emphasis on family planning by leaders at all levels and rapid economic development, which lowered couples' fertility aspirations.[31] Believing that the problem was not the policy itself but poor enforcement, Peng was successful in winning support from the leaders at the top to order leaders at every level to be responsible for the implementation of family planning work (*diyi bashou qinzi zhua*).[32] They were required to conduct meetings to receive reports on population and family planning and to discuss the strategies necessary to carry out family planning work. Starting from 1991, the CCP and State Council held a symposium on family planning every year conducted by Jiang Zemin and Li Peng, demonstrating the importance attached by the national leaders to this matter. Furthermore, failure in family planning could veto success in other works (*yipiao foujie quan*). This new 'responsibility system' placed the duty of birth control in the hands of provincial or county governors and party secretaries and not their deputies. This also elevated the importance of the achievement of population goals to a level equal to that of economic goals.

The emphasis of the current family planning programme can be summarized as a 'three-three' approach.[33] The first 'three' stands for the three directives that will continue to remain in force: first, the overall family planning policy; second, the national population target; and third, the directive that the top local party and government leaders are responsible for efforts in family planning. The stability of the policies is deemed important to the success of the family planning programme. The rough journey of the past experiences, notably that in the 1950s and 1960s, testifies to this claim. As an outside critic observed, 'the success of the Chinese family planning programme is due to a clear enunciation of goals and a precise definition of action strategies'.[34]

Priority, as stressed by the State Family Planning Commission, will be given to the second 'three', which are the 'three priorities' (*san weizhu*) in the work style of implementing family planning. Introduced in 1983, the 'three priorities' approach stresses regular work using education and propaganda to promote the use of contraception in order to limit births. Experience in implementing the policies, particularly in the 1980s, points to the problems arising from the 'cycles of coercion'.

Emphasis is put on work styles which can ease the tension between the cadres and the masses, thus making the goals and methods of family planning more acceptable. As an official in the State Family Planning Commission noted, China's low fertility level is mainly achieved and maintained by a strong executive mechanism which creates a lot of conflict between the cadres and the masses.[35] Furthermore, the fertility level will not be stable if it is maintained only by external social control. A change in the social structure is needed to cultivate an environment conducive to low fertility. The next 'three' approach is designed to fulfil this goal.

The final 'three' approach refers to the 'three combinations' (*san jiehe*) which aim to integrate family planning work with rural economic development. Apart from adopting the 'three priorities' in work style, Peng Peiyun also promotes the 'three combinations' (*san jiehe*) approach, which has had great success in some provinces such as Jilin, Sichuan and Jiangsu. This is an integrated approach which combines family planning programmes in rural areas with developing the local economy, helping peasants to become better off through hard work, and building progressive and happy families. Instead of relying on coercive measures, this approach offers economic incentives for peasants to have fewer children. Local governments have preferential policies in allocating loans and providing scientific consultancy to farmers who opt for fewer children. Therefore, though the policy is relaxed, people will prefer to have a lower fertility when the economy is developed. Low fertility can be achieved by an external social control, but it has to be maintained by a change in the aspirations for children, which can be brought about only by a change in the social structure.

In short, family planning policies and work should be stabilized, perfected and be integrated with other development programmes so as to achieve the 'two transformations' (*liangge zhuanbian*) which make up the major theme of the national family planning work conference in 1997. The first transformation is changing from doing family planning work for the sake of family planning alone to integrating it with other social and economic development programmes. The second transformation is changing the family planning work from relying on an external social control mechanism to a basically internal benefit-driven mechanism, assisted by external social control.

Economic development can provide a social structure which is conducive to low fertility, but the level of fertility expected by the government may be still somewhat lower than that which a Chinese peasant is willing to attain. With an increase in their income, the peasants are willing to pay the fines in order to have more babies. As noted by a *New York Times* correspondent, 'in many parts of China, the one-child policy is melting away'.[36] Faced with improving economic conditions and new challenges, will the Chinese government lift the restrictions on the number of babies her people can have?

CONCLUSION

The progress of China's family planning programme has not been smooth, but it has accomplished its mission to bring down China's fertility rate. Today the mortality and fertility rates are both low, and at levels such that China can be regarded as having completed her demographic transition. The Chinese government is particularly proud of this and usually refers to this as an achievement 'in advance' of the economic condition. However, this success does not come without problems in its wake.

There are two major demographic consequences accompanying the fertility decline. One is the rapid ageing of the population which is an unavoidable consequence of rapid fertility decline. The problem is particularly acute in China because the speed of the fertility decline is much faster than that experienced by the more developed countries, but her economy is not sufficiently developed to be able to provide enough old age security to all needy persons in the future. The economic reform further weakens the financial resources of the government, which means that security in old age will become more dependent on individual rather than collective responsibility.

The other demographic consequence is an escalation in the sex ratio of young children, especially of babies, which began in the 1980s, as shown in Table 11.3. This is not a direct consequence of fertility decline. Reasons for this imbalance of the sexes are many, and the major one is under-registration of female births. However, there are also reports that female infanticides occurred in the early 1980s and prenatal sex determination and sex-selective abortion has been practised since the second half of the 1980s.[37] Whatever cause one attributes it to, the underlying reason for this upsurge in sex ratio for young children is the limitation of the number of children one can have in a culture of son preference.

In this respect, the rise in the sex ratio reflects a failure in the implementation of the 'one-child policy'. Though the quantity of children is the focus of this policy, the quality of children should not be neglected or

Table 11.3 Reported sex ratio at birth in China, 1979–1993

Year	*Sex ratio*	*Year*	*Sex ratio*	*Year*	*Sex ratio*	
					Weighted	*Unweighted*
1970	105.9	1980	107.4	1990	–	114.7
1971	105.2	1981	107.1	1991	117.4	116.1
1972	107.0	1982	107.2	1992	117.4	114.2
1973	106.3	1983	107.9	1993	115.6	114.0
1974	106.6	1984	108.5			
1975	106.4	1985	111.4			
1976	107.4	1986	112.3			
1977	106.7	1987	111.0			
1978	105.9	1988	108.1			
1979	105.8	1989	113.9			

Sources: 1. Data for 1970–88 are from Liang Jimin and Chen Shengli, *Quanguo shengyu jieju chouyang diaocha fanxi shujujuan* (Statistics for National Fertility and Birth Control Sample Survey) (Beijing: Zhongguo renkou chubanshe 1993).
2. Figure for 1989 is from *Tabulation on the 1990 Population Census of the People's Republic of China* (Beijing: China Statistical Publishing House, 1993).
3. Weighted figures for 1991–3 are quoted from the report of the 1993 Population Change Survey, *Zhongguo renkou tongji nianjian 1994* (*China Population Statistics Yearbook 1994*) (Beijing: Zhongguo tongji chubanshe, 1994) pp. 3–4. Unweighted figures for 1990–3 are calculated from birth statistics collected by the annual Population Change Surveys published in various issues of *Zhongguo renkou tongji nianjian* (*China Population Statistics Yearbook*) (Beijing: Zhongguo tongji chubanshe, 1991, 1992, 1993, 1994).

even sacrificed in order to achieve the quantity goal. The current tactic of holding leaders at every level responsible for family planning may have exerted pressure on these leaders to produce faked data or to emphasize the quantity at the expense of the quality of births. There are already discussions among Chinese scholars on this issue. It has been proposed to lessen the over-emphasis on quantity, though there is also a counter-proposal which argues for the importance of number.[38] The former group favours a relaxation of the family planning policy in order to avoid some of the negative consequences caused by this stringent policy. The latter argues for a continuation of a tough policy to avoid an out-of-control surge in childbearing. John Aird, a former chief of the China Branch in the United States Census Bureau and a long-time China observer, also suggested when he gave testimony to an Australian parliamentary committee in 1995[39] that the 'one-child policy' might be relaxed due to growing public resistance.

Will China change its policy on family planning? Replies given by government officials are negative.[40] On many occasions national leaders declare firmly that the policy will not change. The themes of two of the annual family planning symposiums of the CCP and State Council conducted by Jiang Zemin clearly state that population control is the job of a government and should not be left to the market.[41] Peng Peiyun, the Minister of the State Family Planning Commission, further insists that family planning is not an individual affair and thus will not be left to be regulated by the market – as, by contrast, is the case with the economy.[42] In his report delivered at the Fifteenth National Congress of the Communist Party of China on 12 September 1997, Jiang Zemin restated that population growth had caused great strains on resources and the environment. Thus he stressed that the CCP 'should stick to the basic State policies of family planning and environmental protection, correctly handling the relationship of economic development versus population, natural resources and the environment'.[43]

Given that the per capita concept still prevails, all indicators in economic development will be influenced by the absolute size of the population. In order to maintain a prosperous growth in the economy, at least on paper, the Chinese government will be very reluctant to alter its family planning policy, not to mention the release of state control to the people on this issue. Therefore, it is unlikely that there will be any drastic change in China's family planning policy, even though Chinese society has changed a lot due to the economic reforms. In this regard, a statement presented by an American demographer to the Congress of the United States in 1991 still holds:

> Whereas future leadership or regime changes may lead to more fundamental economic or political reforms, relieving the contradictions between plan and market, even the most liberal population advisors advocate a two-child limit. Although the particulars of policy may change, China is unlikely to abandon the principle of state-regulated child-bearing for a long time to come.[44]

Notes and references

1. Zeng Yi, 'Woguo 1991–1992 nian shengyulu shifou dada diyu tidai shuiping?' ('Has China's Fertility in 1991 and 1992 Been Far Below the Replacement Level?') *Renkou yanjiu* (*Population Research*), 1995.3 (May 1995), pp. 7–14.
2. The programme in Chinese literally means birth planning. In order to be consistent with the term used in the English literature, the term

'family planning' and 'birth planning' are used interchangeably throughout the text, though these two terms do not mean exactly the same.

3. Editorial, *Zhongguo renkou bao* (*China's Population News*), 15 February 1995, p. 1.
4. Michael S. Teitelbaum, 'Relevance of Demographic Transition Theory for Developing Countries', *Science*, Vol. 188 (May 1975), p. 420.
5. Frank W. Notestein, 'Economic Problems of Population Change', in *Proceedings of the Eighth International Conference of Agri-Economists* (London: Oxford University Press, 1953).
6. Ansley J. Coale, 'The Demographic Transition', United Nations, *The Population Debate: Dimensions and Perspectives: Papers of the World Population Conference, Bucharest, 1974* (New York: The United Nations, 1975), pp. 347–55.
7. Ronald Freedman, 'Overview', in Lee-Jay Cho and Kazumasa Kobayashi (eds) *Fertility Transition of the East Asian Populations* (Honolulu: University of Hawaii Press, 1979), pp. 286–98.
8. Ansley Coale, 'The Demographic Transition', p. 353.
9. For a discussion of this argument, see Kingsley Davis, 'Population Policy: Will Current Programs Succeed?', *Science*, Vol. 158 (10 November 1967), pp. 730–9.
10. Mao Zedong (Mao Tse-tung), 'Bankruptcy of the Idealist Conception of History', *Selected Works of Mao Tse-tung, Volume IV* (Beijing: Foreign Languages Press, 1969), pp. 453–4.
11. John S. Aird, *Slaughter of the Innocents: Coercive Birth Control in China* (Washington, DC: The AEI Press, 1990), p. 21.
12. *Dangdai Zhongguo de jihua shengyu shi ye* (*Birth Planning in Contemporary China*), (Beijing: Dangdai Zhongguo chubanshe, 1992), p. 6.
13. Liu Shaoqi, 'Tichang jieyu' ('Promoting Birth Control') in *Zhongguo renkou nianjian 1985* (*Almanac of China's Population 1985*) (Beijing: Zhongguo shehui kexue chubanshe, 1986), pp. 4–5.
14. Xiao Zhenyu, 'China's Population Policy and Family Planning', in China Financial and Economic Publishing House, *New China's Population* (New York: Macmillan, 1988), p. 217.
15. Shi Chengli, *Zhongguo jihua shengyu huodongshi* (A History of China's Birth Planning Activities) (Urumqi: Xinjiang renmin chubanse, 1988), p. 142.
16. *Zhongguo renkou nianjian 1985* (*Almanac of China's Population 1985*), (Beijing: Zhongguo shehui kexue chubanshe, 1986), p. 14.
17. Xiao Zhenyu, 'China's Population Policy and Family Planning', p. 218.
18. Shi Chengli, *Zhongguo jihua shengyu huodongshi*, pp. 156–7.
19. *Zhongguo jihua shengyu nianjian 1986* (*Almanac of China's Family Planning 1986*) (Beijing: Zhongguo weisheng chubanshe, 1986), p. 4.
20. Li Kangmei, 'Zhongguo de jihua shengyu' ('Family Planning in China'), *Zhongguo weisheng nianjian 1983* (*China's Public Health Yearbook 1983*) (Beijing: Renmin weisheng chubanshe, 1984), pp. 160–6.
21. Xiao Zhenyu, 'China's Population Policy and Family Planning', p. 219.
22. Western scholars also noticed the importance of this essay and a translation was published in *International Family Planning Perspective*, Vol. 5, No. 3 (September 1979), pp. 92–101.

23. For a detailed discussion, see Ansley Coale, Wang Feng, Nancy E. Riley and Lin Fu De, 'Recent Trends in Fertility and Nuptiality in China', *Science*, Vol. 251 (25 January 1991), pp. 389–93.
24. For example, *Zhongguo qingnian bao* (*China's Youth*), 9 November 1982, p. 3, and 5 February 1983, p. 2; *China Daily*, 9 April 1983, p. 3; *Nanfang ribao* (*Southern Daily*), 7 February 1983, p. 2.
25. For example, Zhao Ziyang, 'Report on the Sixth Five-Year Plan' made in the fifth session of the Fifth National People's Congress, 30 November 1982, and Zhao Ziyang, 'Government Work Report' made in the first session of the Sixth National People's Congress, 6 June 1983.
26. See John S. Aird, *Slaughter of the Innocents: Coercive Birth Control in China*, particularly Appendix A, 'Family Planning Infanticide'.
27. Susan Greenhalgh, 'Shifts in China's Population Policy, 1984–86: Views from the Central, Provincial, and Local Levels', *Population and Development Review*, Vol. 12, No. 3 (September 1986), p. 493.
28. Notable examples are Ma Bin, *Lun Zhongguo renkou wenti – renkou zhanlue, renkou guihua, renkou zhengce* (*On China's Population Problem: Strategy, Plan and Policy*), (Beijing: Zhongguo guoji guangbo chubanshe, 1987); and Liu Jingzhi, 'Zhangguan yizhi de ganrao shi chushenglu huisheng zhongyao yuanyin' ('Interference by Officials is an Important Reason Why Birth Rate Has Risen Again'), *Guangming ribao* (*Bright Daily*), 6 March 1988, p. 2.
29. *Renmin ribao, haiwaiban* (*People's Daily*, Overseas Edition), 22 February 1989, p. 4.
30. For a discussion of the 'loosening or tightening up' of the family planning policy during this period, see Karen Hardee-Cleaveland and Judith Banister, 'Fertility Policy and Implementation in China, 1986–88', *Population and Development Review*, Vol. 14, No. 2 (June 1988), pp. 245–86; Zeng Yi, 'Is the Chinese Family Planning Program 'Tightening Up'?', *Population and Development Review*, Vol. 15, No. 2 (June 1989), pp. 333–7; and Susan Greenhalgh, 'The Evolution of the One-Child Policy in Shaanxi, 1979–88', *The China Quarterly*, No. 122 (June 1990), pp. 191–229.
31. Susan Greenhalgh, Zhu Chuzhu and Li Nan, 'Restraining Population Growth in Three Chinese Villages, 1988–93', *Population and Development Review*, Vol. 20, No. 2 (June 1994), p. 365.
32. The policy was introduced in the 'Joint Resolution of the Central Committee of the CCP and the State Council on 'Strengthening the Family Work and Strictly Controlling Population Growth' (Document 9), which was issued on 12 May 1991.
33. Zhu Baoxia, 'Three-three Plan to Limit Population', *China Daily*, 12 March 1996, p. 2.
34. Harish Khanna, 'China and Population', *Hindusthan Times* (New Delhi), reproduced in *Populi*, Vol. 14, No. 4 (1987), p. 55.
35. Chen Jian, '1995–1996 nian renkou yu jihua shengyu zhuangkuang' ('Fertility and Birth Planning in 1995–1996') *Renkou Xuekan* (*Population Journal*) No. 1, 1996, p. 55.
36. Seth Faison, 'Chinese are Happily Breaking the "One Child" Rule', *New York Times*, 17 August 1997.

37. For a report on infanticide, see John Aird, *Slaughter of the Innocents*, Appendix A. For a report on the other causes, see Zeng Yi, Tu Ping, Gu Baochang, Xu Yi, Li Bohua and Li Yongping, 'Causes and Implications of the Recent Increase in the Reported Sex Ratio at Birth in China', *Population and Development Review*, Vol. 19, No. 2 (June 1993), pp. 283–302.
38. For arguments favouring quality as well as quantity, see Gu Baochang and Mu Guangzong, 'Chongxin renshi Zhongguo renkou wenti' ('A Reconsideration of Population Problems in China'), *Renkou yanjiu* (*Population Research*), No. 5, 1994, pp. 2–10. For arguments favouring the importance of size, see Yan Meifu and Shi Renbin, 'Cong xinlixue shijiao renshi Zhongguo renkou wenti' ('A Psychological Approach to Understanding the Population Problem in China'), *Renkou yanjiu* (*Population Research*), No. 6, 1995, pp. 7–13.
39. *South China Morning Post*, 28 September 1995, p. 13.
40. For example, see *Ming Pao*, 27 January 1996, p. C3.
41. The two symposiums were held in 1993, see *Zhongguo renkou bao* (*China's Population News*), 24 March 1993, p. 1; and in 1994, see *Zhongguo renkou bao* (*China's Population News*), 23 March 1994, p. 1.
42. *Zhongguo renkou bao* (*China's Population News*), 3 March 1993, p. 1.
43. *China Daily* (*15th Party Congress Supplement*), 23 September 1997.
44. Tyrene White, 'Birth Planning Between Plan and Market: The Impact of Reform on China's One-Child Policy', in *China's Economic Dilemmas in the 1990s: the Problems of Reforms, Modernization, and Interdependence*, edited by the Joint Economic Committee, Congress of the United States (Armonk, NY: M.E. Sharpe, 1992), p. 253.

Index

Note: page numbers in **bold** type refer to illustrative figures or tables.